CO-ALM-368

MANPOWER AND ECONOMIC EDUCATION

A personal
and social approach
to career education.

Robert L. Darcy,
Colorado State University

Phillip E. Powell,
Joint Council on Economic Education

LOVE PUBLISHING COMPANY
Denver, Colorado 80222

All rights reserved. No part of this publication may be reproduced, stored in a retrieval system or transmitted, in any form or by any means, electronic, mechanical, recording or otherwise, without the prior written permission of the publisher.

Copyright © 1973 Love Publishing Company
Printed in the U.S.A.
Library of Congress Catalogue Card Number 73-86162

To Jean Stegman Powell

and

for Tim, Kathleen, Roberta, Laura, Mark, Patrice, Julie and 80 million other young Americans who will come of age during the 1970s and 1980s.

Contents

Contents

UNIT THREE
THE MANPOWER MARKET
173

Contents

Illustrations

UNIT THREE

UNIT FOUR

UNIT FIVE

UNIT SIX

Tables

UNIT ONE

Tables

Case Studies

UNIT ONE

UNIT THREE

UNIT FOUR

UNIT FIVE

Case Studies

Foreword

Five years ago the Joint Council on Economic Education had the privilege of facilitating dissemination of the experimental *Manpower and Economic Education* materials. These materials grew out of a curriculum development project co-sponsored by the U.S. Office of Education and carried out under the direction of Robert L. Darcy and Phillip E. Powell. Extensively revised materials were developed for students and teachers by Dr. Darcy and Professor Powell especially for the public served by the Joint Council.

The original *Manpower and Economic Education* text and teacher manual have been used in a variety of experimental programs in school systems throughout the nation. The materials reflect a fine blend of information that orients the student to the world of work as it will be in the future, economic concepts that underlie this developing career outlook and the importance of continuing education to meet new demands being made by society and the economy. Credibility has been established through the involvement of both the schools and community, and the program has been acclaimed by educators and leaders from business and labor. A major contribution has been made by the authors to the evolving concept of career education.

Success of this curriculum effort required a revision of the materials to keep them in tune with new developments in the American scene. The entire text has been updated and revised, material has been added, and the text has been reorganized around six basic themes that comprise the content of world-of-work economic education. The experience of the many teachers and students who participated in five years of use of the materials is reflected in this revision.

The success of the original materials encouraged the Joint Council to carry out a two-year dissemination project (1973-74) involving educational leaders from every state and our network of affiliated State Councils and college and university Centers. The availability of these revised materials will have a major impact on the continuing effectiveness of economic education and career education. The authors have earned the plaudits of all who are concerned with more effective educational programs for the youth of America.

We appreciate the cooperation and initiative of Love Publishing Company in making *Manpower and Economic Education* available for wider dissemination.

April 1973   M.L. FRANKEL
                                          President
                                          Joint Council on Economic Education
                                          New York City

Preface

This book was written to help young people develop an understanding of the economic process and the role that work plays in the lives of men and women. It suggests ways for increasing future employability, productivity, earnings and work satisfaction by investing in the development of one's own knowledge, skills, motivation and patterns of behavior. It has the twin goals of *manpower understanding* and *manpower development*.

Manpower and Economic Education: A Personal and Social Approach to Career Education is not a standard economics textbook in the sense of being a comprehensive study of "Social Economics" or "Consumer Economics." Written from a human resource perspective, the focus is clearly on *man* and *manpower* in the American economy, now and in the future.

In writing this book, we have kept two things in mind. First, our economy is changing. The changes are fundamental, the rate of change is both rapid and increasing every year, and the changes will create both problems and opportunities for Americans in the 1970s and beyond. Second, young people can do a better job of preparing for the future—for full participation in the economic life of our nation—if they are given an opportunity to learn more about the economy, its changing technology and the increasing importance of human resources.

Economic affairs significantly influence our lives. But money, goods and work are not the most important factors in human

15

experience. Numerous lessons in this book are designed to help young people explore the broader social environment and begin to define the role that work should play in their lives. Our hope is that education and work, instead of being burdens and a bore—or tedious means to elusive ends—may themselves bring a larger measure of personal satisfaction and self-fulfillment to the men and women coming of age in the 1970s and 1980s. A strong note of humanism is combined with relevant economic analysis throughout these materials, focusing on questions of values and institutional change. The intellectual orientation is multi-disciplinary, drawing on the insights of sociology, psychology and philosophy as well as economics.

The book consists of 72 lessons organized into six units. Each lesson begins with a concise abstract outlining the central topic or theme to be studied. The function of this introductory paragraph is to focus the reader's attention on key ideas and facts that will be developed in the lesson and also to indicate why an understanding of the material can be useful and relevant. Next comes the main text of the lesson containing descriptive and analytical information, statistical data (in charts and tables) and case studies drawn from real life. At the close of each lesson is a summary paragraph called *Lesson in Brief* which recapitulates and emphasizes the most essential understandings that readers hopefully have gained from the lesson.

There are more facts and ideas in these lessons than most readers will comprehend and remember. Much of this content can be regarded as enrichment material that supplements the basic concepts, facts, information and analysis identified in the abstract and summarized in the Lesson in Brief. Keep in mind that this book is designed to create student awareness of significant forces at work in our economic and social world and to stimulate inquiry, discussion and discovery. The lessons provide material for economic and occupational exploration as a part of a continuing career education learning experience.

Some of the lessons are more sophisticated than others. Many are appropriate for study not only by high school and college students but also by adults who are already pursuing work careers.

Our assumption is that young readers are on their way to becoming mature men and women and will benefit greatly from exposure to the economic, social and psychological topics included in this book, however challenging and complex they may be.

It should be emphasized that although the units are carefully structured the book is not a self-study course. Teachers should play an active role in stimulating and guiding discussion and providing concrete examples based on personal experience and local circumstances. Students can learn a great deal from hearing views expressed by their classmates. Well-prepared and imaginative teachers can adapt the materials to meet special needs of their own students. Guest speakers and other community resources can be used to illustrate problems and issues in the real world.

In the ten years that have passed since the basic ideas about world-of-work economic education began to take shape in our minds, fundamental changes have occurred in educational philosophy and strategy. Widespread support has developed for career education as a theme around which the school curriculum can be restructured—from kindergarten through high school and beyond. The purpose of career education is to prepare young people for productive and satisfying lives, including the ability to participate successfully as human resources in the economic life of our nation. It is our hope that *Manpower and Economic Education* will make a limited but valuable contribution to the emerging career education curriculum as well as promote the long-standing objective of economic education—raising the level of economic literacy in America.

May 1973   ROBERT L. DARCY
                                                 PHILLIP E. POWELL

Acknowledgments

The authors would like to express appreciation to a number of individuals and organizations for the advice, encouragement, cooperation and assistance which they have variously provided over the years. During the past decade, we have participated in programs and activities within the broad area of world-of-work economic education which have entailed financial sponsorship or other forms of support from the U.S. Office of Education, U.S. Department of Labor, Joint Council on Economic Education, Ohio Council on Economic Education, Ohio University, Martha Holden Jennings Foundation, Arkansas State Council on Economic Education, Henderson State College and Colorado State University.

Grateful acknowledgment is expressed for the assistance and encouragement given by Jacquie Darcy, Vicki Williams, M. L. Frankel, George L. Fersh, Jack A. Wilson, Philip R. Teske, Bessie Moore, Nat Goldfinger, Thomas M. Bruening, John G. Odgers, David W. Winefordner, Joseph W. Duncan, Byron L. Hollinger, Dean L. Hummel, Robert M. Boyd, Paul A. Games, Harry B. Crewson, Ann E. Murphy, James A. Schobel, William Papier, Edwin Fultz, Calvin Patterson, Ginger Uthmann and numerous others.

We are indebted to the school officials, teachers, guidance counselors and students in Zanesville, Lancaster and Columbus, Ohio, for their cooperation in field-testing, during the 1967-68 school year, the original instructional materials from which *Manpower and Economic Education* evolved, especially: James R. Brown, Leroy A. Cranz, Wallace E. Blake, Ralph Storts, Thomas Leidich, Gerald Woodgeard, Joel Mullin, Robert Mathias, Donald Phillips, James Lawrence, Richard Nash, Dean Nusbaum, Richard Beck and David Thompson.

Finally, we are gratified by the positive response of the thousands of students and scores of teachers in Arkansas, Ohio and other states throughout the nation to the rather nontraditional ideas and format found in our program.

UNIT ONE

The Individual and the Nature of Work

For most Americans, work is no longer a matter of making a living by the sweat of the brow. Yet even today, approximately one-third of all the waking hours in an adult's life are spent on the job. Work continues to play a central role in man's life though the conditions and even the purposes of work have changed a great deal in the past century. Today, men and women work to help produce goods and services, to earn an income, to satisfy social and psychological needs, and to develop their human potential.

What will the world of work be like in the 21st century? To whom does the future belong? Since the turn of the century is less than 30 years away, these questions are both interesting and relevant to young people for very practical reasons. Many readers of this book will be in the prime of their productive lives in the year 2000—or could be if they prepare themselves wisely through education and career planning.

The lessons in Unit One focus not so much on what the individual can do for the world of work but on what the world of work can do for the individual. Although career success cannot guarantee a happy life, it can contribute to happiness by enabling the individual to meet certain human needs and to avoid insecurities and frustrations. Furthermore, sound preparation for the world of work involves developing one's "human capital" or acquired capabilities. This process not only makes the individual more productive as a human resource but also more effective as a citizen, a consumer and a self-fulfilled human being.

Self-discovery ... job satisfaction ... mental health ... justice ... value conflicts ... personal integrity ... the price of success—many of the ideas and concerns discussed in this unit may seem out of place in a book entitled *Manpower and Economic Education.* Bear in mind, however, that economics is the social science that studies the satisfaction of human wants. Its grand theme is not individual ιprofit-making, but society's search for a higher quality of life. Money, goods and services are desirable. But, to mix an old aphorism with modern slang—the Man does not live by bread alone.

The Future of Work in American Society

The world of work in America is changing. The amount and direction of change will influence the role and the significance that work will have for young men and women in the future. An individual's chances of finding meaning and satisfaction in a job will be affected by the future dimensions of work. Knowing some of the possible ways that work may change will be helpful in planning and preparing for a future career.

Let's examine 3 views of what the world of work may be like in the future as suggested by a government manpower specialist in the *Monthly Labor Review*, a U. S. Department of Labor publication. Each sketch presents a somewhat different picture of American life in the future. Reading about these possible alternatives will be helpful in planning and preparing for a career in the settings described—though these are outlines only, not blueprints or predictions of what really will happen. Consider, also, that every individual can play a role in creating and shaping the actual future world of work. Many of the terms and concepts mentioned in the sketches probably are unfamiliar. They are explained in subsequent lessons of this text.

Future Sketch 1/DOING YOUR OWN THING

Technology—the number and complexity of automated and cybernetic machines are increasing rapidly, spreading from blue-collar production and distribution activities into white-collar and service occupations. *Skills*—new and more complex skills are needed by workers; increasing numbers of people are discovering their skills are inadequate to get or keep jobs. *Production of goods and services*—output is continuing to grow based on cybernation and a high level of market demand for goods and services. *Employment and unemployment*—job opportunities for highly trained workers such as cybernetic engineers are increasing, but millions of lower-skilled jobs are being eliminated and employment is declining to low levels. *Income*—separation of work and income is nearly complete; all members of this type of society are sharing in the consumption of goods and services through guaranteed income plans and other institutional arrangements that assure a high level of demand. *Role and significance of work*—work is losing its traditional importance because economic security is no longer a reason for working; desire for material affluence is gradually being replaced by concern for personal and social improvement in nonwork settings. *Values and lifestyles*—the majority of Americans are oriented to consumption as their basic economic role; a wide range of personal and expressive lifestyles is possible.

Future Sketch 2/EMPLOYMENT IS STILL THE NAME OF THE GAME

Technology—the current gradual trends in automation and cybernation are continuing. *Skills*—new and more complex skills are needed by some workers but, since technological change is more controlled by public policy, the skills of workers are not becoming obsolete as rapidly; training is provided to equip workers with new skills. *Production of goods and services*—output is increasing because of expanding capacity and the government's full employment policy. *Employment and unemployment*—the unemployment rate is low because job barriers based on discrimination are reduced; there is an adequate supply of appropriately trained persons willing to work; local, state and federal governments are employing more workers to attack difficult social and environmental problems. *Income*—workers' incomes are rising because of improvements in the manpower market and a full employment policy. *Role and significance of work*—employment remains the chief source of income; workers continue to be motivated by concern about economic security; work is still viewed as an important means of satisfying personal economic and noneconomic needs. *Values and lifestyles*—more people are benefitting from employment and the opportunities that careers offer for personal satisfaction.

Future Sketch 3/HUMANIZING WORK

Technology—there is continued improvement and application of automated machinery and cybernetic processes to meet the growing needs of society. *Skills*—new skills and greater proficiency are required of workers. *Production of goods and services*—output is determined more by nonmarket cultural values than in the past; since more workers are involved in service occupations where productivity increases slowly, output is rising only moderately. *Employment and unemployment*—there is a growing demand for such highly trained workers as technicians and engineers, public advocates or ombudsmen, public and personal services, craftsmen and artisans, and workers in the experience industries where recreation and educational opportunities are packaged to appeal to the interests of an increasingly affluent and educated population with more leisure time; the percentage of workers engaged in goods production is lower. *Income*—employment still is the key factor in determining the amount of income a person receives; workers' incomes are increasing more slowly than in the past. *Role and significance of work*—work and leisure are beginning to merge into a wholeness they did not have in the past; the difference between work and leisure is becoming more difficult to identify; there is more stress on work as a means of increasing opportunities for personal growth and fulfillment; work tasks are being adapted to fit the needs of the individual; the work place is becoming a more humanized setting. *Values and lifestyles*—change is gradual with more emphasis on individual freedom, dignity and quality of life.[1]

These sketches of the future world of work pose certain questions. What difference does it make what the future of work will be like? Which of the proposed alternatives is most likely to occur? What facts or other evidence can be presented to support this view? Which one of the future worlds of work described do young people prefer? Why?

Lesson in Brief

The world of work is changing. These changes will affect the role and significance of work in the lives of Americans. The actual future of the world of work will be influenced by the values, decisions and actions of the American people.

---

1. These 3 sketches are based on ideas contained in Denis F. Johnston, *Monthly Labor Review*, May 1972, pp. 3-11.

Education and Work: 2
A Means of Discovering Oneself

Education and work experiences can help a person learn more about himself and the goals he wants to achieve in life. Economic and manpower understanding can be useful in planning a career. Knowing how the economy operates—and the roles that people play as workers in economic life—can be valuable in attaining personal goals.

The case studies in this lesson are true. They involve real people and illustrate some of the problems and opportunities young people may face in the next few years. The case studies indicate what the workers did or did not do to create the situations in which they found themselves.

NO LOVE FOR THE IRON HORSE

"When I finished high school, I heard they were hiring people at the automobile assembly plant. I figured I'd get a job there. Then, with the vocational training I got in school, I could work my way up to a good position. The idea of making cars sounded like something really important. My luck was good, and I got a job as spot welder. The job didn't amount to much. I learned it in a week. Later, I got drafted. After my discharge from the Army, I tried to get an electrician's job at the plant, but there wasn't any openings. So I went back to the assembly line—we call it the iron horse— as a welder. I've been there ever since.

"My job is to weld the hood to its metal underbody. I take a job off my bench, put it into place and weld the parts together. The job is all made up, and the welds are made in certain places along the metal. There are exactly thirty spots that have to be welded. The line runs according to schedule. Takes me two minutes and twenty-five seconds for each job. The cars differ, but the job is almost the same every time. Finish one car and another one is looking me in the face.

"I hate working on the line. Nobody likes to work on a moving assembly line. You can't beat the iron horse! Sure, I can keep it up for an hour or so, but it's tough doing it eight hours a day, five days a week, all year long.

"When I'm working, there isn't much chance to take a break. Sometimes the line breaks down. When that happens, all the line workers are really happy. But as long as the line keeps moving, I've got to stay up with it. A few jobs on the iron horse allow the guys to work up the line if they want to. Then they can do a little loafing. On most jobs you can't do that. If I get a few seconds ahead, the next model will have more welds to it, so it takes a few seconds more. You can't win for losing. You're always behind the eight ball.

"I'd like to have a job where I could feel I'm doing something important. When everything's laid out before you and the parts are all alike, you can't feel like you're doing much. The thing that bugs me most is the constant pace of the line. I can't control the iron horse. It controls me!

"It's hard to feel that you're doing a good quality job on the line. There's a steady push, at high speed. You may get better after you've done your job over and over again. But you never get to a point where you can feel that you've done one right. If I could do my best I'd get some satisfaction out of my job, but I can't do as good work as I know I can."

The above case describes a certain kind of economic activity and how a particular worker feels toward his job. The case also provides a basis for a young person to imagine how he might react to working on an assembly line.

THE DROPOUT WHO DIDN'T GIVE UP

Joe has 25 scars on his hands to prove that he is a street fighter. By the time he was 20, he had flunked out of high school several times, had been kicked out of the Marines and had lost about 30 jobs. The second oldest of 7 children, Joe always wanted to achieve; and in his neighborhood, an achiever had to know how to use his fists. A veteran of more than 100 rumbles, Joe was put on probation by a juvenile court after one very bloody street fight. When he was in his first year of probation, he flunked out of high school. Not long afterward, he enrolled in another high school at night—he failed there also. In a third attempt at high school, he didn't last the semester.

At 14, Joe began trying his hand at various jobs. He set a record for failing which was worse than even his school record. On his first day of work at a bleach factory, he attempted to carry 10 gallons of bleach to a truck he was loading and dropped all 10. Joe later worked in a clothing factory, where he was awakened from sleep one afternoon by the president of the company. Joe had another job opportunity when a furniture company advertised in the newspaper that they were seeking ambitious young men who were looking for responsibility. After a month of aligning wheels of teacarts, Joe got tired of responsibility.

Joe enlisted in the Marines when he reached 18 but could not take the discipline and rebelled. He fought with recruits, rioted in the mess hall and tried to go over the hill. Judged an incorrigible by the Marines, he was booted out with a general discharge. Back home, he was a hero to his old street-gang buddies. But within himself, Joe felt ashamed. At 20, he realized that his only chance for a better life was to improve his education. So for the fifth time he returned to high school. He attended at night and worked days in a grocery store. After two years, Joe graduated with the highest average in the night school's history.

Despite only fair results on college extrance exams, Joe's grades got him admitted to a university. At first, he felt he had nothing in common with the college youths who talked about summer vacations and beach parties—things he didn't know about. But he stuck it out and in his senior year was elected president of the student body. After graduating with honors, Joe went back into the Marine Corps for two years, feeling that he had to make up for his past record. He did. This time he became a platoon leader, the highest scorer in athletic competition and had his general discharge changed to an honorable one.

At 30, Joe graduated as valedictorian of his class from a famous law school. He received several offers to work for major law firms; instead, he chose to serve a term as an assistant U.S. attorney.

Joe's case illustrates some changes in attitudes and values that young people may have as they finish high school and become aware of the job opportunities and economic rewards available in the American economy.

SKILL AND SATISFACTION

"I'm a die designer. We draw the prints when someone gets a bright idea for a new die. Dies are tools that are used in the plant for shaping material for machine production. The management goes to the planner and asks him whether or not we ought to work on it. Then they give it to us, and we have to design a die that is as good as one they might get from an outside firm.

"I used to make dies, that's how I got started. I came to the company for my apprenticeship right after high school. In those days jobs were hard to find. But I had a friend whose father was a foreman, and he told me about a job opening and managed to help me get hired. I didn't start at tool and die work though; they put me on the assembly line. But after I was in the plant for a while and I looked around at the various jobs, I thought I'd like to get into die work.

"You'd go into the die shop, and it was always so clean and neat. They clean the machines every weekend. Well, one of the die shop supervisors thought I could learn the trade so he took me on as an apprentice. I had to take a cut in pay, but it was worth it. I had to start at the bottom. Along with the work on the job, you had to go to school at night. We took what they called a 5-year course. I finished it up in 2,800 hours. That meant some rough going. They taught us what an engineer learns, but from a practical point of view.

"I always try to do the best job I can. My company has been very good to me. I'm going to stay with them until they foul me up. If the work I do isn't satisfactory, well, that's tough. I always do the best work I know how.

"When I got back to the plant from my Army service, I thought I should have a more responsible position. But I never said anything about wanting a better job. One day the boss called me into his office, and he asked me if I'd like to become a die designer. I'd never done great at mechanical drawing in school, but I figured I'd give it a try. Well, today I'm a designer. I'm one of only eight in the whole plant. What I design and draw in 8 hours creates enough work to keep our production men busy for 50 to 60 hours.

"The engineers in our company, all of them smart college graduates, often come to me to ask questions. I don't take anything away from them—they know all about stresses and strains. But when they want something done, they have to come to me. Now that's something I'm very proud of."

These case studies and other ideas and information included in these lessons will be helpful when thinking about the world of work and American society. By posing some key questions about attitudes and work satisfaction, we hope young men and women will become interested in learning about the changing economy, the role that work plays in life and the relationship between economic activity and human development.

Lesson in Brief

Work and education can be a means of understanding oneself and developing one's human capabilities. Knowing how the world of work operates can help an individual understand an important part of his environment—modern technology, the role of human resources, and the social and economic forces that influence life. This base of understanding, in turn, can prove useful in achieving life goals. The chances of finding meaningful employment and building a life of purpose and fulfillment will be greater if one prepares now for tomorrow's opportunities.

... the changing shape of the world of work is the economic challenge before the American economic system.

Robert Heilbroner

Throughout history, men have had many different ideas about the nature and importance of work. To some people work is a necessary evil, or a way to make a living, or a means to express oneself. Let's review what work has meant to man through the years and the functions that work can serve.

What is meant by the term work? The dictionary defines *work* as an activity in which a person exerts strength or effort (physical and/or mental) to do or perform a task. Work is the labor, toil, duty, function or assignment which is often a part of a larger activity. For example, math homework is part of formal schooling; doing household chores is part of sharing in the productive side of family life.

A *job* is a position in a particular work place, such as a local factory. *Occupation*, however, refers to a group of similar work activities found in more than one place of employment. An occupation requires certain skills. The building custodian in a school and the carpenter helping to build a house are involved in occupations.

A *career* is the sequence of jobs and occupations that a person has for his life work. People who have careers have a pattern to their employment during their lifetime. Careers involve specialized education or training and a series of positions requiring greater and greater skill. For example, a physician has a career in medicine while a brick mason may have a career in construction. Most workers do not have careers! They may have a number of different jobs and occupations, but these do not form a specific pattern of work over a lifetime.

Work has two basic functions that are purely economic: to produce goods and services and to provide the worker and his family with an income.

The first function of work, to produce goods and services, is so important and so obvious from the viewpoint of society as a whole, yet sometimes it is not even recognized. Often, work from the individual's point of view is a means to earn a living. The value of work—or labor, to use the technical term—was considered by economists to be so important that, before the 1850s, they assumed that labor alone determined the value of goods and services. Even today, economists still credit *labor*—defined as all human effort devoted to production—with a much larger contribution to the nation's total output of goods and services than comes from the nonhuman factors of production, capital and natural resources.

For most families in the United States, work is necessary to provide the income needed to maintain their standard of living. About two-thirds of the total income received by families comes in the form of wages and salaries paid for work.

Years ago, for most people work meant hard physical effort which they had to exert to survive. Even today, work means survival to some Americans and to nearly all the people of Asia, Africa and Latin America. More recently, work has become what a person does to earn a living for his family—to be able to pay rent or to send the kids to college.

Ideas about work have changed through the ages. In fact, the very nature of work itself has changed. Some scholars say the notion of work as drudgery is tied up with certain religious ideas, such as working by the sweat of one's brow as punishment for original sin, and for these reasons work has come to be viewed as a necessary evil. Yet work can be a pleasure, as many women and men will report, and may become a means of satisfying some personal, social and psychological needs as well as a source of satisfaction, happiness and fulfillment for the individual.

Increasingly, it is being recognized that work is a means of human development. For example, through activities on the job, new skills can be learned and old skills conserved. Work can offer men and women an opportunity to demonstrate their skills or human capital. Work can also contribute to human development and fulfillment in the broadest sense by helping people express themselves, find meaning in their lives and achieve personal growth.

Work is not only a way to avoid economic insecurity and personal unhappiness but can be a positive experience that opens new horizons for individual awareness and further development. Work may be a blessing rather than a curse.

Figure 1.1
THE CHANGING NATURE OF WORK

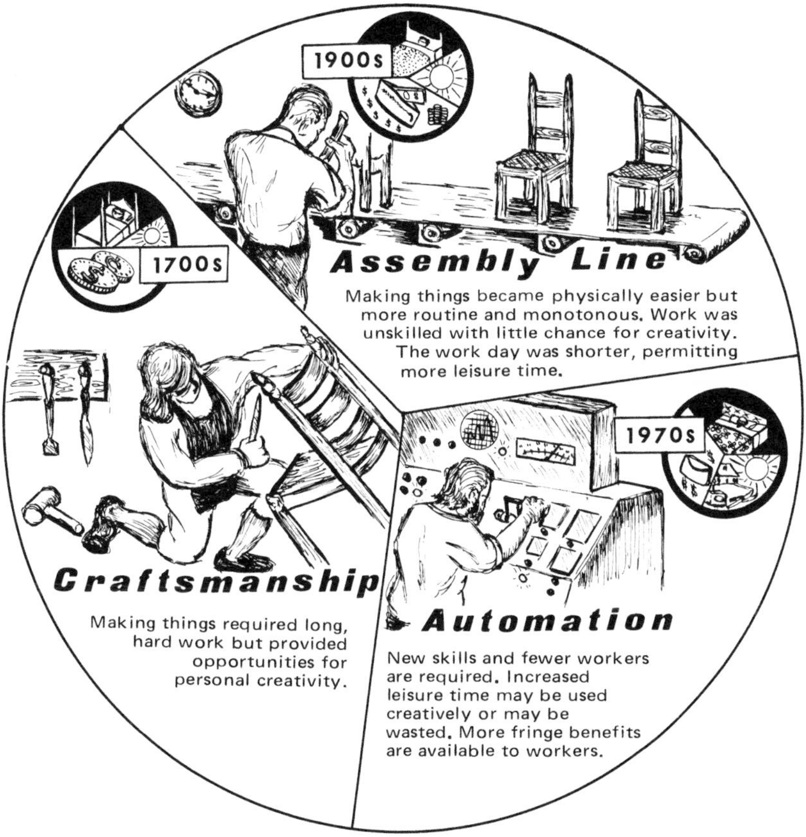

Consider Figure 1.1 which illustrates how the nature of work has changed with time. The first frame depicts the skilled craftsman of the 1700s making a chair, the complete product. With the development of factories and the assembly line, workers started making only parts of a product. Present-day automation provides the modern worker with a set of buttons to push or dials to operate instead of requiring a great deal of manual work. The worker has become more of a highly skilled specialist, and employers need fewer unskilled workers. With man freed from much of the difficult manual labor and repetitious tasks through the use of machines, the worker of the future will use his talents in very different creative ways.

The pie charts in Figure 1.1 represent estimated divisions of work, sleep and leisure in a worker's 24-hour day. Note that the working day has been cut from 12 hours in the 1700s to about 8 hours in the 1970s. Does this mean that workers are better off today with modern technology, specialized skills and increased leisure than they were in the 1700s?

Lesson in Brief

The nature of work has changed through the years. Today, work continues to have 2 important economic functions—to help produce goods and services and to provide the opportunity to earn income so workers can maintain an adequate standard of living.

Work has other important functions as well—to help satisfy workers' social and psychological needs and to aid human development in terms of workers' skills and personal growth.

The Job: Satisfaction or Disappointment? 4

An important factor to consider when thinking about an individual's future as a worker is whether he will find satisfaction or disappointment on the job. Will his job really satisfy his needs?

How many people ever stop to think about the kinds of satisfactions different jobs offer the worker? A few examples of satisfactions and dissatisfactions that workers experience are friendship, a sense of accomplishment, pleasure from the physical environment of the work place, frustration, nervous strain, boredom. For most jobs, workers will have both positive and negative feelings.

The following 12 factors suggest some qualities different people may want or need to get from their jobs. The extent to which these needs are fulfilled will help determine how satisfied a worker is with his job. Which factors seem most important?

1. Economic security—the need to feel assured of a continuing income and adequate standard of living
2. Recognition and approval—the need to have one's work and other activities known and approved by others
3. Mastery and achievement—the need to perform well according to one's own standards and abilities
4. Dominance—the need to have some power or influence and control over things and people
5. Socioeconomic status—the need to provide one's family with money and material goods that measure up to community standards
6. Self-expression—the need to have personal behavior consistent with one's self-concept
7. Affection and interpersonal relationships—the need to have a feeling of acceptance by and belongingness with other people, to be liked and loved by others

8. Moral values scheme—the need to feel that one's behavior is consistent with some moral code or structure in order to feel good and worthy
9. Dependence—the need to be directed by others to avoid feeling alone and totally responsible for one's own behavior
10. Creativity and challenge—the need to meet new problems requiring initiative and imagination and to produce new and original works
11. Social well-being or altruism—the need to help others, to have one's efforts result in benefits to others
12. Independence—the need to direct one's own behavior rather than to be completely controlled by others

It is obvious that jobs give economic rewards for work through earnings. But consider also how other needs are met through certain jobs. When co-workers elect an individual union representative or chairman of a committee, when a person's family appreciates him, when one has friends—these individuals gain recognition and experience satisfying interpersonal relationships. When a girl sews an attractive dress or builds a beautifully-styled wooden stool or bookcase, she feels mastery, achievement and self-expression. When a policeman exerts influence by controlling the flow of traffic and preventing people from breaking the law, he fulfills his need for dominance.

The truck driver feels a sense of mastery, achievement and dominance over machines when he backs his huge truck and trailer into a narrow place. The medical doctor gets social satisfaction from helping sick people. The teacher feels creative and challenged after designing and presenting a lesson that is both interesting and meaningful to her students.

The writer, the advertising designer and the sculptor often experience creativity and challenge, mastery and achievement when working. Independence is expressed by the man who owns his own business, by the executive who directs the activities of several departments, by the secretary who is also an office manager.

Lesson in Brief

Each individual brings needs, desires, feelings and skills to the job. He wants to earn money, but he has other needs as well. The amount of satisfaction or need fulfillment received from a job depends on the individual and the opportunities his job provides for self-expression and achievement of his goals.

A job is more than a means to earn a living. The long arm of the job reaches out to influence the worker's total life. What work he does, why he does it, where, how and with whom he performs his job will greatly influence his whole lifestyle. The job helps shape personal behavior patterns and establish beliefs in certain ideas, values and attitudes.

THE LONG ARM OF THE JOB

What is meant by the following statement? *What a man is, both in his own mind and in the eyes of others, is closely involved with the work he does.* The statement indicates that the kind of work a man does and how well he does it influence the formation of his personal identity.

Decisions regarding career choice made by young people during their school years will have a great effect on their total future life. For example, a person must decide whether he will graduate from high school. After making that decision, he needs to decide where to go from there—shall he join the armed forces; get a job; get married; attend a technical school, a business school or a college?

Consider a few of the ways an individual's choice of occupation and career might affect his future. His selection may determine whether he is employed or unemployed. The choice will influence whether he enjoys or hates his work. It can affect his whole style of living. It may even determine his success or failure in life. How does a person's job, occupation or career influence each of the following:

—his work atmosphere and surroundings
—his co-workers
—the clothes he wears
—the car he drives
—the state, town, neighborhood and house he lives in
—the people who become his friends
—the clubs and organizations he joins
—his hobbies and recreational activities
—his political ideas
—the books and magazines he reads
—the schools his children will attend
—his accomplishments and contributions to society

Lesson in Brief

A job creates a style of life for a worker. Its influence extends beyond his place of employment and the length of his work day. The long arm of the job reaches into his home and family, affecting his total way of life—his ideas and ideals, attitudes and interests, manners and clothes.

> Work is seldom all good or all bad for the worker. Most jobs have both positive and negative aspects. If the positive factors are great enough, the job can make a major contribution to the satisfactions the worker gets from life. Wise career planning will increase one's chances of finding positive values in work and life.

When reading the following biographical sketch about Dr. Braunwald, think about why she works, what satisfactions she gets from her job, what limitations her career places on her family and social life. Are these same considerations present in a man's career?

MOTHER IS A SURGEON

In every sense of the word Nina Braunwald is a specialist in affairs of the heart. A devoted wife and mother, the slender, brown-eyed brunette was the first woman in the United States to be certified by the American Board of Thoracic Surgery (specializing in heart, lungs and esophagus) and one of the few women doing open-heart surgery in the 1960s.

In September, 1963, the National Institute of Health Clinical Center at Bethesda, Maryland, dedicated its new two million dollar heart and brain surgery wing. While the dedication ceremonies were going on, two delicate operations were in progress on the third floor—one performed by Dr. Andrew G. Morrow, Chief of Heart Surgery, the other by Dr. Braunwald.

Dr. Braunwald cut open the chest and leg of a young woman, attached a heart-lung machine, stopped the patient's heart and replaced a constricted mitral valve. She then surgically sewed into the patient a small metal cage containing a white plastic sphere resembling a miniature Ping-Pong ball. On a wall in the observation room, electronic instruments recorded such vital data as blood flow rates, blood pressure, heartbeats, blood loss and body temperature.

Spiked waves moved across screens adjacent to each set of records. Thus, the audience of topflight surgeons could observe the progress. It must have been a dramatic moment, even to eminent surgeons, to observe the skill of the brilliant young woman performing this difficult operation. The evening after surgery Dr. Morrow's and Dr. Braunwald's patients, each of whom suffered rheumatic fever during childhood, were reported doing well.

It takes courage to have a life in your hands. Nina Braunwald is among the courageous American women who remove barriers and help pioneer in the new fields developing in this fast-moving age.

Although the crusade to allow women to pursue medical education to practice medicine in the United States began as recently as 1845, women actually have been physicians from earliest times. In medieval Europe, women studied at most universities and were professors at some schools. In sharp contrast, King Henry V of England ordered that any woman practicing medicine would be imprisoned.

During our Civil War and the two World Wars, when many physicians were called to the battlefields, the acceptance of women into medicine was accelerated. Women doctors have contributed their time and skills to many branches of medicine. The world's first clinic for mentally retarded children opened with a woman doctor as administrator. Women physicians also administer and staff programs for the deaf, the crippled and the poor who are ill.

Ever since high school, Nina Starr had a career goal. Her father and uncle were practicing physicians, and the world of medical interests and contacts was her environment. It seemed natural for her to go into medicine.

But what prompted Nina to choose, of all branches of surgery, one of the newest, most difficult and challenging? Medicine, she explains, is like writing. While there are magazines, novels and newspapers, all writers are usually lumped together. It is only when one is in the field of writing that one recognizes the differences in mediums.

After completing high school, Nina Starr enrolled in college. After graduation, she went on to medical school at New York University. After meeting a fellow medical student, Eugene Braunwald, the pattern of both her professional and future personal life was quickly established. Their dating was no conventional round of youthful pleasures and activities. Instead of going to movies, the theater or dinner, they studied together, helped each other and just enjoyed being together. They were married in 1952.

Later the Doctors Braunwald successfully intermingled their personal and professional lives. Both have been associated with the National Heart Institute at Bethesda, Maryland—Nina in heart surgery and Eugene as Chief of Cardiology (the study of the heart and its actions and diseases).

Nina began her early work in surgery at Bellevue Hospital, New York City, where she served her internship. She then joined the surgery staff of Georgetown University in Washington, D.C., where she served first as Senior Assistant Resident, then as Chief Resident of Surgery.

The following year marked the beginning of her association with the National Heart Institute, one of seven National Institutes of Health at Bethesda. At the age of 29, she became one of three full-time staff members of the Surgery Branch of the Institute, working under Dr. Andrew G. Morrow, a pioneer in the field of open-heart surgery.

Research is the major interest of the Institute, and Nina has spent considerable time in the Animal Experimental Laboratory. She has worked on several research projects; one involved a new substance to control bleeding inside the heart.

One of her most notable medical achievements was her early success, in association with two male heart surgeons, in completely replacing a patient's diseased mitral valve with an artificial device that works like a normal cardiac valve to prevent the return of blood to the auricle.

Nina does not recall the exact number of operations she performed at the Institute. She estimates that during the past few years she has averaged three operations a week. Approximately half of her patients are adults and half are small children. Because she is a woman and mother, her bedside manner makes her a great favorite with the youngsters.

Nina's achievements have been widely recognized. She is a member of the American Society for Artificial Internal Organs and a Fellow of the American College of Surgeons. She also has served as a Clinical Instructor in Surgery at the Georgetown Medical School. She has been featured in newspaper and magazine articles. In 1962 she was included in *Life* magazine's list of One Hundred Most Important Young People in the Country. That same year she received the popular Golden Plate Award from the Academy of Achievement, a nonprofit organization dedicated to the education and inspiration of youth. More honors were in store. Early in 1963, Nina was named the Woman of the Year by the Business and Professional Women's Clubs of Silver Spring, Maryland. This honor is given in recognition of achievements, character and a sense of responsibility in civic affairs and public service.

A typical busy day for the Doctors Braunwald begins at 8:30 a.m.

When not operating or engaged on research projects, Nina's crowded calendar includes frequent visits to the bedsides of her patients and working on medical papers in her office. She is so pressed for time that frequently her lunch consists of a quick sandwich at her desk.

There are days when the Doctors Braunwald, in spite of the nearness of their offices, do not see each other at work. While their hospital day is over at 5 p.m., their professional work day does not end. With new knowledge and facts emerging daily, doctors must constantly keep themselves abreast of medical information by continuing study. The Braunwalds normally bring home scientific papers to keep up with developments in their respective fields. Their homework is done after their children have gone to bed.

Nina has firm convictions about working mothers. In the case of a highly educated and trained woman, working is not only a career, it is a way of life. She feels strongly that a woman who has earned a medical degree is obligated to continue her work on behalf of society. She knows that there are many sides of life; and, in order to fulfill herself, she must arrive at a reasonable compromise between her life's work and her family.

An admirable sense of balance and maturity is evident in her provision for her children. They are not deprived of their normal family life even though mother is a heart surgeon. Their pleasant suburban home in Silver Spring, Maryland, has an atmosphere of happiness that she and her husband have created for their two girls, Karen and Denise.

How is this achieved? Nina, who admits that she does not really enjoy cooking, rises at seven and prepares breakfast for her family so they can start their day together. At home she always dresses for comfort. When she washes dishes, she wears rubber gloves to protect her surgeon's hands. As is true of other workers, surgeons feel the need for relaxation. Nina shows an artistic side to her nature by painting and sculpturing in the gardenhouse of the Braunwald home. She has had no formal training in sculpture, but believes that by studying medicine one learns so much about anatomy that sculpture is just a natural consequence. She finds it particularly relaxing to paint abstracts in oil, which satisfies her love for color.

Nina also feels a debt and responsibility to society. About three-fourths of the cost of medical training is paid by the medical school, not by the student. Many people feel there ought to be a return to society for the expensive investment supported by private and public funds. There can be no doubt that Dr. Nina Braunwald's debt to society is being repaid several times over. Frequently, the Doctors Braunwald return to their offices or to the laboratory in the evenings to keep up with their work. Besides, like most physicians, they are always on call. Even their vacations are affairs of the heart, since they generally try to include attendance at a conference on heart research.

Despite their many activities, the Braunwalds still find time for an occasional horseback ride together in the natural woodlands of Rock Creek Park or Potomac Park. Much of their home life centers around their two daughters.[2]

Dr. Nina Starr Braunwald's work is in many ways an affair of the heart. To a great extent she pursues her career as a heart surgeon for the personal fulfillment this work gives her. Nina's story illustrates the kinds of satisfactions that women and men can get from employment and life. It also suggests that a worker may have to pay a price for being successful.

Lesson in Brief

Most jobs have both positive and negative aspects for a worker. If the positive values are great enough, the job can make a major contribution to the satisfactions the person gets from life. The individual who plans his career wisely will increase his chances of getting greater satisfaction from work and from life.

---

2. Adapted from *Profiles in Success: Forty Lives of Achievement*, by Lily Jay Silver, pp. 47-53.

A person's job requires him to do certain things and, thus, to a certain extent molds him to "fit" the job. But the worker does have some control over his job. He may define the nature and meaning of his job through his ideas and attitudes toward his work. Often, he can make something important and personally satisfying out of his job by the way he approaches and carries out the work.

A janitor in a hydroelectric plant was asked to explain his job to the people attending a conference. Consider his statement carefully.

THE JANITOR WHO CARES

"I represent the janitors. We believe that a clean plant is an efficient plant. Other workers in the plant seem to like a clean plant to work in. It helps to create better working conditions. This makes it possible for them to be more efficient and produce inexpensive electric power and better flood control. We are creating a better life for the people in this area."

This man views his job in a way that might seem surprising to some people. Why does he have this positive attitude toward doing clean-up work? In part, his attitude may reflect the way his employer values his work. Personal involvement not only makes the job more satisfying but also encourages this janitor to do a better job.

When reading the following statement made by an aircraft worker, contrast how this man views his job with how the janitor looks upon his job.

THE HOLE DRILLER

"You take this here thing—I don't know what they call it. My job is to drill a few holes in a triangle shape. All I do is set my pattern on the plate and drill the holes. They tell me it fits somewhere in the wing section. Sanchez, the shop foreman, was giving me some bull about how the airplane would come apart without my holes. Well, ain't that something! Look, all I want is my $5.50 an hour. If a few holes in a triangle will do it, that's fine. If they want 'em in a square, I don't care. Just give me the pattern and I'll do what they ask, just as long as I draw my $5.50."

What interests this worker? Does his job have meaning for him? Aspirations and occupational goals influence a worker's performance on the job. A supervisor will probably promote a worker to a more complex and responsible job if his attitudes indicate he will be productive and valuable.

The following report shows another example of the attitudes some workers have toward their jobs. Consider the types of jobs that give workers some control over the work they do and how they do it.

BUCKING THE LINE

Often men who work on assembly lines dislike the mechanical monster they serve. They seek to buck the line and, in some small way, introduce variety in their jobs. They want to make their own work rhythms. One way is to build banks, that is, to accumulate a number of items they are working with. They also beat the line by working very fast. Either way lets them take a break. The most popular jobs in a plant are usually those of utilitymen, foremen and repairmen—those least resembling assembly line jobs. The utilitymen, who act as substitutes for the line men at various times, like getting an idea of the whole line, of meeting and talking with different workers and of knowing all the jobs. The difference between a job with a few operations and one with several or between a job taking 2 minutes to perform and one taking 4 might not seem like much. However, the assembly line worker attaches great importance to even very small changes in his immediate job experience.

Do workers get bored doing small repetitive tasks? Do they want to influence in some way how they go about doing their jobs? Do workers need to feel they are of value and that they can use their brains to control parts of the operation?

44

Lesson in Brief

A person is able to influence and control his job to some degree by his attitudes and behavior. The 3 case studies in this lesson reflect various attitudes that workers have toward their jobs. Workers' attitudes affect how enthusiastic they are about their work and how well they perform their jobs.

"A Sure Sense of His Own Usefulness"   8

At the close of his 1967 Manpower Report, the late President Johnson said that one of the most important national goals is to offer every citizen "a sure sense of his own usefulness." Do all workers feel useful and get satisfaction from their jobs? Do professionals and highly skilled workers get more satisfaction from their jobs than unskilled workers, or is it the other way around? How do workers rate various factors concerning their jobs?

Whether a job provides a means for finding a sure sense of one's own usefulness depends upon what happens in the work place. The types of experiences encountered in the world of work are related to the changing technology, resources and institutions. (These terms are explained thoroughly in Unit Two.) This lesson raises basic questions about the meaningfulness of work that men and women perform and is concerned about what, if anything, work adds to the dignity of man. Increasingly, Americans are talking about changing the ways to use resources (especially human resources) and technology to produce the nation's output of goods and services. Americans are calling for improvements in institutions in order to create a world of work in which all the needs of man will be considered.

Table 1.1 is based on a national sampling of 2,460 normal, stable American workers and gives a summary of their personal attitudes and evaluations regarding their jobs. Professionals and technicians (such as doctors, lawyers, accountants and engineers) hold high prestige jobs requiring considerable education and/or training. Skilled workers have specialized training for particular jobs but are not usually as highly trained as professional workers. Unskilled workers are assigned relatively simple tasks which do not require specific training. Each person, however, brings different needs and different skills and abilities to the job.

The information given in Table 1.1 suggests that some workers probably have more control over their jobs—they plan what to do, supervise others and decide how to do the work. Having control over one's job may determine how satisfied one is with the job. Unskilled workers are less satisfied with their jobs than professional and technical workers.

Certain working conditions seem to be more important to some workers than to others. Studies have been made of factors which seem important to different groups of workers.

Table 1.1
RELATIONSHIP BETWEEN OCCUPATIONAL GROUPS
AND JOB ATTITUDES AMONG EMPLOYED MEN

How Workers Rated Themselves	Professionals & Technicians %	Skilled Workers %	Unskilled Workers %
OVERALL JOB SATISFACTION			
Very Satisfied	42%	22%	13%
Satisfied	41	54	52
Neutral	11	16	19
Dissatisfied	3	7	16
REPORT OF WORK PROBLEMS			
Had problems	36	25	21
Had no problems	64	75	78
FEELINGS TOWARD OWN PERFORMANCE ON THE JOB			
Very good	37	24	17
Little better than average	46	45	31
Just average or not very good	13	29	38

Source: G. Gurin, et al., *Americans View Their Mental Health*, p. 163.

Note: Data are excerpted from a larger table; therefore, percentages do not total 100 in all cases.

Table 1.2 gives the results of studies made of 325 women factory workers, 100 men and women department store employees and 150 miscellaneous men and women workers.

Table 1.2
IMPORTANCE OF CERTAIN FACTORS
TO DIFFERENT GROUPS OF WORKERS

Factors	Factory Workers (women)	Department Store Workers	Miscellaneous Workers	Average (combined data from 3 studies)
Steady work	1	2	2	1
Comfortable working conditions	2	8	8	7-8
Good working companions	3	7	7	6
Good boss	4	5	5	4
Opportunity for advancement	5	1	1	2
High pay	6	6	6	7-8
Opportunity to use own ideas	7	3	3-4	3
Opportunity to learn a job	8	4	3-4	5
Good hours	9	9	9	9
Easy work	10	10	10	10

Source: Norman Maier, *Psychology in Industry*, pp. 472-473.
Note: Each worker was asked to rank these different job factors "1,2,3...10" on the basis of how important he judged each to be.

Note the following implications of the information in Table 1.2:

1. Steady work is important for all groups, perhaps because it helps satisfy the need for economic security.
2. Good hours and easy work, on the other hand, are relatively unimportant suggesting that workers do not

insist on having everything arranged to suit their personal convenience.

3. Employees are willing to do a good day's work. However, in return, they want fair treatment, security and a reasonable opportunity to improve themselves.
4. Women more than men seem to value comfortable working conditions and pleasant working companions.
5. Many factors vary in importance among workers, depending upon the type of work and work situation.

Other studies show that union members often feel that fair adjustment of grievances and better safety standards are highly important. Nonunion members rank these factors somewhat lower.

Lesson in Brief

Some people are more satisfied in their work situations than others. Workers in the same type of job get different kinds and amounts of satisfaction, in part because they rank their needs differently. Research studies show that professional and technical workers feel more satisfied with their jobs, while the unskilled feel they have fewer problems. Workers who have a greater chance to use their own skills and initiative seem to be happier about their job performance. Finally, steady work and opportunity for advancement seem more important than high pay.

Since good health—both physical and mental—ranks high as a life goal for most Americans, mental health is important to workers, their families and their communities. What is meant by mental health? How does a person's job affect his mental health? What problems are created for workers in today's industrial society?

Workers know they are likely to enjoy better physical health if the work place meets proper standards of safety, lighting, temperature, ventilation and other environmental factors. But what factors influence mental health?

Good mental health for an individual requires a realistic belief in himself and in what he is doing. He needs the feeling that his life has meaning and purpose. By accepting himself (including his limitations) and by confronting and solving his problems as best he can, the individual will maintain good mental health.

A person is mentally healthy when he has the ability to handle emotions and problems that arise in the real world. All people have ups and downs, the blues, moments when they want to strike out at others, or times when they may feel unwanted and lonely. The difference between the mentally healthy and unhealthy person is that the healthy one usually snaps out of periods of blues and frustration quickly without special help or treatment.

To adapt to change and to direct aggressive energy into creative and constructive outlets are two signs of good mental health. The state of an individual's mental health depends on his total personality and character in the setting of his total environment.

Certain conditions, activities and situations promote good mental health, while others cause poor mental health. Individuals, too, react differently to various circumstances. One man's meat is another man's poison.

Let's consider how certain aspects of a job and the work situation can affect an individual's mental health. Table 1.3 presents some data about skills, age and the mental health of workers. The data reveal, for example, that over half (58%) of the young skilled workers have good mental health, while only 1 out of 10 (10%) young workers doing repetitive, semiskilled jobs was judged by psychologists to have good mental health.

	Table 1.3	
	MENTAL HEALTH OF FACTORY WORKERS	
Skill Level	**Young Workers with Good Mental Health** %	**Middle-Aged Workers with Good Mental Health** %
Skilled Workers ⎫		56%
High Semiskilled ⎬	58%	41
Ordinary Semiskilled	35	38
Repetitive Semiskilled[a]	10	26

Source: Arthur Kornhauser, *Mental Health of the Industrial Worker, A Detroit Study*, p. 85.

Note: This study was based on men working in automotive companies.

[a]Pace of these jobs is closely tied to the demands made by machines.

The data in Table 1.3 suggest there is a relationship between skill level and mental health. Does this conclusion apply equally to both age groups?

Studies done by psychologists have shown that the mental health of workers is better if their jobs provide opportunities for them to use their abilities, to feel they are performing worthwhile functions, to find interest in their work, to feel they are competent human beings and to gain a sense of accomplishment and self-respect. In other words, workers will have better mental health if various psychological needs are satisfied by their jobs. Certain aspects of some jobs, however, often make it difficult for the worker to satisfy his needs. And individuals respond differently to the various pressures encountered on the job. Often in a particular work situation, one worker will lose control of his emotions while another will deal with the same problem in an effective manner.

What problems are created for workers by the conditions of an industrial society? The following case shows how work-related problems affect the lives of the worker, his family and his fellow workers.

HANK, THE HUNG-UP WORKER

After graduation from high school, Hank was employed by XYZ Company as a clerical worker in the office. During the next several years he did satisfactory work. At the end of this time he was promoted to the position of bookkeeper. Shortly after beginning work as a bookkeeper in the accounting department he got married. During the next few years, Hank's family responsibilities increased until his salary was no longer adequate to maintain the standard of living that he and his wife wanted. Hank requested a salary increase from his department supervisor and was told that he was receiving as much as a bookkeeper was worth. The supervisor told Hank that the only way he could hope to receive more money was to qualify himself for a higher-rated job. He advised Hank to enroll in an accounting course in a local night school.

Hank had no formal training since high school. His academic work in school had been only average. However, he did enroll for the accounting course. Within a few months, he began to have trouble with his school work. His behavior in the office and at home began to change. At the office he talked loud and long to fellow workers about how the accountants deliberately made work difficult for the book-keepers by insisting upon certain accounting procedures. Hank's behavior at home was also different. Formerly, he had taken interest in his family and enjoyed being with them. He now became unfriendly toward his family and spent much of his spare time away from home.

Instead of working on his lessons for night school, Hank began spending a great deal of time hanging around a local beer joint. He drank a lot and planned various schemes to get a job that would make him rich. However, he made no effort to carry out any of these get-rich-quick schemes.

Hank's case is not as unusual as one might think. Studies have documented the plight of thousands of workers who face similar difficulties in their careers. What can society do to help these unhappy and frustrated workers?

Lesson in Brief

Good mental health is an important goal for all members of society. Studies by psychologists and sociologists show that a worker's mental health is influenced by his job and work situation. Workers enjoy better physical health when they have proper ventilation, heating, lighting and safety standards on the job. They also enjoy better mental health when the job provides them with opportunities to satisfy their needs for interesting and worthwhile work activity.

Ah, but a man's reach should exceed his grasp,
Or what's a heaven for?

Robert Browning

Aspirations are the hopes and dreams of men and women. They are
the goals people set, what they want from life and what they strive
to achieve. What are the forces that determine goals and aspiration
levels? How do aspirations develop and change? How do notions of
success and failure depend on values and goals?

Along with ability and action, aspiration and achievement are
requirements for success. This lesson explores the first A—
aspiration—which must be combined with ability and action to
produce achievement. Aspiration includes not only what a person
says he wants to accomplish but also his determination to work
toward his goals.

What factors affect the goals people set? Some of the
things that influence an individual's goals are his past achievements, experiences that were successful, interests, abilities, unique
personal needs, parents' attitudes, peer pressures (standards set by
friends and members of one's age group) and the economic and
social group to which he belongs.

Consider the following advice: *Aim at the sun. You may
not reach it, but your arrow will fly higher than if aimed at
an object on a level with yourself.* How high are an individual's
goals? How does he view his own aspirations? Does he have real
enthusiasm? Is he satisfied with things as they are? If changes are
needed, does he make the effort to bring them about? Do his
interests change as he explores and learns new things about himself
and others? Once he has achieved some goals, does he set others?
Is life exciting because of his different experiences and accomplishments?

Through his job, a worker may fulfill various hopes and
aspirations. Jobs provide the opportunity to be creative and
original, to use special abilities and talents, to help others, to deal
with people rather than things, to work with things rather than

people, to enjoy feelings of status and prestige, to earn a great deal of money and to assure a stable, secure future.

Studies have shown that people's aspirations can be raised by exposing them to new experiences which help broaden their values, motives and attitudes. Upward Bound, a government Economic Opportunity program aimed at raising the aspirations of disadvantaged youth, is an example of this type of experience.

Everyone encounters stumbling blocks that make it harder to reach goals. Success breeds success, but sometimes failures may cause one to work harder. The following examples show that continued effort and action, not ability alone, are required to achieve success:

- —Pierre and Marie Curie performed 5,677 experiments in the discovery of radium (a white metallic element used in the treatment of cancer).
- —James Watt worked 20 years on his steam engine.
- —It took George Stephenson 15 years to perfect his railroad locomotive.
- —Noah Webster labored on his dictionary for 36 years.
- —William Harvey worked day and night for 8 years determining how blood circulates before publishing his findings.
- —Charles Goodyear endured unbelievable hardships for 11 years in order to perfect his rubber-making process.
- —Cyrus W. Field experienced one disheartening failure after another in his attempt to lay a telephone cable across the Atlantic; however, he kept trying and finally succeeded.
- —Thomas Edison reported that only one of his inventions, the phonograph, came accidentally. The others were the result of repeated experiments and everlasting effort. For example, Edison and his staff worked 10 years on the electric storage battery, making more than 10,000 experiments before the results seemed encouraging.

Some people believe that the formula for success is 1 part inspiration and 9 parts perspiration. Is this formula accurate? Where does aspiration fit in?

Lesson in Brief

We've considered the importance of aspiration in achieving success and noted some of the ways aspirations are formed and how they change. To think about personal goals and how they might be achieved through work is well worth the effort.

"I'm a—Physical, Social, Psychological—Person"

> For purposes of career planning, a young person should look at himself as the end product of his biological-social-psychological situation. By identifying the physical, social and psychological parts of his make-up—and seeing how these develop over a period of time—he can gain valuable insights. For example, he can learn what particular characteristics he brings to a job and how certain jobs may affect him.

Some of the interesting theories and explanations to explain the many sides of man suggest that a person's physical or biological body contains characteristics inherited from his parents and ancestors on both sides of the family. When these traits combine, the resulting individual is unique, not a carbon copy! The individual then grows and develops using air, food, drink and activity and has physical characteristics including health, strength and manual dexterity (the ability to use one's hands).

An individual's social being is influenced by his surroundings and experiences with all people with whom he comes in contact. Social characteristics include communication skills, ability to get along with other people, poise and confidence.

Psychological characteristics are influenced by the physical body and social experiences. Each individual has a distinct personality and character with unique attitudes, values and feelings. He sets his own goals and works toward them.

Physical development takes time as people grow from helpless babies to mature adults. Their psychological-social development also takes place over many years. Let's consider how and when the various psychological-social characteristics are acquired.

1. Sense of trust—results from receiving love and protection and from having one's needs met. Example: loving care from parents. Birth to 1 year.
2. Sense of autonomy—results from the development of one's own separate and distinct personality. Example: "I want to do it myself!" 1 to 4 years.

3. Sense of initiative—results from the vigorous testing of reality. Example: "Is it true? Let me try it!" 4 to 5 years.
4. Sense of duty and accomplishment—comes from taking on real tasks and either accomplishing them or learning from mistakes. 6 to 11 years.
5. Sense of identity—develops as one's self-concept emerges. Example: "I am friendly and reliable." "I am insecure and ineffective." 12 to 15 years.
6. Sense of intimacy—results from the ability to establish close personal relationships with members of both sexes. Examples: friends, a marriage partner. 15 years to adulthood.
7. Parental sense—comes from providing love, training, material things and security for one's children. Being able to earn a good income from employment is important. Adulthood.
8. Sense of integrity—results from the establishment of one's own values and unique personality, the ability to deal with life and people. Adulthood.

An individual is fulfilled as a human being in the sense that he develops as fully as possible his physical, psychological and social capabilities. Knowing the stages of psychological-social development can help a person deal with his problems, recognize his current level of development and move on to the next stage of personal development.

Each person seems to develop and fulfill himself best when he has a purpose to his life. By striving to accomplish something, he becomes somebody. Work is one activity that provides this sense of purpose by allowing the worker to test his ideas and skills and achieve some of his goals. With purpose and enthusiasm, he can face new challenges. It takes a long time to develop the various biological-psychological-social characteristics and skills, and even these change with time. Growth, development and new challenges can create a new individual from the old.

We have analyzed the 3 separate parts (psychological, physical and social) of the individual. Now let's put him together again and consider the whole person. This is one meaning of the term personal integrity. It is important to view the individual as a total person because, when employed, he brings to the job his whole personality—all his social, psychological and physical characteristics. Undoubtedly, he wants to be himself on the job, just as he does away from the job. However, he may have to put up with conditions and do things on the job that make him unhappy and frustrated. Often, the job may force him to pretend to be somebody he really is not.

An important question to consider is whether the job will help develop one's human potential? What if a person brings physical strength and vigorous energy to a job that requires him to sit at a desk all day? What effect will this have on his personality? If an individual likes to compete and be a leader, will he be satisfied following detailed instructions and conforming to the demands of an assembly line? How will he react? If an individual does not have an opportunity to talk to people while he is working, how will this affect him away from the job? Heat, foul air and loud noises on the job bother some people. Should men and women spend their lives working on a job that clashes with their personal characteristics?

Some specific types of physical, psychological and social conditions which can have good and bad effects on work satisfaction are:

—Adequate light (physical)
—The opportunity to work at one's own speed (physical and psychological)
—Friendly fellow workers (social)

—Very loud noise (physical)
—Supervisors who constantly check one's work (psychological)
—Fellow workers who gripe continuously (social)

If a person does not have a job in harmony with his total self, he is unlikely to be happy, successful or even healthy. Jobs that do not make enough demands on people's talents are just as likely to cause unhappiness as are those jobs that require more than workers are capable of providing. Each worker needs to ask: Am I getting the full rewards of work? Or am I being short-changed?

Lesson in Brief

Men and women bring to jobs what they have gained through their total life experience—their biological, psychological and social development. Physical, social and psychological factors continue to influence people both on and off the job. The way these factors affect them will determine not only the satisfaction or disappointment a job brings but also the kind of people they are becoming.

Work: Test Site of Human Relations   12

Work in modern society usually involves group activity. In a predominantly service-producing economy, a worker's ability to get along with his employer, fellow employees, clients or customers is extremely important. The work place is becoming a test site for the worker's communication and group relations skills. Success in the manpower market, now and in the future, will to a large extent depend on these human relations skills.

Why has work become a group activity? One basic reason is the high degree of specialization and division of labor in the economy. No longer does one worker alone produce all the food and other items that his family needs. Instead, he helps produce a limited range of goods and services or only one small part of a single good or service and *depends on others* to provide the rest of the goods and services necessary for consumption. What happens when a worker fails to do his part of the job? The cost to the individual and to the group can be high—for example, work interruptions on an assembly line, reduced output, defective goods.

This interdependent relationship among workers suggests that an individual must be able to cooperate with other people in the work place. He must have social skills. What are some of these human relations skills? Included are the abilities to get along with people, to accomplish group goals, to communicate with others by having understanding and compassion. Possessing social skills is almost a must to get and keep a job. Industrial relations studies show that more people lose their jobs because they cannot get along with co-workers and employers than for any other reason.

Since work today involves group activity, it can satisfy some of the social needs for interpersonal relations. For reasons of increased productivity as well as noneconomic rewards such as enjoyment based on association with fellow workers, social skills are necessary on the job.

The increasing social nature of work in a modern economy is reflected in the manpower market. Interpersonal relationships are a very important part of the work in many of the occupations and industries where employment is growing the fastest. For example, technicians must communicate effectively with the scientists and other professional people with whom they work. Nurses should have agreeable relationships with their patients. A helpful relationship between salesman and customer is crucial in retail trade. There is a strong trend for more workers to be employed in the production of services than in the production of goods. Jobs in service-producing industries usually require more social skill on the part of the worker than employment in the goods-producing sector of the economy.

Certain personality and character traits help maintain good interpersonal relations on the job. There are people who think that work today is so social in nature that the worker must be "one of the herd" to get along with co-workers. In some specific occupations, such as the ones mentioned above, social skills are extremely important for success.

The observation that work is social in nature and a potential source of need satisfaction for the individual is supported by evidence gathered by industrial psychologists and sociologists. What does the following actual case study reveal about the social aspects of work?

WAITING AT THE GATE

At a firm which retires its women employees at age 55, many of the retired workers may be seen standing by the factory gates every evening waiting for their friends to get off work. These retired women continue to attend social events held by the firm. When part-time work is available, they are always ready and willing to work. These women look upon the factory as a social center.

Another way to illustrate the social nature of work is to show that worker morale is not totally dependent upon the physical conditions of the job. In fact, as the following case shows, the social aspects of the job are much more important to the workers than are the physical conditions in the plant.

HAPPY WORKERS IN THE SLAUGHTERHOUSE

In a slaughterhouse where pigs were killed, there was a small room in which the internal organs were sorted and washed prior to using them for other purposes. The room was below ground level, poorly lighted, cold and damp. Its floors were covered with waste which smelled extremely unpleasant to an outsider. It was a perfect example of a work place environment that most people think they would not want.

Yet, in these surroundings, six cheerful women worked laughing and singing throughout the day. A new company doctor visited this room and was shocked by the surroundings. He immediately recommended that the women be replaced by men and transferred to other departments. But this well-meaning recommendation brought such protest from the women that it was withdrawn. They wanted to know what was wrong with the way they were doing their work. If management was not satisfied with their work, why not say so and give the women a chance to do something about it?

These employees made a happy work team and liked each other. They believed that they were doing a good job, and they had a supervisor who let them work at their own speed and gave them a lot of praise.

The 2 cases illustrate the social nature of work and show how the job can be a source of personal need satisfaction.

The next case summarizes a famous study made in the late 1920s. It reveals another dimension of the social nature of work.

THE HAWTHORNE EXPERIMENT

The Hawthorne plant of the Western Electric Company near Chicago, Illinois, was the site of a famous industrial psychology experiment. The purpose of the experiment was to see what effect changes in wages, hours and working conditions have on worker productivity (their efficiency in assembling telephone parts). Six girls (regular employees of the company) whose jobs involved putting together small telephone parts were the subjects of the experiment. For five years they worked under the observation of a scientist, doing their regular job completely isolated from the rest of the plant. At first, for about two months, they worked a 48-hour week, including Saturday, and turned out 2,400 parts. Then for weeks at a time, the conditions of the job—the hours, working conditions, methods of payment—were changed many times. Each time a change occurred, the output of the girls was carefully recorded to see how the new situation affected their productivity.

At the end of the five years, the girls had turned out hundreds of thousands of parts, and the psychologists had discovered some important facts. When the girls were put on a piecework basis, their output rose. This was logical, for their pay went up accordingly. When they were given coffee breaks in the morning and afternoon, their output went up again. That made sense because they went back to work rested and refreshed. When coffee breaks were made longer, output continued to rise. Now the psychologists began to be puzzled. They cut the working day to 7 hours, the week to 40 hours, then to 35. And each time the weekly output was higher than ever! Had something gone wrong? What kept pushing the output up, above 2,400 units, no matter how many changes were made in hours, wages and working conditions?

The researchers decided to start over again from the beginning. For three months the girls worked their original 48-hour week—no piecework, no coffee breaks, no Saturday holiday. And they turned out 3,000 parts each week, a record for the company! The psychologists were now really puzzled. It took months to discover the explanation of the amazing production record of the girls. What was the answer?

Because the girls were a work team whose activities were being studied by outside experts, they sensed how important the experiment was to the psychologists and the key part they themselves played. No matter what the hours, pay or working conditions, they tried to do their best. Over the five years of the experiment, the girls consistently improved their productivity in their desire to please the psychologists and show how capable and cooperative they were!

Ever since this experiment, scientists conducting social research have been aware of the so-called Hawthorne Effect—that is, the outcome of an experiment involving human subjects is likely to be influenced by the fact that the people are aware of their participation in an experiment and, therefore, may change their behavior simply because it is being studied!

Lesson in Brief

Work in a modern economy is social in nature and may fulfill many social needs a person has, such as the need for interpersonal relationships. Social skills like personal communication and group relations are increasingly important in a service-producing economy. Work places are becoming human relations test grounds. Workers whose social skills measure up to the demand of the changing manpower market will probably achieve the greatest success and personal satisfaction.

Reason, justice and fair treatment do not always exist in the work place. Employers, supervisors and fellow workers—like men and women everywhere—may behave in unreasonable and even inexcusable ways. People do not always think, feel or behave rationally toward their jobs, fellow workers or employers. Knowing what to expect in the world of work improves the individual's ability to deal with difficult, on-the-job situations.

Do reason, justice and virtue always triumph in the work place? Do the good guys win over the bad guys? Do the most deserving workers always get the highest pay and the quickest promotions? Unfortunately, the answer is no. Often the decisions and behavior of fellow workers, supervisors and employers reflect such factors as anger, group morale, envy, favoritism, prejudice and even hatred. In addition, it may not always be easy to identify what is reasonable and just in the work place as the following cases illustrate.

THE GLEE CLUB

In an automobile plant, a group of workers sang while they worked on the assembly line. They were led by a big, middle-aged man with a booming bass voice. The men would work in silence for awhile, then their leader would sound the first note, and they would sing in rhythm to the repetitive motions of the line.

When a new plant manager was appointed, the outgoing manager oriented his replacement in a routine manner. He explained the organizational chart, the policies and the procedures. He did not mention the singing since it was not in management's official procedures or policies.

The new manager had hardly moved into his office when the singing started. He called in his assistant and demanded an explanation. The assistant told him that the men like to sing while they work. The manager replied, "We're running a factory, not a glee club! The men are here to work! Stop the singing at once!" The order was sent out to the assembly line and the singing stopped. With what result? Never again did the assembly line attain the level of production it had made in the glee club period. Somehow, even though the men were doing nothing but work, not as much work got done.

WHO CARES ABOUT TEST SCORES?

A young personnel assistant carefully administered tests to several applicants for an important secretarial position in the office. He also gathered data about the prospective employees' educational background, training, work experience and references. Combining the test scores with the background information, he eliminated all but two young women.

The serious-minded personnel assistant then assembled all of the test scores, applications and letters of reference and took them to the personnel director. He told the director that two women seemed equally qualified for the position. He asked the director for an evaluation of the applications, to which the director replied: "Who cares about test scores and application forms. Hire the one with the prettiest legs."

Many people may feel that the plant manager and personnel director in these 2 cases acted in an irrational and unjust manner. Good supervisors try to find ways to assure rational treatment and justice for their workers whom they regard as human beings and not merely factors of production. But is it always easy to decide what is fair and reasonable in the work place? Consider the whole range of feelings, ideas and behavior that people have on the job. The following cases involve differences in opinions about what is reasonable and just.

POLITICS ON THE JOB

Alex Smith was a maintenance man with a very good work record. One day, a witness before a U.S. Congressional committee charged that Smith had once been an active member of the Communist Party. Soon after Smith appeared before the committee and pleaded the Fifth Amendment, he was fired by his employer. The company maintained that Smith's presence on the job caused disharmony among employees, many of whom refused to work with him.

Smith protested his firing. He said that his refusal to testify before a Congressional committee was none of the company's business. He had a very good work record and had done nothing on the job to justify his being fired. The resentment against him by some of the employees was not his doing. Smith maintained that he had a right to plead the Fifth Amendment under the Constitution of the United States. Even if that made him unpopular, it was not a good enough reason to get rid of him. He said that his employer should judge him on his work ability and not his political views.

Consider, however, that publicity about an employee's political activities and ideas may create real problems for the employer. Was the employer justified?

THE RIGHTS OF SENIORITY

Being shorthanded one day, the plant foreman asked Roosevelt Brown, who had been with the firm for several years, to take on some extra duties—marking and packing some boxes. The work was outside Brown's regular and usual duties, but would take only about an hour and a quarter.

Brown refused to do the extra duties. He said that it was company practice to give such menial labor to newer employees, not old-timers like himself with many years on the job. The management had gotten similar refusals from other workers. This time they decided to make an issue out of Brown's questioning of what they felt was their right to assign work. In arbitration proceedings (a method of settling disputes involving a third party) that followed, the company argued that there were not any job descriptions in the plant. Therefore, Brown could not claim any violation of company policy when he was given any kind of work. Management pointed out that the plant-wide seniority system applied only to layoffs and recalls. The company admitted it usually assigned newer employees to do the type of work that Brown refused to do. However, this practice was not a rigid policy. The company argued that management had to be flexible in assigning jobs in order to keep the men working efficiently.

Brown maintained that other workers had refused such menial assignments before. He had a right to do the same. Brown also emphasized his long period of service to the firm and argued that the foreman should assign newer workers to do the menial chores.

Is it reasonable for an employee to be allowed to refuse menial work assignments on grounds of his seniority? This is the type of situation which may arise in the world of work. As we shall discuss later, conflicts of this type are sometimes resolved through use of grievance procedures set up by labor unions and management.

THE BEST MAN FOR THE JOB

Last month, Lee Chan completed his 15th year of loyal service to the Ace Products Manufacturing Company. He is a hard worker, never misses a day from the job, helps new employees get settled in their work. Rather on the quiet side, Lee is known and respected by everyone as a good, reliable man. Pete Gonzales came to work for the company several months ago and was assigned to Lee's department. Pete is likeable, a good bowler on the department's team, but something of a goof-off. He can be counted on for an amusing story of why he missed a day's work. He lets Lee help the new men learn their jobs while he entertains them with his endless supply of jokes. Everybody likes Pete, including the boss, who is also a member of the department bowling team.

An opportunity opens up for a new supervisor's job, and the boss has to pick the best-qualified man for the job.

Who gets picked, Lee or Pete? The way this decision is actually made will reveal something about reason and justice in the work place.

Lesson in Brief

Injustice does exist in the work place. The ideas, attitudes, values and behavior of workers and employers reflect irrational responses to the work place and the job. It is not always easy to know what is appropriate and fair in each work situation. Men and women who come to their jobs knowing they will find some irrationality and injustice may be better able to deal with the situation.

Man Is More Than a Means of Production

14

Man is not only the end, but also the means of production. Out of his dual capacity arises a conflict between his activities as a producer and his interests as a man—a clash between life and work.

Sumner Slichter

Man is constantly making value judgments about what is good and what is bad in the work place and in other areas of his life. Conflicts of values arise within oneself, with other individuals and with institutions. These conflicts exist because each individual has his own values which differ somewhat from the values of others. Only the individual can decide which values he will hold and how he will rank them. The satisfaction a person receives from his work will be closely tied to his ability to resolve value conflicts that arise in the work place.

What are the causes of value conflicts that exist in the work place and society? Previous lessons discussed the basic needs of man as well as differences in needs among individuals. For example, all humans need food and water, but the amount of creative expression each person needs varies. This difference in needs among individuals may create value conflicts. Also, because different human needs can be fulfilled in various ways (even the same need can be fulfilled in many ways), conflicts in values arise.

An example of a conflict in values that might exist because of the individual's different needs involves security and personal integrity. In order to satisfy a need for economic security, a person may adopt the practice of playing it safe—not getting involved in anything controversial. However, playing it safe may clash with his value of standing up for what he believes (personal integrity).

Value conflicts also arise because a person performs many different roles (often at the same time) during his life. The individual is many different things to various people. Some of these roles are economic in nature—worker, consumer, citizen. Other roles are social—student, husband, wife, father, mother, son, sister, community volunteer worker, homemaker.

70

Traditionally, American society has emphasized that the worker is important because he is a valuable resource that helps produce goods and services. But can a worker fulfill his needs as a unique human being if he is viewed by others as a means of production? A society which views work primarily in terms of output—how much is produced and how efficiently—is likely to create value conflicts. Why? Because many people are primarily concerned with work from a personal standpoint. Workers want a pleasant and satisfying life doing interesting and worthwhile things. They want more than high wages, job security and fringe benefits. But what happens to the worker's nonmonetary needs if jobs are designed to maximize output and profits rather than satisfy the needs of the worker? Conflicts of values occur!

Let's examine the 3 kinds of value conflicts a worker may have to deal with.

Conflicts arise within the individual. What a person has to do to be successful on the job may conflict with his other values. To climb the ladder of success, an individual may feel that he has to take advantage of his fellow workers while at the same time try to be a practicing Christian. What he values as a husband and father may clash with what he values as a worker. If a person wants to get ahead on his job, he may have to work long hours leaving very little time to spend with his family. A young mother who is offered employment may feel torn between working (to satisfy financial need or her desire for expression and professional activity) or staying home to care for her children. Will the children receive adequate care while she is gone? Will the income she earns contribute more to her family's well-being than being a full-time mother and housewife?

Conflicts develop among workers in their interpersonal relations. Differences in attitudes about smoking cigars on the job may lead to conflict. Boris refuses to stop smoking cigars in the office even though it makes Julie and the other people in the office ill. Naomi is energetic and productive although her co-workers do as little as possible. As a result, some hard glances and unfriendly comments come her way. In this situation, what should she do? Please the easy-going group or be her own person?

Can a worker get fired for being too efficient? Impossible? Let's read the following true case study.

HARRY, THE GO-GETTER

Harry went to work as an auto mechanic in a downtown garage. After a few days, the boss told him he liked his work and hoped he would be working there a long time. However, when Harry went to get his first pay check, he was told that he was fired! Why? His boss said that he was so energetic and ambitious that the other employees around the garage seemed slow in comparison. Harry's energetic work routine made the others so angry and upset they complained to the boss. The boss told Harry that obviously he could not fire everybody else. So he had to fire Harry!

Conflicts arise when the values of the individual worker differ from the values of the organization. A worker may believe that honesty is the best policy and never consider cheating or being dishonest. His organization's values may be somewhat different. Suppose the boss directs Alice to falsify some office records in order to reduce the amount of tax to be paid. Whose values should she follow—hers or the organization's?

Lesson in Brief

Values are ideas about what is good and bad, right and wrong. Value conflicts arise in the work place. These conflicts occur because individuals have different needs and different ways of fulfilling needs and also because they have many roles to perform in their lives. Conflicts of values arise within oneself, among co-workers, and between the worker and the organization. Each individual must decide what values he will live and work by and what costs he is willing to bear for choosing certain values. In the world of values, as in the world of economics, there is no such thing as a free lunch.

If a man does not keep pace with his companions, perhaps it is because he hears a different drummer.

Henry David Thoreau

Many Americans believe that success is a very important goal worth striving for. What is success? Is it money, power, social status? Or is it something entirely different? How is success achieved? What is the price some people pay for success? Answers to these questions can help an individual establish goals and values and also aid him in understanding the behavior of other people.

Success is a goal that is sought by many Americans. It has been called the great American dream. But what is success?

In one view, success is the proper *ambition* that almost all parents have for their children. It has been called the national vice and the national virtue of Americans. The desire for success spurs personal activity, drives industry, fosters intellectual and moral change. It provides the individual with incentive and the nation with drive. It makes people both active and restless, hard working and overworked, generous and greedy.

Politicians identify success with *power*. Public relations men see success as *fame*. Teachers and ministers rate themselves successful when they *influence* the minds and characters of others. Creative men strive for *self-actualization*. Humanitarians equate success with *service*, reformers with bringing about *improvements in society*. The concept of success which appeals to many Americans is *making money* and enjoying the highest possible standard of living. For a large number of people, success is *contentment* and *happiness*.

Each of these definitions has merit. Success in life begins by determining one's own significance and deciding what is truly important. A person must examine his values and specific goals in order to define success for himself.

Money and success are linked together in the minds of some Americans. Who are considered great Americans? Names like George Washington, Thomas Edison, Abraham Lincoln, Henry Ford, Eleanor Roosevelt, John D. Rockefeller, Helen Keller,

Andrew Carnegie and Martin Luther King immediately come to mind. While America's heroes have been active in every field from politics to education, a large number have achieved fame and fortune in business. Many Americans believe that any man can achieve fortune through hard work and wise use of his money. The office boy who becomes the head of a great business firm making millions of dollars in the process is one example.

The importance many people attach to money can be demonstrated by some of the following ideas and attitudes:

Money talks. If you're so darn smart, why aren't you rich? Money isn't everything, but it's way ahead of whatever's in second place. He's as sound as a dollar. Money isn't everything, but it helps. You can't live on good will. Money may not buy happiness, but it sure prevents a lot of misery.

The role that money plays in the individual's definition of success is important because money-getting and money-spending will have a deep impact on his life. Money determines the standard of living he can maintain. The income and wealth he possesses are likely to influence his status in the community. Even his personal feeling of self-worth may be affected by the amount of money he earns.

Defining success is one thing. Achieving it is something else. Is it true, as some psychologists and sociologists have said, that to be a success an individual has to "market" or "sell" himself—to shape his identity in order to become a package that is demanded in the manpower market? Are work and life a stage on which men and women merely play roles? In a race to achieve financial success and the status, prestige and power that go with it, does man lose sight of what is really important? Does he lose control of his own life?

We have suggested that many Americans think of success as a good and worthy goal. Status, prestige and power are the rewards Americans give the successful—especially those who are financially successful. Though people tend to identify success with making money, there certainly are other definitions. Concern with financial success, whether or not it is achieved, may affect many areas of life since money often serves as a measuring stick for society to judge and evaluate the worth of a person. In hot pursuit of success, an individual can lose sight of some of the more important things in life and become different from the person he intended to be. But, recalling this lesson's opening quotation, if a person does march to the beat of a different drummer, he undoubtedly will discover there is no such thing as a free lunch. Although he is not forced to pursue the goal of high income and great wealth, the cost of pursuing nonmonetary values may include both material sacrifice and a certain loneliness that results from not keeping pace with one's companions.

Serious questions may be raised about some of the traditional goals and values of the American people. Whether or not one personally accepts these values, these are the kinds of questions that should be discussed in an open society.

Lesson in Brief

Success can be defined in various ways. Many Americans identify it with money and material possessions. Often this concern with financial success influences their outlook and values. The way an individual defines success will have a significant effect on his life.

UNIT TWO

The Economic World:
An Important Part
of Our Social Environment

The 2 oldest and most basic functions of work are economic in nature: (1) to help produce goods and services, and (2) to earn an income. Because the world of work is part of the economic world, workers and future workers need to learn how the economic system operates. Another reason for studying economics is that it is a useful way of approaching an understanding of any social system, such as the world of work.

Many of the "big ideas" of economics, once learned, can be readily transferred to a study of the world of work. For example, it is generally agreed that economics is the study of the interaction of resources (productive inputs such as manpower and capital), technology (knowledge of how to make and use tools) and institutions (established patterns of social behavior). Certain techniques or tools of thinking—theory, statistics and history—are necessary to understand economic problems and trends. And there are 3 basic problems facing every economic society: (1) how much employment and production there will be, (2) what kinds of goods and services to produce, and (3) how to divide the nation's income. Most people care a great deal how these problems are solved. They want the overall level of employment and production to be high and to increase steadily over the years. They want a mix of goods and services that meets the demands of consumers, business firms and government, all of whom have reasonable freedom of choice. They want equality of opportunity, economic security and a distribution of income that is fair and just.

Economists use a 5-step approach to the solution of problems. First, define the problem (using theory, statistics and history). Second, identify the goals to be achieved. Third, consider the different possible ways of solving the problem and achieving the goals. Fourth, study the probable benefits, costs and other consequences of adopting the alternative solutions. Fifth, choose the best course of action in terms of the goals to be achieved.

Economic education involves a study of all the topics mentioned above and more. World-of-work education also involves the study of the interaction of resources (especially manpower), technology (including skills) and institutions (such as the supply and demand for workers, the effect of labor unions and the various kinds of government programs to aid disadvantaged workers). Understanding the world of work requires mastery of the basic theory of production, manpower statistics and historical evolution of work and economic life. People care about such things as full employment, high production, economic growth, freedom of choice, equality of opportunity, economic security and distributive justice. These are the very same goals that individual workers want to achieve.

Men and women, pursuing their own personal goals, can benefit from the systematic way that economists study economic problems. Career planning, for example, requires the individual to define his problem (choose an occupation), establish goals (career aspirations), consider the alternative ways to achieve the goals (high school, college, apprenticeship, post-secondary technical institute), study the benefits, costs and other consequences of alternative courses of action (time, money, effort, sacrifice) and, finally, choose the best course of action (in terms of the individual's own personal goals).

The economic world is an important part of the social environment. The world of work is an important part of the economic world. To understand today's work setting—to see the forest as well as the individual trees—a knowledge of the economic system is essential. The lessons in this unit are designed to provide some of the economic literacy and social perspective required for participation in today's and tomorrow's world of work.

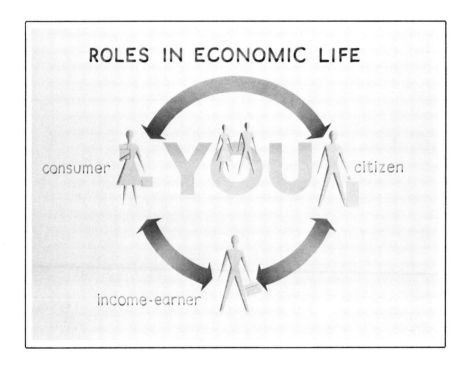

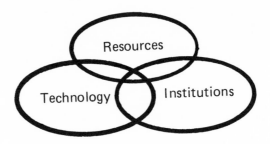

"The time has come," the Walrus said,
"To talk of many things:
Of shoes—and ships—and sealing wax—
Of cabbages—and kings. . ."

Lewis Carroll

Economics is the study of how society organizes to develop and use its productive resources (manpower, capital goods and natural resources) to satisfy human wants. Economics is concerned, therefore, with resources, with technology, with social institutions— and how these 3 sets of forces interact to determine how well off a society is in terms of the goods and services that it has.

Lewis Carroll's verse gives an impression of what economics is all about. It suggests that economics is concerned with many different things—clothing, transportation, business supplies, food and government. It is possible, of course, to add to the list almost without limit because economics is concerned with a very large part of the life of man. Economics has been called the study of "man in the everyday business of life" and the study of "how man makes his living." Economics includes the study of money, business, personal finance, the stock market, farming, labor unions, profits, taxes, department store sales and much more.

But what is the basic subject matter of economics—the theme that puts all of these specific subjects under the heading of economics? *Economics* is the study of *how society organizes to develop and to use its productive resources to satisfy human wants.*

Resources

What does this definition of economics really mean? First of all, *resources* are those things that can be used to produce goods and services. *Goods* are material things that can be used to satisfy wants or to help produce other things. A hamburger sandwich is a good; a TV set is a good; a bulldozer is a good. *Services* are activities that satisfy wants, such as a haircut from a barber, a tooth pulled by a dentist, the minister's church sermon on Sunday morning. These terms, goods and services, are important; they are part of the technical language of economics.

Generally, economists divide all the things that can be used to produce goods and services into 3 groups: labor, capital and natural resources.

Labor is the human effort (work) used in production and includes physical and mental effort as well as any other kind of effort used. Some examples of what labor (sometimes called manpower or human resources) contributes to production include digging ditches, operating machines in a factory, pumping gasoline at the corner service station, and supervising the stock clerks and checkers in a big supermarket.

Capital includes all the tools and equipment used in production. Sometimes the word capital is used to mean money. We'll use this term to mean capital goods. It is important to remember that capital goods are produced by man and are real things used in further production, not used to satisfy people's wants directly. Examples of capital goods include a farm tractor, the Brooklyn Bridge, a factory that produces automobile tires, and a school building as well as the books and classroom equipment that it contains.

Natural resources includes land, minerals, rivers and forests— all the things that are available in nature and can be used in production. Sometimes the term *land* is used as the general name for this type of resource. This may seem strange since land or natural resources refers to such productive resources as water (for river transportation or generating hydroelectric power), oil reserves still under the ground and trees growing in the earth.

Technology

One of the most important principles of economics is that resources are determined by technology. Whether something can be used in production (usefulness is what makes it a resource) depends on whether people know how to use it and have the necessary skills and the equipment to use it. Back in the 1930s, a mining company in Colorado was producing molybdenum (a metal similar to chromium) and throwing away another substance also found in the same rock. The substance was not valuable as a productive resource because industry had no important use for it. In the 1940s, however, a scientific and technological discovery sent the miners digging frantically to recover the "unwanted substance." It was uranium ore, and scientists had found it useful in producing atomic energy.

Technology refers to the knowledge of how to make and use tools. Technology is one of the most important forces at work today in the economy, the chief cause of economic progress and the basic reason for the high productivity of the American economy. Much more will be said later about technology and its cousins, "automation" and "cybernation."

Institutions

Patterns of social organization and behavior are called *institutions. Economic institutions* are the behavior patterns that influence the way resources are used and developed.

Institutions are the "coordinating systems" of the economy. They are the methods and organizations (and traditions) that control the use of resources. The wage system, for example, is an institution ("invented" during the Middle Ages) by which men and women exchange some of their time and effort for money, then exchange the money for goods and services. Another institution is money itself—which is really not so much a "thing" as it is a system of behavior. People agree to accept pieces of paper (currency and checks) in exchange for services or goods, even

82

though the pieces of paper have no value in themselves. They are valuable only for what they can buy, and this depends on the institution of market exchange.

The heavy emphasis economics places on the subject of institutions is perfectly natural, since economics is a social science. Economics is "social" because it is chiefly concerned with how groups of people behave. Economics is a "science" because it makes use of the scientific method of checking its theories by making predictions and testing them carefully with the facts.

Lesson in Brief

Economics is the study of how society organizes to develop and use productive resources to satisfy human wants. It is a social science that focuses attention on resources, technology and institutions. The 3 types of resources are manpower, physical capital and natural resources. Technology refers to tool-making and tool-using skills. Institutions are patterns of social organization.

Every economic system deals with 3 basic questions. What should be the total level of production? What particular kinds of goods and services should be produced? How should the total income of the society be shared among its individual members? These 3 basic problems must be solved by every human society in the world—whether it is primitive or advanced, whether it is a capitalistic, socialistic or mixed system.

An economic system (or economy) is simply the way that a society of people is organized to develop and use its resources. The American economy is the total economic system of the United States including all of its institutions, technology and resources. Later, we will describe in detail some important features of the economic system. Now, however, let's turn to the question of what an economic system must do—the functions that all economic systems must perform.

Every economic system, whether it is the socialist economy of the U.S.S.R. or the market economy of the U.S.A., must answer 3 basic questions:

1. What should be the *total level* of production? How much should be produced, in total? How big will the nation's "economic pie" be, in total? The answers to these questions include the answers to some related questions. For example, when the total quantity of goods and services to produce is determined, whether to make full use of the economy's available resources is also decided. Setting the total output, therefore, involves determining the overall level of economic activity for the entire system.

2. What particular kinds of goods and services should be produced? Given the overall size of the "economic pie," what is its *composition?* (Given a giant 20-inch pizza pie, the next question is, What's in it? How much cheese, tomato sauce, sausage, mushrooms? What mixture of

which different things?) A nation's output can be described as consisting of "guns and butter" (economists use these terms to represent the division between military goods and civilian goods); or capital goods and consumer goods; or gadgets and necessities. The actual composition of output in the real world, of course, is far more complex.

3. How is the total income of the society to be *shared* among its individual members? That is, once the goods are produced, who gets how much of what? How is the nation's "economic pie" going to be sliced? How is income to be distributed among families and individuals?

These 3 questions always will be answered, in one way or another, through the institutions that make up the economy. The problems will be solved, more or less satisfactorily. The actual patterns of production and income distribution always will be worked out in some manner.

The people who make up the economic society may or may not like the way these problems are solved, depending on whether the outcomes are consistent with their goals and preferences. (More will be said later about economic goals.) If people like the way their economic system answers the 3 basic questions, it can be said that the system is performing well. To the extent that people do not approve of the actual level of production, the kinds of goods and services that are produced or the way income is shared, they can attempt to change the resources, technology and, especially, the institutions in such a way as to get results more to their liking.

The economic system of the United States of America is basically a *private enterprise* system, in which individuals and groups of people own most of the productive resources and decide how they should be used. They have private property rights concerning natural resources and capital goods. The Union of Soviet Socialist Republics is a socialist or "communist" system, in which most of the natural resources and capital goods are owned and controlled by government. The United Kingdom of Great

85

Britain and Northern Ireland has an economic system that is often described as "democratic socialism"—with some of the basic productive resources owned and operated by the government. Yet, this birthplace of industrial capitalism is still largely a private enterprise economy. And the same is true of France, Germany and Japan, among other countries.

In some ways, the economic systems of the United States, Russia, Japan and Britain are very much alike. They all make use of money and prices, their methods of production are technologically advanced, they use billions of dollars worth of capital equipment, they are all highly productive, and they are among the richest nations in the world.

But their economies differ in the way they are organized to use (and to develop) their resources. One of the most interesting subjects in economics is the study of Comparative Economic Systems, which focuses attention on how these different types of economies answer the 3 basic questions of How Much, What and For Whom to Produce.

Lesson in Brief

In this lesson, discussion has centered on what an economic system is and the 3 basic questions it must answer: (1) how much should be produced, (2) what kinds of goods and services should be produced, and (3) how should the total output be shared among members of the society?

Economic Institutions: 18
The World As It Really Is

> An "institution" is an established pattern of group activity—a set way of doing things. Institutions may be formal organizations like schools (for education) and courts (for law enforcement) that provide a structure for carrying on activities. But an institution can exist without a formal organization to go along with it. Economic institutions are the habits, procedures and established ways that people (or a nation) follow in using productive resources. Some important economic institutions are the labor market, the money and banking system, private property rights, progressive income taxes, labor unions and the business system. Institutions change over time, growing and adjusting gradually to changes in technology and production.

Economics is a study of 3 sets of forces—resources, technology and institutions—and how they interact with one another. The quantity and quality of labor, capital and natural resources together with technology will always set the upper limit to what a nation can produce. However, it is the society's *institutions* that will determine the actual level and pattern of production by determining how the resources are used. The important thing to remember about institutions is that they depend on the beliefs and behavior of people. Most scholars agree there are no "natural" institutions, only man-made institutions.

John Stuart Mill, an English philosopher and economist, pointed out more than a century ago how important institutions are in determining the distribution of wealth and the sharing of income. "The laws and conditions of the production of wealth partake of the character of physical truths," he wrote in *Principles of Political Economy*.

> There is nothing optional or arbitrary in them . . . . It is not so with the distribution of wealth. That is a matter of human institution solely. The things once there, mankind individually or collectively can do with them as they like. They can place them at the disposal of whomsoever they please, and on whatever terms. Further, . . . any disposal whatever of them can only take place by the consent of society . . . . Even what a person has produced by his individual toil, unaided by anyone, he cannot

> keep, unless by the permission of society. Not only can society take it from him, but individuals could and would take it from him, if society only remained passive . . . . The distribution of wealth, therefore, depends on the laws and customs of society. The rules by which it is determined are what the opinions and feelings of the ruling portion of the community make them, and are very different in different ages and countries; and might be still more different, if mankind so chose.

The economies of different countries, such as the United States and Soviet Russia, may seem very much alike in their resources and technology—as indeed they are. But when one considers the economic institutions of the 2 countries, important differences can be noted. For example, "private property" is a key institution of the American economy. According to this institution, individuals and groups are allowed and encouraged to own capital goods and natural resources and use these "means of production" to further their own economic self-interest. It should be noted that property is not a "thing" like a factory building or oil well but is a bundle of legal rights concerning the use of economic resources.

In Russia, the institution of private property for the most part is outlawed. Basically, the means of production—capital and natural resources—are not owned by individuals or private organizations such as business corporations but are owned collectively by the government. Note that capital (man-made goods used in production) is found both in the capitalistic U.S.A. and the socialistic U.S.S.R. The big difference between capitalism and socialism is an institutional difference, centering on the organization of the use of capital goods and other resources.

In the U.S. economy, the prices of most goods and services are set by the market forces of "supply and demand" or, in some cases, by the decisions of business corporations and labor unions. With few exceptions the government controls prices only during emergencies, such as wartime or periods of serious inflation. But in Russia prices are set by government planners practically all the time, and consumers must adjust their buying decisions to whatever these prices happen to be. This is an important institutional difference between the 2 systems.

One final example of an economic institution which merits discussion is "acquisitive behavior"—a fancy name for the profit motive or desire to "get ahead in the world." Many writers and businessmen speak of this desire to make money and build up a stockpile of material goods as "the American dream." In certain other countries, people are not motivated by this acquisition drive in their economic lives. A typical villager in India, for example, would not dream of changing his job or moving 100 miles away in order to increase his wages by 15%. The South Sea islanders, who built airfields for the U. S. Air Force during World War II, worked 8 to 10 hours a day for as little as 25 cents per day. When the Air Force raised their pay to 50 cents a day out of generosity, many of the natives decided to work only half a day. Others worked 3 days, then took the rest of the week off to go fishing or just to loaf. Earning as much as one can may be typical behavior for Americans, but it was not the islanders' habitual way of behaving. Acquisitive behavior is not an institution of their economic system as it is in the United States.

An interesting exercise involves listing a number of current American economic institutions (such as the 40-hour work week, TV commercials, September-to-June school year, AFL-CIO, inheritance of wealth, etc.) and then asking the following questions about each:

—Where did the institution come from?
—What function does it serve?
—Should it be changed?

Institutions have their roots in the past. Because society inherits its institutions from earlier times, many people feel the institutions should not change. Before the 1930s some people argued against a Social Security system to provide government pensions for retired workers because there had never been one in the past. Free public education for everyone was criticized when the plan was first suggested in the early 1800s as was universal adult suffrage (letting all grownups, including women, vote). Labor unions and collective bargaining by workers were bitterly opposed by business, the courts and government until the 1930s.

Because they have their roots in the past, many institutions are slow to change. But when technology changes and economic growth takes place, a basic problem arises. Can society adjust its economic institutions quickly and smoothly and fairly to keep pace with technological progress and economic growth?

For example, automation (a form of technological change) is eliminating the need for certain kinds of workers. A few years ago, many claimed that automation was destroying 40,000 jobs a week in this country and the "cybernation revolution" would create mass unemployment by 1975. What happens to the people who lose their jobs when machines take over? Sometimes they can simply go out and find a new job, using the same skills they used on the old job. But in the case of coal miners, farmers and railroad firemen, they cannot transfer their skills so easily. New institutions—manpower training programs and temporary unemployment compensation—may be required to meet the needs of people whose jobs and lives are disrupted by technological change and economic growth. During the past 20 years, 75% of the jobs in coal mining were wiped out. In agriculture and railroading, the number of jobs was cut in half. Millions of workers were displaced.

Is automation a problem today? Should society halt the spread of automation or encourage it? Why? How to adjust economic institutions so that the burden of change will not rest too heavily on particular individuals and groups is a major economic challenge today.

Lesson in Brief

Economic institutions are the established patterns of group behavior that influence the way resources are used. Institutions are man-made, rooted in the past and often very slow to change, even when technology is advancing rapidly and the size and structure of the economy are radically altered. How to accomplish wise institutional change is one of society's biggest continuing problems in a growing economy.

Capitalism: "The Anatomy of Free Enterprise"

19

The economic system of the United States is a mixture of private enterprise and government, of competition and monopoly power, of tradition and of the market mechanism. But even though it is a very complicated mixture of many things, the American economic system remains basically a capitalistic system built on the foundation of private property, the profit motive, free enterprise, competition and market prices.

The economic system in the United States is known by many different names—free enterprise, market system, capitalism, profit system, price system, private enterprise, free competition, mixed capitalism, and others—some of which are more complimentary than others. Each of these terms suggests something about the way the economy is organized and how it operates. What is the correct name for the kind of economy America really has?

Of course, the answer is that the system is very complex and there is no "right" name for it. Many economists agree that terms like "mixed capitalism" or "mixed economy" or "basically private enterprise" are fairly accurate to describe the present-day economy. But where do all these labels come from? What do the terms imply?

If the economy is "mixed," one may well ask, A mixture of what? Basically, the mixture consists of "pure capitalism" and those factors such as monopoly power and government intervention that inject "impurities" into the system. These impurities are not necessarily bad or harmful; sometimes they are exactly what the people desire and may have very good effects on the economy. But they do change the economy from a pure to a mixed breed.

Let's consider the anatomy of pure capitalism or the theoretical model of a free enterprise system. Pure capitalism has 5 distinctive features; that is, there are 5 important institutions in a capitalistic system.

—Private property
—Profit motive
—Free enterprise
—Competition
—"Free market" prices and wages

These institutions were first explained in 1776 when Adam Smith, a British philosopher and economist, published his famous book *The Wealth of Nations.*

Private property is the basic institution of capitalism, the core and the foundation of the whole system. Without the legal institution of private property, capitalism could not exist. What, then, is meant by private property? Simply, *private property* is the legal right to own capital goods and natural resources and the right to use and dispose of them. Private property is not a thing, like a coal mine, but rather "a bundle of legal rights" that prescribe how the coal mine may be used. Because private property is an institution in the United States, individuals and groups of individuals are allowed (and encouraged) to own coal mines (and other resources) and to decide how they should be used in production.

How should coal mines be used under a system of private property? This is where the profit motive, the second feature of pure capitalism, comes in. In a capitalistic system with the institution of private property, resources are supposedly used by their owners in such a way as to make the largest possible profits. The *profit motive* is identified as the driving force that activates and allocates resources for use in production. The desire for money gain is the main incentive in a capitalistic economy. Of course, not only owners of land and capital but also business firms, workers and consumers are motivated to do as well as they can in the economy. Economists refer to behavior that is aimed at getting the most that one can get as "rational" behavior.

Free enterprise, another feature of pure capitalism, means that an individual or group is free to start a business, to come into existence as a producing unit. It is a "natural" outcome of the legal right of private property and the profit motive in the sense that setting up a business enterprise is a good way to take advantage of profit opportunities in the economy.

A fourth characteristic of pure capitalism, emphasized by Adam Smith in *The Wealth of Nations*, is competition. According to the theory of pure capitalism, *competition* is not the same thing as rivalry or "trying harder" but is the absence of market power (sometimes called monopoly power). Competition is a necessary feature of capitalism because it forces producers to be efficient and to charge prices that are close to the actual costs of production. It guarantees that consumers have real freedom of choice. Without real competition in the market, businessmen might take unfair advantage of consumers—charging high prices and selling shoddy merchandise. Without competition among sellers, consumers would have no freedom of choice. They would have to take whatever was available and pay the prices set by business.

Fifth and finally, under pure capitalism *prices and wages* are determined by supply and demand forces at work in free, competitive markets. Large numbers of independent buyers and sellers come together in free markets, and prices are automatically set by supply and demand. Whenever prices are set by monopolistic businesses or by labor unions or by government commissions or bureaus or boards, as they sometimes are in the real world, the system is not pure capitalism.

Is the American economy of the 1970s "pure capitalism"? To answer the question, check each of the 5 features listed above. Do Americans own private property? Do the American people respond to the profit motive? Is there free enterprise in the sense that people can start up any legal kind of business they want? Is there competition in the market for consumer goods? Is there competition for resources? Finally, how are prices and wage rates set? By supply and demand in competitive markets? Or by big business, big labor unions and big government?

The answers probably suggest at least 3 reasons why the American economy today is not pure capitalism. First, there certainly are some monopolistic (noncompetitive) markets. Big corporations and big labor unions do have some market power to influence wage rates and the prices of goods and services. Second, government does step in and regulate prices and production in certain industries such as farming, public utilities, steel, railroads and sometimes (as President Nixon did with his Wage-Price Freeze in 1971) in the whole economy. Then, too, people are not always well-informed. They do not always act "rationally." When consumers and other economic decisionmakers fail to act rationally, the system does not work according to "the model." If consumers, workers and business firms are not well-informed, rational, competitive and if they are not willing to make rapid adjustments in order to increase profits and incomes, then the system of pure capitalism breaks down.

Actually, pure capitalism has never really existed—except in people's minds and in some economics textbooks. But something very close to this system did exist in Britain, the United States and some other European and English-speaking countries of the world during the 1800s and early 1900s. Today, however, most countries of the world have mixed economies. The American economy probably has more features of pure capitalism than any other nation's in the world. The system is growing and changing. Thirty years from now, we predict it will be different from what it is now. But today, and in the year 2000, the term "mixed capitalism" probably describes the economy pretty well. For this reason, an understanding of today's actual American economy requires basic knowledge of the structure and functioning of theoretical capitalism or "the market model."

Lesson in Brief

The economic system of the United States is a mixture of pure capitalism and a set of other forces such as monopoly power, government intervention and "imperfect" market behavior. Key features of pure capitalism are private property, the profit motive, free enterprise, competition and free market prices.

The Circular Flow of Economic Activity

20

In every economic system, decisions are made concerning the amounts and kinds of goods and services produced. Who makes these decisions in a market-type economy? How are they made? For the most part, economic decisions in a capitalistic system are made by consumers, business firms and owners of productive resources. The decisions are linked together and coordinated by flows of money and flows of goods and services in a system of markets.

Figure 2.1 is an economic "model" and is a simplified representation of the private sector of the economy, leaving out the role of government. This private sector accounts for nearly four-fifths of all the goods and services produced in the economy each year. The model would be more realistic (and also more complicated) by including the role of government and converting the model from one that describes pure capitalism to one describing mixed capitalism.

What does this diagram represent? First, the 3 *decisionmaking units*—consumer households, business firms, resource owners—are listed. They make important economic choices in the private (nongovernment) sector of American economic life.

Second, *flows of money* (represented by broken lines) and *flows of goods and services* (represented by solid lines) are diagramed. The flows of goods and services are influenced by money flows. Because the system is a "market" economy based on spending, goods are produced to meet market demand. (A *market* is a pattern of exchange relations, where things are bought and sold.)

Third, some details of the *input market* are shown. This is the market for productive resources, where labor, natural resources and capital are sold to business firms. The money that business firms pay for these resources becomes the income of the resources owner.

Finally, the *output market*—where goods and services are bought and sold—is closely linked to the input market.

Figure 2.1

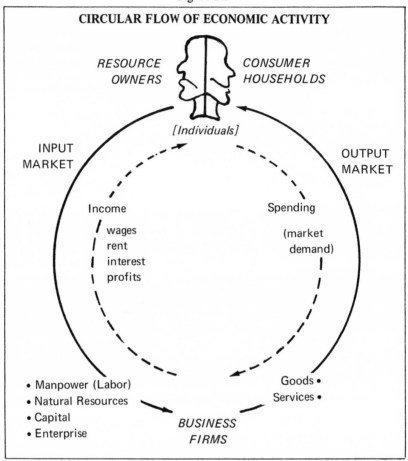

The smiling face on the right-hand side of the two-headed character at the top of the diagram represents individuals in their capacity as consumers. Every person in the economy is a consumer (over 200 million mouths to feed) and belongs to a "consumer household." There are more than 50 million consumer households in the United States having 2 or more members, plus an additional 15 million having 1 member.

Consumer households make economic decisions in the output market. They decide whether to buy particular goods or services, what quantities to buy, whether to buy from a certain business firm or from its rival. Consumers spend money to buy goods and services in order to enjoy consuming them (and that is why the face on the right is smiling).

The face on the left represents individuals in their capacity as resource owners. Not all individuals own productive resources, but most of the consumer households in the economy have at least 1 resource owner—a person who has manpower to exchange for money in the input market.

There are 90 million men and women in the American labor force. Because that many people are owners of their own labor, that means there are at least 90 million resource owners. In addition, there are people who own natural resources (such as oil wells and farmland) and people who own capital goods (factories, stores, etc.). All in all, there are about 100 million resource owners in the U.S. economy (without double counting). Although many people really enjoy their productive activity, the frown on the left side of the two-headed individual suggests that contributing to the input side of production is perhaps less pleasurable than consuming the output of goods and services.

When the resource called manpower makes its services available to business firms (say, for 8 hours a day, 5 days a week, to help produce automobiles), what does manpower get in return? All those people who contribute human effort to production receive a payment that economists call *wages* which includes hourly wages, monthly salaries, sales commissions, tips, fringe benefits and all the other direct and indirect payments for work.

Owners of natural resources who allow their land or materials to be used in production are paid something called *rent*. Note that this is not the same as the rent families pay for the houses or apartments they live in. That rental payment really includes a payment for labor services and capital goods (the house and its fixtures) as well as the use of land itself.

Owners of capital who allow their buildings and equipment to be used in production receive a payment called *interest*. Actually, they often receive this interest for letting people use their money, which in turn is used to buy capital goods (i.e., the buildings and equipment).

Finally, in addition to manpower, natural resources and capital, a fourth factor of production (or type of resource) sometimes included in the circular flow model is called *enterprise*. It is the economic function of making basic policy decisions (not day-to-day supervising and managing) for a business and bearing risk. The payment made to the enterprise, when the business is successful, is called *profits*.

Using the circular flow diagram as a model of a capitalistic economy (with government temporarily left out), one can see how money flows in one direction and goods and services in the opposite direction. Consumers spend money in the output market to buy goods and services from business firms. These expenditures are like dollar votes that give signals to business, telling them what to produce (more transistor radios, nylon sweaters, houses, cars, rock music festivals). The market is actually a communications system, with the signals given by the dollars that people spend.

When the business firms receive signals in the output market from consumer households, they can decide what and how much to produce. And they can turn to the input market and buy the resources they need to produce the goods and services that are demanded by consumers. At times, business firms hire resources (for example, the services of advertising agencies) and use them to influence consumer demand.

Resource owners receive money income in payment for the labor, natural resources and capital they provide. This income is available to be spent on consumer goods. Individuals take in money as resource owners and then spend it as consumers. That is, they earn wages in the manpower market and then spend their wages in the output market.

Although buying and selling are not the most important kinds of economic behavior—production is the more basic economic activity—they are very important. The circular flow model depicts who it is that makes the buying and selling decisions in a market system, what impact these decisions have in guiding resources into productive use, and how goods and services are "rationed" to consumers who have the desire and the ability (dollar power) to purchase them in the marketplace.

The model shows that the basic purpose of business is not really to satisfy human wants but to make profits by producing the goods and services that people effectively demand (pay for) in the market. In a market economy, human wants are satisfied as a by-product of the profit system.

Lesson in Brief

About four-fifths of the economic activity of the United States is based on decisions made in the private (nongovernment) sector of the economy. There is a circular flow of money spent by consumers and business firms in one direction and a corresponding flow of goods and services from resources owners and business firms in the opposite direction. These flows show how the input market and the output market are joined together to coordinate and determine how resources are used in a basically private enterprise economy. (The role of government is considered in Lesson 29.)

Long ago men and women learned they could produce more and better goods and services by working together as a team rather than working alone and trying to be a "jack-of-all-trades." Adam Smith, the "father of economics," sang the praises of the division of labor and argued that it was the best way to increase the nation's wealth. Specialization of labor on the basis of comparative skill advantages increases not only total production but also the economic interdependence of all members of society.

The circular flow model (Figure 2.1) illustrates how the productive resources of labor, capital and natural resources are combined by business firms to produce goods and services. In this way, inputs of manpower, machinery and materials are converted into outputs of food, clothing, cars and TV sets to satisfy the wants of millions of consumers.

Of all the resource inputs, nothing is more important to the economy than the quantity and quality of its manpower. To understand how important labor is in the economic process and what factors influence the productive powers of labor, let's go back in history nearly 200 years and see how these questions were answered by one of the first great English-speaking economists, Adam Smith.

Improvements in the "productive powers of labor" was the first topic covered in *The Wealth of Nations*. Published in 1776, Smith's book is considered to be one of the most important ever written. The author, a professor of philosophy and economics from Scotland, is generally considered to be the "father of economics." Many of the theories he explained in *The Wealth of Nations* are still taught to students of economics here in the United States and all over the noncommunist world. The ideas of Adam Smith mean as much to people in the English-speaking countries of the world as the ideas of Marx, Lenin and Mao mean to Russian and Chinese Communists.

The first lesson Adam Smith taught about manpower efficiency is that "division of labor is the great cause" of increased productivity. The example he used was a pin factory that made ordinary straight pins like those used in sewing and packaging clothing.

> A workman not educated to this business, nor acquainted with the use of machinery employed in it, could scarce make one pin in a day, and certainly could not make twenty. But in the way in which this business is now carried on, not only the whole work is a peculiar trade, but it is divided into a number of branches, of which the greater part are likewise peculiar trades.
>
> One man draws out the wire, another straightens it, a third cuts it, a fourth points it, a fifth grinds it at the top for receiving the head. To make the head requires two or three distinct operations; to put it on is a peculiar business; to whiten the pins is another. It is even a trade by itself to put them into the paper.
>
> The important business of making a pin is, in this manner, divided into about 18 distinct operations. I have seen a small factory of this kind where 10 men were employed, and where some of them consequently performed two or three distinct operations. But though they were very poor (and did not have the best of machinery) they could, when they exerted themselves, make among them about 12 pounds of pins in a day. There are in a pound, upwards of 4,000 pins of a middling size. Those 10 persons, therefore, could make among them upwards of 48,000 pins in a day. Each person, therefore, making a tenth part of 48,000 pins, might be considered as making 4,800 pins in a day. But if they had all worked separately and independently, they certainly could not each of them have made 20, perhaps not one pin in a day—that is, not even a small part of what they are at present capable of performing, because of a proper division and combination of their labor on different questions.

Smith explained why the division of labor resulted in greater production. First, being able to work at a single task helps the worker improve his skill. Second, there is a big gain by saving time that would otherwise be lost in moving from one sort of work to another. And third, division of labor makes it possible to develop and use specialized machinery (i.e., capital goods embodying improved technology) that helps workers turn out greater quantities of goods and services.

The principle of *specialization and division of labor* means that a greater total output of goods and services can be obtained by organizing the job in order to save time, by taking advantage of each worker's skills and by benefitting from the use of machinery and tools. This principle, which plays an important role in economic analysis, means that the output of the community, the nation and the entire world can be increased by having individuals and businesses specialize in producing the goods and services that they are particularly good at producing and by letting other people produce goods and services that they, in turn, produce more efficiently.

In a modern society, division of labor and the principle of specialization are often so extreme that a worker may not even know what he is producing or where his contribution fits into the overall picture. A factory worker who tightens bolts on a truck wheel as it moves past him on the assembly line may never see what the finished truck looks like. But production managers have discovered that the assembly line method is a very efficient way to organize the job and divide the labor. Since the efficiency criterion stands so high in the American system of values, use of assembly lines and other highly impersonal methods of mass production are widespread.

Along with specialization of labor comes *economic interdependence.* Just as an assembly line worker is depended upon to tighten bolts on trucks, he in turn depends on hundreds of other people to provide food, housing, clothing, schooling and other goods and services for him and his family.

The greater the division of labor, the greater the productivity; but more specialization means more interdependence. Consider how Americans depend on the farmers to plant and harvest enough crops; the electric companies to produce and transfer electric power to light homes and keep refrigerators running (not to mention furnaces and kitchen ranges); the oil companies to refine gasoline and maintain adequate supplies in thousands of service stations; and state and local governments to provide educational services for young people. The occasional crop loss, power failure or work stoppage in a key industry make people

102

realize just how dependent they are on other members of economic society.

This high degree of interdependence, which is the other side of the coin of specialization and improved productivity, is one reason why economics is such an important subject. Since everyone is part of an interdependent economic system—as producers and consumers—everyone needs to know more about how the system is organized, how it operates, how personal decisions and behavior affect other people and how their decisions will, in turn, affect the individual.

Lesson in Brief

One of the most important causes of increased labor productivity (that is, the power of labor to produce goods and services aided by capital goods and natural resources) is the division of labor. But specialization in production also causes economic interdependence. As the economy becomes more specialized, each individual and each family becomes less and less self-sufficient.

The economic world is so complicated and confusing—millions of people making tens of millions of decisions affecting the production of billions of dollars worth of goods and services—that individuals could not even begin to understand it without simplifying and carefully organizing the subject matter. In order to study and explain how the economy functions, scholars have developed analytical frameworks, simplified models and economic theories. Although some of these models and theories are very simple, they can be useful for explaining and predicting economic behavior.

One of the great economic educators of the 20th century was Joseph Schumpeter, an economics professor at Harvard University. Schumpeter believed that it was possible to identify people who really know what they are talking about in the field of economics by testing their knowledge and skills in 3 areas: theory, history and statistics. Many people have opinions about such economic topics as taxes, poverty, inflation and labor unions. But, according to Professor Schumpeter, what separates the truly competent economist from all the other people who think, talk and write about economic subjects is command of the 3 reasoning skills.

In this lesson, we discuss theory. Later, we will introduce history and statistics to show how important they are for sound economic reasoning.

In the American economy there are nearly 70,000,000 consumer units, about 100 million resource owners and more than 10 million business firms. There are approximately 250 "working days" in a year (52 weeks times 5 days in a week less 10 holidays). Most households make at least 1 economic decision (for example, to buy a loaf of bread from the store) every working day. Multiply 70,000,000 consumer units by 250 decisions, and that comes to more than 17 billion individual consumer decisions made in the United States economy during the year. Add the decisions made by resource owners and business firms, and the total number of decisions becomes enormous!

How are all these decisions coordinated? How could anyone possibly explain or predict the patterns of decisionmaking and economic behavior? The answer is by simplifying and by organizing the important facts systematically in order to study and analyze them.

Let's consider how economists simplify and organize facts and ideas to help explain economic behavior and, specifically, how we have done so in this book. What did we do first? We set up an *analytical framework* for studying economics. We divided all the factors that concern the economy into 3 groups and called them "Resources," "Technology" and "Institutions."

Next, we went beyond this analytical framework and developed simple models. One was the circular flow model (Figure 2.1) which helps explain how the market is organized and how it operates. The model tells something about how the economy behaves and shows relationships among important factors. The circular flow model shows how consumers buy goods and services in the output market, how resource owners sell their productive services in the input market and how business firms buy in the input market and sell in the output market.

A *model* is a scheme or gadget that represents reality, just as a globe is a spherical model (or map) of the earth and a planetarium is an elaborate model of the heavens. Most of the models used in economics are limited to pictures, graphs, numbers and words.

What about theories? For some people, theory is a scare word. Yet, an economic theory is just a more specific kind of model. A *theory* describes a set of specific relations among economic forces. It tells something very specific about the world of facts. The "supply and demand theory of market price" for example, states that the price of a good is determined—when there is competition in the market—by the interaction of supply and demand; that an increase in supply, with no change in demand, will cause the market price to fall; that an increase in demand, with no change in supply, will cause the market price to rise.

A theory contains certain assumptions and definitions, makes predictions and shows how experimental tests can be conducted using facts in the real world. Many so-called theories are not really scientific-empirical theories because there is no possible way to check whether they are valid.

For most people interested in acquiring an elementary knowledge of how the economic system works, there is no need to learn all about economic theory or even to learn the supply and demand theory of market price. More advanced courses offer the opportunity to study these. The important thing now is to understand what a theory is and how economic theories can be used to explain how the economic system functions in the real world.

Let's consider 2 more important questions about models and theories. First, when is a theory a good theory? Consider the statement, "That's all right in theory, but it doesn't work in practice." Actually, if a theory does not work in practice, then it really is not "all right." In fact, if it does not work in practice, then it is a bad theory. Theories, like all tools, are supposed to be useful—to help one do a job. If a theory can be used to make accurate predictions about economic behavior, it is a good theory. If a theory does not help do the job of predicting and explaining behavior, then it is a bad theory.

In economics, lots of things really cannot be explained or predicted very well—such as, the number of skilled carpenters to be employed in Denver, Colorado in 1980. But economics is a fairly young science, and improvements are being made all the time. It took physicists a long time to solve the mystery of atomic and nuclear energy. Meteorology still is not an exact science. A discipline such as economics which tries to understand and explain the behavior of people in their complex and continually changing economic life can be expected to be "inexact" and far from perfect. But, remember, economics does have some excellent theories, some very useful models and an analytical framework that helps explain the American economic world.

Finally, there is the question, How important are theories, anyway? One of the most famous economists of our time, John Maynard Keynes (an Englishman who died in 1946), wrote that "the ideas of economists and political philosophers, both when they are right and when they are wrong, are more powerful than is commonly understood. Indeed, the world is ruled by little else."

If evidence is needed to support this claim, consider the ideas and theories—and their impact on today's world—of men like Aristotle, Darwin, Pasteur, Freud, Smith, Marx, Lenin and Mao Tse-tung.

Lesson in Brief

In order to be competent in economic reasoning, a person must have command of 3 sets of analytical skills: theory, statistics and history. To explain economic behavior, economists make use of analytical frameworks (to organize the subject matter systematically), simplified models and economic theories. Theories that are "all right in theory, but don't work in practice" are not really all right. A theory is good only if it can be used to give an accurate explanation of the behavior of economic forces.

Statistical thinking will one day be as necessary for efficient citizenship as the ability to read and write.

H. G. Wells

The *gross national product* (GNP) of any nation is the total value of all the goods and services that its people produce in a particular year. GNP statistics are useful because they reveal important facts about the overall level and composition of current production and indicate how the economy is behaving. Other economic indicators that are useful in measuring the performance of the economy include the consumer price index and the unemployment rate.

Economics is a social science in which scientific methods are used to study the subject matter. People who want to read, think and talk intelligently about economic questions have to master certain skills. They must become competent in using the techniques of theory, statistics and history.

Because most of the economic facts of interest come in the form of statistical data, individuals study *statistics*—numbers that describe what is happening in the economy in terms of production, employment, spending and all sorts of other activities and conditions. The numbers come from business firms, labor unions, farm groups, private research organizations, and state and federal government agencies. Studies have been made of government statistics by unbiased experts, and their judgment over and over again has been that the data generally are accurate, honest and complete (though by no means perfect, conceptually or statistically).

Many people share a strange attitude toward statistics. This attitude is revealed by a number of often-heard sayings. "There are three kinds of lies," they say, "plain lies, damned lies and statistics." "Figures don't lie, but liars figure." "I make up all of my statistics. Where do you get yours?" There is even a book entitled *How to Lie with Statistics.*

This skeptical attitude would be healthy if it caused people to be very careful about the way they used statistics. But, unfortunately, some people go beyond caution. They refuse to believe any statistics at all! This attitude comes close to saying, "Don't bother me with the facts. I'll make up my mind without them."

Let's look at one very important set of economic statistics—the gross national product accounts. Table 2.1 shows the gross national product of the United States for 1971.

Table 2.1 **GROSS NATIONAL PRODUCT** **OF THE UNITED STATES, BY SECTORS, 1971**	(billions of dollars)	(percentage distribution)
Personal Consumption Expenditures (C)	$ 665	63%
Gross Private Domestic Investment (I)	152	15
Net Exports of Goods & Services (X_n)	1	—
Government Purchases of Goods & Services (G)	233	22
TOTAL GNP = C + I + X_n + G =	$1,050	100%

Source: U.S. Department of Commerce, *Survey of Current Business*, July 1972, p. 7.

What do these figures mean? They show that the market value of the total output of final goods and services in the United States in 1971 amounted to more than a trillion dollars! The dollar value of all the thousands of different goods and services produced that year—cars, breakfast cereal, missiles, TV sets, haircuts—totaled $1,050 billion. How is the total computed? Simply add all of the money that consumers spent to buy goods and services during the year ($665 billion), plus the investment spending by business firms on new equipment and buildings, etc. ($152 billion), plus the excess of goods produced in this country and then shipped overseas above and beyond what foreign countries produced and sent to the United States ($1 billion), plus the money spent by local, state and federal government agencies to buy goods and services ($233 billion). The total of these sums is $1,050 billion. GNP = C + I + X_n + G. This is the total *market demand* for newly produced goods and services, and it is the dollar value of what was *supplied*.

GNP is the total spending for final goods and services during the year, eliminating the double counting of goods that are bought and sold by businesses in the process of production. Another way to look at GNP is to realize that it is the total money value of the goods that the nation produces. GNP = Price x Quantity. GNP equals the quantity of goods and services produced multiplied by the average price at which the goods and services were sold.

The 4 terms in the GNP formula reveal 4 major spenders in the economy: consumers, businesses, foreigners and government. Altogether, they purchase the entire output of the economic system.

There is no need for students to become experts in GNP accounting. The important thing to remember is that GNP is a measure of the *total output of the economy*. When GNP goes up, after adjusting for change in prices and the value of money, then production has increased. If GNP remains constant year after year, the economy is not expanding. If GNP goes down, a recession is under way. GNP is the most important single measure of economic performance available. Students of economics will find it very useful to know what GNP is and how to interpret the statistics.

There are 2 other important statistical indicators used to measure the economy's performance. One is the consumer price index. The other is the unemployment rate.

The *consumer price index*—the so-called cost of living—is a number that measures changes in the buying power of the dollar. When the consumer price index (CPI) rises, that means the general level of prices is going up for the goods and services that consumers typically buy. When prices go up, the purchasing power of the dollar goes down. One reason why *inflation*—defined as an increase in the general level of prices—is considered a bad condition is that people with a given number of dollars (such as retired workers living on fixed-income pensions) are unable to buy as many goods and services as they could before price inflation occurred.

The consumer price index is figured on a base of 100 in 1967. By June of 1972, the CPI stood at 125. This meant that in mid 1972 it took $1.25 to buy the same "package" of goods and services that could have been purchased in 1967 for $1.00. Because of inflation—as measured by a 25% increase in the consumer price index—the value of the dollar declined to only 80¢ as compared with the base year. During the 5-year period from 1967 to 1972, the consumer price index rose an average of 5 percentage points each year.

Is the American economy always faced with a serious inflation problem? Not at all. During the 5-year period 1960 to 1965, for example, the CPI rose only a little over 1% each year. The general level of consumer prices was almost perfectly stable.

The *unemployment rate* is an indicator of unused manpower in the economy, measuring the number of men and women who are able to work and actively seeking employment but have no job, as a percentage of all persons in the civilian labor force.

The civilian labor force is made up of all persons 16 years and over who are able and willing to work (except those in military service or in institutions such as prisons). The size of the civilian labor force is growing every year, and in 1972 it averaged more than 85 million workers. Nearly 5 million of them were jobless that year. Therefore, the national unemployment rate was almost 6%. This was one of the highest unemployment rates in the past 20 years and was a cause for great concern. During the Great Depression of the 1930s, the unemployment rate averaged nearly 20%! Since World War II, however, unemployment has never approached even half that level.

When dealing with unemployment statistics, do not make the mistake of looking only at gross averages. To understand what is happening in the manpower market, it is necessary to observe the *structure* of employment and unemployment. In 1971, for example, when the nation's overall unemployment rate (UR) was

5.9%, the rate for Negro workers was 9.9%. The UR was 5.3% for all male workers in 1971, but 6.9% for women. For men (white and nonwhite combined) age 35 to 44, the UR was 3.1%; but for male workers 18-19 years of age, the rate was 15.0%. In ghetto areas in some large cities, unemployment rates of 30% or higher have been recorded.[1]

Statistics on the labor force, employment and unemployment are not perfect, but they are valuable indicators of the use made of resources in the economy. When the unemployment rate for labor increases, unemployment rates for capital goods and natural resources are also rising. When this happens, the potential output that the economy is capable of producing is not reached resulting in wasted resources and lost goods and services. In addition, the economy fails to provide jobs and incomes for people dependent on the manpower market for their livelihood.

Lesson in Brief

Ability to understand and use economic statistics is necessary in order to read, think and talk intelligently about economic questions. Three important statistical indicators used throughout this book are gross national product, the consumer price index and the unemployment rate.

---

1. Data in this lesson taken from the *Monthly Labor Review* (October 1972) and the *1972 Manpower Report of the President*.

America's present-day industrial system is quite different from what it was 50 or 100 years ago. Today's economy is the product of evolving technology, resources and institutions. A process of continuing economic development and change is going on right now and can be expected to transform man's life in the future just as the original Industrial Revolution changed man's economic and social world in the 19th and 20th centuries.

In addition to theory and statistics, another tool of thinking that promotes understanding of economic problems is *history*. This lesson illustrates the historical way of looking at important changes that occur in the economic process.

What was economic life like 1,000 years ago or even 300 or 400 years ago—say in 1600, in Europe, where capitalism and the industrial system first developed? People worked, they produced goods and services, and they consumed. They also paid taxes. But how they worked, what they produced and the quantity and quality of food, clothing, housing and other goods and services that they were able to consume—these were all vastly different from today.

Economic life during the Middle Ages (approximately 500 A.D. to 1500 A.D.) and for roughly 250 years afterward was pre-industrial. Most men worked as farmers. Some were craftsmen. A few were merchants. Production was mainly for subsistence (just enough food and other necessities to live). There were no huge corporations or bustling factories with power-driven machinery and armies of wage earners. Transportation and communication were primitive—no railroads, automobiles, airplanes, telephones, radios, TV. People lived in small isolated villages and towns, never knowing comfort, convenience, economic security or what life was like 10 miles away. Their life span was half as long as 20th century Americans.

Then, something happened. Over the decades and centuries, technology gradually and continuously was changing. Transportation methods improved. Productivity in agriculture and industry increased. Trade and commerce expanded. Like a snowball gaining both force and speed as it rolls downhill, the process of revolutionary change transformed the old feudal system of Europe. In its place arose the modern industrial world that now characterizes Europe, the United States and other economically advanced areas scattered around the world.

What happened in the mid 1700s and early 1800s has come to be called the Industrial Revolution. It started in England and Western Europe and later spread to America and other parts of the globe. Some say it is still going on. Others believe a second industrial revolution has begun.

The term *Industrial Revolution* is used to describe that period of history when the pace of economic development was so rapid and the changes so dramatic and far-reaching that social and economic life was revolutionized. But more specifically, what are the historical facts about the Industrial Revolution? Why is the history of the Industrial Revolution significant for Americans living in the 1970s?

The Industrial Revolution was a process of technological and economic change that took place first in England and later in other countries of the world in the period after 1750. Machines were invented. Water and steam power were harnessed to operate the machines. Factories were built. Large cities mushroomed. And men, women and children were employed by a new class of "industrial capitalists" to produce goods for sale in markets throughout Europe and around the world. The key to the industrial revolution was the use of new machines and new methods to produce textiles, iron, pottery and hardware, machinery, and other goods. Rapidly improving technology was used to expand production; the whole pattern of social and economic arrangements was disrupted and restructured in the process.

Examples of technological advances are the inventions of John Kay, James Hargreaves and Richard Arkwright in the spinning and weaving of cloth. Abraham Darby and Peter Onions found better ways of making iron. Thomas Newcomen and James Watt developed the steam engine. In America, Eli Whitney invented the cotton gin in 1793 and, a few years later, used interchangeable parts for the mass production of guns.

Before the introduction of these new machines and factories to house them, the production of clothing and other goods was done primarily in workers' homes or small shops under the "domestic system." With the growth of factories, workers left their homes and workshops and began selling their labor in the industrial manpower market. Many books have been written describing conditions of the early factory workers in England and in the United States. What the factory system did was to bring equipment—machines operated by water power, then steam, and later electricity and the internal combustion engine—under the supervision and discipline of industrial managers. One result was vastly increased production. There were other results, too. For example, the new system created certain problems for workers who now became completely dependent on industrial employment to make a living.

Now consider the second question posed about the Industrial Revolution—why is it significant for Americans living in the 1970s? Briefly, the 18th century Industrial Revolution created today's world. The process of technological development and institutional change that started after 1750 created what is now called the "industrial system" forming today's economic and social environment.

Understanding the Industrial Revolution is important because it shows the process of technological progress and economic growth. This process is still going on today at a faster rate than ever before. By looking back at the impact of industrial development during the past 200 years, one can see more clearly what exists in the present and what is likely to come in the future—not perfectly, of course, not in full detail, but at least the general outlines. One can see how machines affect the work that men and women do, the goods and services they consume and the kind of world they live in. Using this knowledge of the past, one can make plans and adjustments to ease the burdens of future change and find ways to take fuller advantage of the opportunities and rewards of continuing economic growth, not only as a consumer but also as a worker and a member of society.

Lesson in Brief

A third important tool of economic reasoning is history. This includes an understanding of technological change, social evolution and information about present-day institutions. The American industrial economy evolved from the past. The process by which this evolution took place was revealed in the Industrial Revolution that began in England after 1750 and spread throughout Europe and America in the 1800s. The process of technological progress and institutional change will continue in the future and will re-shape people's lives just as the Industrial Revolution transformed the lives of their forefathers.

Scarcity, Opportunity Costs and Choice 25

If all the world were apple pie,
And all the sea were ink,
And all the trees
Were bread and cheese
What would we have to drink?

Children's verse

It has been said that words are the vehicles upon which ideas ride. The ideas that ride on the 3 terms included in the title of this lesson are among the most important in economics. Because of scarcity, economic choices have to be made; and every choice involves a cost. What do these terms mean, and how can the ideas be used to make wiser decisions?

It has been said that, if food and other goods and services were available just for the asking, there would be no economic problems and no need to study economics. Note that, even if money grew on trees, the same old problem of finding resources to be used to produce the goods and services that people want would remain. A private money tree might be great for the individual. But if everybody had a money tree, money would be worthless. After all, money cannot be eaten, only traded for something that has value in use.

Looking at the world economy as a whole with its 3.5 billion people, it is apparent that there are not enough goods and services available to satisfy all the wants that men, women and children can think up. In fact, throughout much of the world, there is not enough food to keep people from starving to death. Thousands of people die of starvation every day in places such as India, Africa and the Middle East. For two-thirds of the world's people, life is a desperate and painful struggle for existence, without comfort, without convenience, without progress and without hope. Income per person in the poorest countries is less than $200 per year compared to the annual per capita GNP of $5,000 in the United States!

Very few people starve to death in America. Yet most of the people would like to have more goods and services than they actually get. Well then, why not simply produce more?

The answer is that there are not enough resources—manpower, capital and materials—to produce all of the goods and services that people would like to have. Goods are scarce relative to wants, because the resources needed to produce the goods are scarce relative to physical requirements. *Scarcity* means the amount of resources available is less than the amount required to produce all the things people would like to have.

Because resources are scarce, their use must be economized. That is, people must choose how to use the limited resources to provide the goods and services they value most highly. They need to plan and make choices to get the most from what they have. For an individual or a family, the same problem exists. Because money is limited, one must plan the spending of money in the most economical way. In this way, one gets the greatest benefit from the limited money available.

Since it is a fact of life that resources are limited (or scarce), *choices* must be made concerning the use of available resources. Are there any ideas, skills, concepts or analytical tools that can be learned from the science of economics to help people make wiser choices? One concept, called opportunity cost, is especially useful. Consider the case of a young consumer, age 13. To help him (or her) decide how to spend a weekly allowance of $1.00, think of some possible alternative uses for the money. He may buy 5 cans of pop or go to the movies once or buy 4 chocolate milkshakes (or save the dollar). To illustrate the concept of opportunity cost, let's pose the following question: What is the real cost of 4 chocolate milkshakes?

Assuming a price of 25¢ per milkshake, the total cost of 4 shakes would be $1.00 (25¢ times 4). Or, thinking in terms of the other things the young consumer would have to give up if he spent his dollar to buy 4 shakes, the opportunity cost of the shakes is 5 cans of pop or 1 movie ticket. The *opportunity cost* of buying (or producing) a good or service is the alternative goods and services that must be sacrificed (foregone) in order to obtain the particular goods selected.

The opportunity cost of national defense to the American people is all the houses, cars, hospitals and schools they cannot have because so many productive resources are used for bombs, missiles and nuclear submarines. The opportunity cost of having 8 million young men and women in college is the value of the goods and services they could have produced if they were employed on jobs instead of going to school. From the viewpoint of an individual student, the opportunity cost of spending 4 years in college is the amount of income he could have earned if he were employed on a full-time job during those 4 years. Add to this the tuition and other direct costs in order to compute the total costs of a college education.

Opportunity cost is an important concept and a very practical one. By providing a basis for comparing the benefits of different uses, wiser decisions concerning the way resources are used can be made. In the above example if the 13-year-old consumer feels he would enjoy the benefits of 4 milkshakes more than 5 cans of pop—or some other attainable combination of goods and services (such as 2½ cans of pop plus 2 milkshakes)— then he can have more confidence that he is spending his allowance wisely. He not only knows what he is getting from using his resources in a particular way but also what he is giving up. When people realize the many alternatives that $10 million worth of manpower, capital and materials can produce, then they, as citizens, are in a better position to choose what they consider to be the best combination of goods—the best composition of the nation's income.

Lesson in Brief

Resources are scarce in the sense that the country does not have enough manpower, capital and natural resources to produce all the goods and services that people would like to have. Because resources are scarce relative to needs and wants, choices among alternative uses must be made. The concept of opportunity cost helps people make these choices by showing the amounts of other goods and services that must be given up when the decision is made to devote available resources to one use rather than to another.

One of the basic facts of life is that one cannot get something for nothing. One particular person might get it for nothing, but somebody pays. In economics, the output of goods and services (like cars and candy and clothing) depends on the input of productive resources (such as labor, equipment and raw materials). There are always costs involved in the production of goods and services.

Economic activity does not begin with buying and selling but with production—the use of resources to produce goods and services. To produce chickens, eggs are needed. To grow corn, soil, fertilizer, the services of a tractor and much hard work are required. To build a bridge, steel, heavy equipment, iron workers and engineers are needed.

Several years ago the economics editor of a national news magazine spoke to a group of professional economists on the topic, "The Teaching of Economics." He began by listing, partly as a joke, "some simple, basic economic truths that everyone should be taught." His first truth was "there is no such thing as a free lunch." (Years ago, taverns advertised "Free Lunch" to attract customers. The sandwiches and pretzels were free; customers had to buy the beer.)

What the speaker meant was that goods and services are never "free"—that is, they must be produced and must be paid for. The free lunches might be provided to the customers without charge, but costs were involved. (The tavern owner had to pay for the pretzels, bread, meat, pickles and mustard. Wheat and rye had to be grown to provide the flour to make the bread, and livestock had to be fed and marketed and processed by meatpackers to produce the meat. All this involved costs of production.) For every unit of output, there must be inputs—materials, manpower and capital. Not only must these inputs be paid for by someone, but remember too that if they were not used to provide "free lunches" they could be used to produce some alternative goods and services. There are opportunity costs.

Let's look at the output of the U. S. economy for 1971 and see what inputs of resources were necessary to produce the goods and services.

In 1971, the total output (GNP) of the American economy amounted to $1,050 billion. The economy produced $665 billion worth of goods and services for consumers (such as food, cars, clothing, books, vacation trips, and so forth). The economy produced $152 billion in capital goods for business investment (such as new machinery, office buildings and inventories of goods). One billion dollars worth of goods and services (in excess of the imports from other countries) were exported. Two hundred thirty-three billion dollars in goods and services were produced, for use by local, state and federal government agencies.

A simple formula to remember for counting the nation's total output of goods and services is

$$GNP = C + I + G + X_n$$

(Gross National Product is the total of all spending for Consumption plus Investment plus Government Purchases plus Net Exports).

Table 2.2 shows the total output for 1971 and how it was divided among the 4 groups of buyers in the economy.

Table 2.2
**PURCHASERS OF THE
U.S. GROSS NATIONAL PRODUCT, 1971**

	(billions of dollars)	(percentage total GNP)
Consumer Goods and Services (C)	$ 665	63%
Gross Private Investment (I)	152	15
Net exports (X_n)	1	—
Government Purchases of Goods & Services (G)	233	22
State & Local Governments	(135)	
Federal Government	(98)[a]	
TOTALS	$1,050	100%

Source: U.S. Department of Commerce, *Survey of Current Business,*
    July 1972, p. 7.
[a]Federal purchases for purposes other than national defense totalled
$26 billion.

What were the inputs that were used in producing all those goods and services?

The input of manpower is seen in the figures on labor force employment. During 1971, there were 82 million men and women employed in producing goods and services. This number includes all the unskilled workers, the technicians, the managers, self-employed doctors and lawyers, members of the armed forces, and everyone else who was employed during the year. In total, they contributed more than 2 billion man-hours of work to the U.S. economy.

The input of capital is a little harder to measure. Table 2.3 gives a rough idea of the capital input. It shows, for example, that every worker in the chemicals industry had an average of $77,000 worth of equipment, buildings and tools on hand to help him get the job done.

Table 2.3
CAPITAL INVESTED PER EMPLOYEE
IN MANUFACTURING, 1962

Industry	Amount
Chemicals	$77,000
Motor Vehicles	22,000
Petroleum (refining, extraction, pipe lines)	27,000
Printing & Publishing	11,000
Manufacturing (all industries—average)	$16,000

Source: National Industrial Conference Board, "Road Maps of Industry" #1526, 1965.
Note: Amount represents total investment divided by all employees, including clerical and supervisory.

The input of natural resources is even harder to measure than capital. The input of natural resources may be illustrated by noting that some years ago (according to the President's Materials Policy Commision) each man, women and child in the United States used 18 tons of materials each year. Each consumer used 7 tons of fuel for heat and energy, 2 tons of building materials, 3 tons of food and other agricultural materials. He consumed 150 gallons of water per day in household consumption. An additional 1,250 gallons per person per day were used in industry and agriculture. (Compare this total water use of 1,400 gallons per person each day in the United States with a total of only 50 gallons per person per day in Europe.)

Large amounts of manpower, capital and natural resources were required to produce more than a trillion dollars worth of goods and services in 1971. With only 6% of the world's population and not quite 7% of its land area, the United States each year produces about one-third of total world output. Of all the raw materials used up in production each year in the entire world, the U. S. economy consumes more than half. The output is fantastically great, but the input of resources is also large. Some people are deeply concerned over the rate at which materials are being used and feel that the conservation of natural resources is a national problem demanding urgent attention.

Economists call the relationship between inputs and outputs a *production function*. A production function tells what kinds and amounts of resources are needed to produce a particular good, assuming that a certain method of production is used. Technological progress and automation, of course, bring about changes in production functions.

Note one final point concerning the idea that there is no such thing as a free lunch. Sometimes people make the mistake of thinking that goods and services coming from the federal government are free. Citizens often vote against a local tax increase for schools because they do not want to pay the cost. Then, acting under a fiscal illusion, they tell their Congressmen in Washington that they prefer federal financing of education— because they think they are getting something for nothing. But federal money also comes from taxes (though not necessarily the same kinds). In the same way, colleges often receive gifts from business corporations for scholarships or to pay for new buildings. Are the new campus buildings free? Obviously, somebody pays for them—the stockholders in the corporation, consumers who paid higher prices than would have been necessary to cover the costs of production, employees whose wages might have been higher if the corporation's extra money had gone to them rather than to a college. This does not mean that it is wrong for corporations to

125

give money to colleges and universities (or for the federal government to finance schools). It simply means there is no such thing as a free lunch.

Lesson in Brief

One of the first lessons of economics is that it takes inputs (of manpower, capital and materials) to get output. There are costs involved in producing goods and services, and somebody must pay these costs.

Economic Goals of the American People

Just as individual men and women have aspirations and goals, it is also true that groups of people set goals for the whole society. In the area of economics, some important goals of the American people are full production, stable growth, freedom of choice, economic security, distributive justice and international balance. When the economy comes reasonably close to achieving these goals, it is considered to be performing successfully.

When he was President of the United States (1953-61), Dwight D. Eisenhower appointed a special Commission on National Goals to work out a set of goals for the American people in various areas of national life. The Commission was made up of leaders from the fields of education, business, labor and other professions. In 1960, after much study and discussion, the Commission published a report entitled *Goals for Americans.* The report contained ideas about what the nation should do about technological change, education, the individual, economic growth and the kind of economic system that would best serve the needs of the people.

Setting goals, and then working to achieve them, is a sign of maturity and responsibility in a society just as it is a sign of maturity in an individual. What economic goals have the American people set for themselves? How well are these goals being achieved?

One important goal that the American people have set for their economy is *full production*—the full and efficient use of available labor, capital and natural resources. Americans feel so strongly about the importance of this goal that Congress passed a law—the Employment Act of 1946—making it the responsibility of the federal government to "promote maximum employment, production and purchasing power."

How well is the goal of full production (and full employment) being achieved? Let's use manpower statistics as a tool to study this economic question.

In the 1930s the unemployment rate averaged nearly 20%. Year in and year out, 10 million people who were able and willing to work were jobless. In contrast, during World War II and the Korean War, the United States came very close to having full employment. Between 1954 and 1965, the rate varied but remained high. From 1966 through 1969, unemployment dropped below 4%. With an average of less than 3 million jobless workers during those 4 years, the United States could claim to be achieving its goal of full employment and full production.

The nation cannot realistically expect to provide jobs continuously for all of the 90 million men and women who are able and willing to work. There will always be some unemployment, roughly 2% to 4% of the labor force. But when millions of people are unnecessarily unemployed, it means they are not making a productive contribution to the country and they are not earning an income. For this reason, the economic goal of full production is one of the most important.

A second major goal is *stable growth*—the economy should become "bigger and better" through the years. The amount of national output of goods and services is measured by looking at the gross national product statistics. Economic growth means a steady increase in GNP per person—that is, total GNP divided by the size of the population. The goal is to have GNP increase more or less at a steady rate of about 4% or 5% each year and to avoid economic recessions (which cause unemployment) and rapidly rising prices (inflation).

Since 1929, America's GNP has more than tripled. In the last 20 years, it has grown at an average rate of 4%. Growth has not been steady, however. In some years GNP went down, which happened in the recession years of 1954, 1958 and 1970. From 1960 to 1969 the economy grew rapidly, and real GNP rose nearly 50%.

Production, employment and growth are all fairly easy to measure. Other economic goals, however, must be discussed in more general terms.

Freedom of choice is a goal that practically everyone would include high on the list. But what does it mean in concrete terms?

Economists have pointed out that freedom of choice is important for consumers, for workers and for business. *Freedom of consumer choice* means that consumers will be able to select the goods they want to buy from a fairly wide range of alternatives according to individual needs and preferences. Americans are not satisfied with a system where the consumer is told "You can have any size and color hat you want—as long as it's medium and black!"

Freedom of occupational choice, an important area of economic freedom, enables men and women to choose jobs that will provide adequate earnings and personal satisfaction. In order to exercise real freedom in choosing a career, men and women must have opportunities to acquire formal education and the other qualifications required by the job. They also need to develop an understanding of how the industrial system functions, where the best career opportunities exist and how the world of work influences the lives of workers. Only then can people make wise career choices.

Finally, an important aspect of freedom of choice is *free enterprise*—the opportunity for people to start their own businesses and use the factors of production in such a way as to make a profit. Much of the American economic system is built on the foundation of this particular freedom.

If all people are to enjoy freedom of choice in the American economy, reasonable equality of opportunity must be assured. Indeed, a major challenge facing the nation is the provision of real freedom of choice to all consumers, workers and enterprisers regardless of their race, sex, ethnic background, age or other characteristics.

The goal of *economic security* means that the members of the economic society want to have enough money to be able to buy adequate food, clothing, shelter and other necessities. In a rich country like the United States where the personal income per person is more than $4,000 per year (over $16,000 for a 4-person family), it seems unnecessary to have people living in poverty and fear. Thus, the American people established a Social Security system in the 1930s, declared a "War Against Poverty" in 1964 and began talking in the 1970s about providing a minimum level of income for all families.

In 1970, 25 million Americans were still living in poverty. Nearly half of these were children under 18 years of age. Such widespread poverty not only meant failure to achieve the goal of economic security for these Americans but also raised serious questions about the achievement of the goal of *distributive justice*—fairness and equity in the way income is distributed. Not everyone agrees on the meaning of fairness or justice in economic life, although nearly everyone feels the goal is important to define and work toward. The Economic Opportunity Act of 1964 and some of the recent civil rights and other legislation has aimed at improving economic justice for Negroes, Indians, Spanish-speaking people and other groups of Americans.

Finally, there is one economic goal that is not limited to the boundaries of the United States itself but spreads overseas to other countries. This is the goal of *international balance*—the maintenance of a strong and balanced relationship in foreign trade and international payments and in relations with the underdeveloped nations and socialist countries. Failure to achieve this goal not only causes serious economic problems at home and abroad but also increases international tensions and the threat of war.

Lesson in Brief

The following economic goals have been identified as ranking high in the minds of the American people:

1. Full employment and full production
2. Stable growth without inflation
3. Freedom of choice for consumers, workers and enterprisers
4. Economic security
5. Distributive justice
6. International balance

When the economic system comes reasonably close to achieving these goals on a continuing basis, the system is judged to be working well and serving the needs of the American people.

"The Business of America Is Business" 28

Calvin Coolidge, President of the United States in the 1920s, is well remembered for making the statement that appears as the title of this lesson. The business enterprise sector of the economy is a very important part of the economic life of the United States. It accounts for nearly 80% of the nation's total production and income. Business firms, striving for profits, make many of the buying, selling and operating decisions that determine production, employment and distribution. One form of business organization, the corporation, receives nearly four-fifths of all business income and manages two-thirds of the nation's total production.

Business firms play a key role in the circular flow of economic activity, as shown in Figure 2.2.

Figure 2.2

BUSINESS FIRMS IN THE CIRCULAR FLOW MODEL

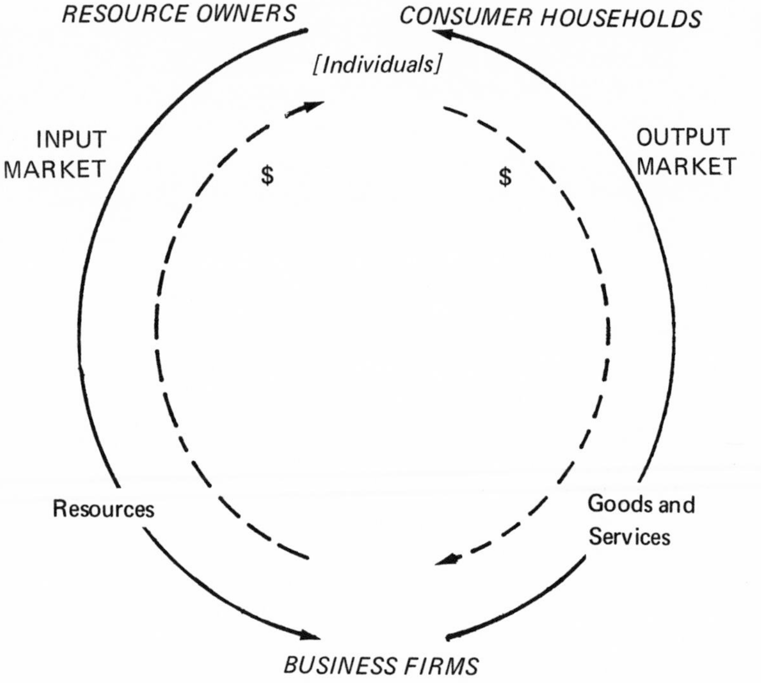
RESOURCE OWNERS
CONSUMER HOUSEHOLDS
[Individuals]
INPUT MARKET
OUTPUT MARKET
$
$
Resources
Goods and Services
BUSINESS FIRMS

A business firm (or "enterprise" or "company") buys resources of labor, land and capital in the input market. It combines and coordinates all these resources to produce goods and services. It then sells the goods and services in the output market.

Why is it that business firms are willing to take on all this responsibility, effort and risk? The answer is they hope to make profits. They expect to be able to sell the finished products for prices that are high enough to cover all their costs of operating the business and still have money left over. (Profit equals Total Receipts less Total Costs).

The incentive of business, the driving force that "makes businessmen run," is the profit motive. Business firms produce goods and services not to satisfy human wants but to sell products in the market in order to make profits for the owners and managers of the business and to provide investment funds for expanding the business. Generally speaking, in order to make profits the firm must produce goods and services that satisfy the wants of consumers. This system of production provides jobs and incomes for workers and for the owners of other resources.

Counting the nation's 3 million farms and all of the self-employed professionals like doctors and lawyers, there are about 12 million business enterprises in the United States. One million firms are organized as corporations. Nearly 1 million are partnerships; and 3 million are sole proprietorships. (If farms and professionals who sell their own services are included, as in Table 2.4, the number of proprietorships would be 9 million and the total number of businesses in the country would be nearly 12 million.)

Most businesses are small, employing fewer than 4 workers. Many of these firms make little or no profits. Thousands of them "go broke" every year. The average life of a business firm in the United States is 7 years. The big corporations, however, are generally much more stable and earn much greater profits.

Table 2.4 shows the business receipts of proprietorships, partnerships and corporations in 1968. Businesses organized as producer and consumer cooperatives are not included in the table.

Table 2.4
BUSINESS FIRMS AND BUSINESS RECEIPTS IN 1968

	Number of Firms	Percentage Distri- bution	Receipts (billions of dollars)	Percentage Distri- bution
Sole Propri- etorships	9,212,000	79%	$ 222	12%
Partnerships	918,000	8	83	5
Corporations[a]	1,542,000	13	1,508	83
TOTALS	11,672,000	100%	$1,813	100%

Source: U.S. Department of Commerce, *Statistical Abstract of the United States 1972*, p. 469; and *The Fortune Directory*, May 1969, p. 2.

[a]The largest 500 industrial corporations had receipts totalling $405 billion.

Some corporations have grown to tremendous size. They are responsible for the production and sales of billions of dollars of goods. Together they employ millions of workers and are "owned" by millions of stockholders. Table 2.4 shows that the 500 biggest industrial corporations actually do far more business than the total sales of all 9 million proprietorships put together!

General Motors Corporation (GM), for example, had assets of $18.2 billion in 1971 and sold $28.3 billion worth of automobiles, trucks, diesel locomotives and a variety of other goods. Three-quarters of a million workers were employed by GM. Profits after taxes totaled $1.9 billion (a 6.8% profit rate figured as a percentage of sales and a 17.9% profit rate figured as a percentage of invested capital).

General Motors is the biggest industrial corporation in the nation. But the Ford Motor Company, Standard Oil of New

Jersey, General Electric Company and International Business Machines (IBM) are giants too. Each had more than $8 billion worth of sales receipts in 1971. The American Telephone and Telegraph Company (AT&T)—a utility rather than an industrial corporation—had assets of $54.6 billion in 1971, operating revenues of $81.5 billion, net income of $2.4 billion. The corporation employed 776,800 workers and had over 2 million stockholders. Four large industrial corporations—General Motors, Ford, General Electric and IBM—had more employees in 1971 than the entire federal government excluding the Department of Defense. General Motors alone handled more money (receipts and expenditures) than the state governments of California, New York, Ohio and Texas combined.

What is a corporation? The simple answer is that a *corporation* is a form of business organization that gives the firm a legal existence that is separate from the people who own and manage the business. Money to set up and operate the business comes from people who buy shares of stock. These people are called *stockholders* and might be thought of as the "owners" of the business. They are risking the money they invest in the corporation. Their hope is to receive *dividends* (regular payments on each share of stock they own) and also to make *capital gains* ("profits" from increased market value of the stock) if and when they choose to sell their shares to somebody else. Under the corporate form of business organization, basic policies are set by the board of directors whose members are elected by the stockholders. The board hires a president, treasurer and other members of *management* to run the corporation.

There is also a more complicated answer to the question, What is a corporation? Some economists believe that the giant corporation is an economic institution that replaces the supply and demand system of market competition because the owners (stockholders) of many large corporations really do not control the business. Small groups of managers have control. Private property rights are sometimes limited by government controls. Corporations are not always free to use and dispose of their capital and other resources any way they please. The corporations do not always behave rationally in terms of pricing and output policy. And they are not competitive in the free enterprise sense. Sometimes they "administer" their prices rather than let the forces of supply and demand set them in the market place. Some experts on the structure of American industry argue that General Motors is really more like a government agency—the Tennessee Valley Authority, or the State of New York or the Department of Defense—than like the corner grocery store, the small tailor shop or the construction firm. If these experts are right, it will be interesting to watch the giant quasi-public corporations during the next 20 or 30 years to see how they affect the nature and performance of the mixed-capitalism economy of the United States.

Lesson in Brief

The business sector of the economy accounts for 80% of the total production. Business firms assume the responsibilities of coordinating production because they anticipate making profits. Some business corporations have grown to tremendous size, handling billions of dollars and employing hundreds of thousands of workers.

The term government, in this study of economics, refers to all of the units of government—local, state and federal. Citizens of the community, the state and the nation use these governmental units to make rules, to engage in activities that influence both the production and distribution of income, and to help stabilize the economy. Government accounts directly for more than 20% of the U.S. gross national product.

What image does the word government bring to mind? A fire truck or police car rushing to the rescue? A teacher instructing an eighth grade math class? The Congress in Washington, D.C.? A job counselor in the State Employment Service? The Tennessee Valley Authority producing electric power? A tax auditor from the Internal Revenue Service investigating a 1972 tax return?

The word *government* is used here to include all units of government—local, state and federal. These are political agencies set up by citizens to handle certain jobs. There is 1 unit of federal government, 50 state governments and more than 80,000 local units of government! Local government includes cities, counties, townships, special districts and school districts. In the 1967 Census of Governments, there were 22,000 separate school districts in the United States, all with the power to levy property taxes.

What kinds of services do these government units perform for their citizens? They put out fires, build roads, fight wars, operate schools and handle hundreds of other assignments. They also collect taxes to pay for all these activities. Looking at government from the viewpoint of the economic functions performed, government activities fall under 4 main headings:

1. Making rules (e.g., civil and criminal laws, public health regulations, antimonopoly laws, city zoning ordinances)
2. Producing goods and services (e.g., building roads, operating schools)

3. Transferring income (e.g., taxing, borrowing, paying social security benefits and welfare assistance to needy families)
4. Stabilizing the economy (e.g., raising and lowering taxes to stimulate employment and production and to prevent inflation)

Government has always played an important part in the economic life of the American people. In the past 40 years, however, government's role has expanded. Taxes and spending at all levels of government have increased greatly. Government purchases of goods and services went up from $8.5 billion in 1929 to $233 billion in 1971 (partly because of inflation). As a fraction of GNP, government purchases of goods and services rose from less than one-tenth to more than one-fifth. Today, government absorbs more than 20% of the total GNP. Approximately 13 million men and women are employed by government. Nearly 4 of every 5 civilian government employees work for state or local government.

Why is government involved in the 4 kinds of activities listed above? The reason that government makes rules and regulations is pretty obvious to most people. They are necessary in order to maintain order and stability for over 200 million people in a huge country stretching 3,000 miles from the Atlantic to the Pacific Ocean and 1,500 miles from Canada to Mexico. As economic and social life becomes more complex, government involvement will probably increase as well.

Why does government get involved in producing goods and services, transferring income and stabilizing the economy? One way to approach this question is to realize that the United States is a democracy. If government gets involved in certain activities, presumably the people want it that way. The citizens of the United States turn to government to help solve certain economic problems because apparently they feel that government can help bring about better solutions than can be obtained without government participation.

What are these economic problems? They are the familiar "basic problems facing an economic society"—how much to produce, what specific goods and services to produce, how to distribute the income.

For example, in order to get a better solution to the problem of how much to produce, the people of the United States (through the Employment Act of 1946 which Congress passed with strong support from both Republicans and Democrats) have made it the responsibility of the federal government to "use all practicable means . . . to promote maximum employment, production and purchasing power." This was done partly because the Great Depression of the 1930s left many people with the idea that the economy would not automatically achieve these goals without active help from the government.

The famous 1964 cut in federal income tax was passed for the stabilizing purpose of encouraging full employment and growth. The 1971 wage-price freeze was adopted for the stabilizing purpose of halting inflation.

Government is also involved in producing highways and schools because the American people want more and better transportation and education than they get individually through the private (market) sector of the economy. Because the federal government is responsible for the "common defense," it spends some $80 billion each year to produce the large Army, Navy and Air Force establishments.

Table 2.5 shows the amount of direct general spending, by function and level of government, for the 1970-71 fiscal year. These figures do not report money which is transferred from federal government to lower levels for such purposes as public welfare and highways until the point where it is directly spent.

Table 2.5 does not show all government expenditure. It leaves out insurance trust funds such as the federal Social Security program, state liquor store receipts and local utility revenues from city-owned water systems. Boxes have been drawn to show that $81 billion was spent by the federal government on its biggest function, national defense and international relations, and that local and state governments spent $16 billion and $43 billion, respectively, on their biggest function, education.

Table 2.5
DIRECT GENERAL EXPENDITURES BY FUNCTION AND
LEVEL OF GOVERNMENT, 1970-1971

Function	Level of Government and Amount Spent (billions of dollars)			
	Local	State	Federal	Total
National Defense and International Relations	$ –	$ –	$ 81	$ 81
Education	43	16	5	64
Public Welfare	8	10	2	20
Highways	6	12	–	18
All other functions including interest on general debt	37	18	62	117
TOTALS	$94 +	$56 +	$150 =	$300

Source: U.S. Bureau of the Census, *Governmental Finances in 1970-71*,
GF71 No. 5, October 1972, p. 22.

Where does all this money come from? Altogether, government collected $232 billion in general taxes in 1970-71, plus $57 billion of insurance trust revenues and $53 billion other miscellaneous receipts. The federal individual income tax alone yielded $86 billion of revenues. Other big money raisers included the federal corporation income tax ($27 billion), state sales taxes ($30 billion), local property taxes ($37 billion) and federal excise taxes ($17 billion). The per capita revenue bill of the American people in 1970-71, including general taxes plus other payments to local, state and federal government, amounted to $1,660.

Government spending and taxing affect the overall level of the economy and also the specific goods and services that are produced. Taxes and spending also influence the distribution of income. *Progressive* taxes such as the federal individual income tax take a higher percentage of income from the high-income family than from the low-income family. Because sales taxes generally are *regressive,* they take a higher percentage of income from poor families. Government *transfer payments,* such as public welfare assistance and unemployment compensation benefits, give more money to the poor than to the high-income families. These transfer payments help reduce some of the inequalities in the distribution of income in the economy.

Government's role in the economy is both important and complicated. Many people disagree about what the government ought to be doing in the economy, and there are many heated arguments on the subject. When reading the newspapers during a political campaign—especially during a presidential election year— notice how important the economic issues can be. In local communities too, note the pro's and con's presented on school bond issues, local property tax issues and other dollars-and-cents issues before voting takes place.

Lesson in Brief

Local, state and federal government play an active role in economic life. Altogether, they handle over 20% of U.S. gross national product. Taxing and spending by government affect the overall level of economic activity, the particular kinds of goods and services that are produced and the way income is divided.

Although labor unions have existed in the United States since the early 1800s, they did not become a solid fixture in the economy until the 1880s; membership was small until the 1930s. Unions were organized to give workers a stronger voice in dealing with employers regarding wages, hours, working conditions and job security. Today nearly 20 million men and women, about one-fourth of all American workers, belong to unions. The AFL-CIO is a federation of labor unions that serves as national spokesman for union members and other workers.

Organized labor (sometimes called the labor movement), an important institution in the American economy, refers to the organization of workers into unions and to the linking together of these unions through cooperation (and sometimes formal organization and federation) to accomplish certain common goals.

A *labor union* is an association of employees. The purpose of unions is to give men and women who work for wages a stronger influence in dealing with employers. Their motto is "Through union, comes strength." They use this strength to gain higher wages, better working conditions, more control over their jobs and improvements in their social and economic lives.

History as well as theory and statistics can help people understand the institution of unionism as it exists today. What was it like to be a worker in America three-quarters of a century ago, about 1900? The following description of the world of work at the turn of the century suggests some reasons why workers felt the need to join together into unions.

- —The average worker made about $10 a week for a 60-hour week. Some textile workers put in as many as 84 hours. More than 2 million children, some only 12 years old or younger, worked long hours frequently at night for which they were paid no more than 60¢ a day.
- —For working 12 hours a day, 7 days a week, garment workers were paid $3.00 or $4.00 a week from which they often had to pay fines to their employers for talking, smiling or breaking needles.

—The only relief from work came as a result of being laid off or fired. Then came the desperate search to find some work, any work, at any pay, just to stay alive.

—Garment workers were employed in dim, damp, disease-breeding places of labor called sweat shops. There were no regular hours, no minimum wages, no paid holidays, no vacations and no human dignity.

The following rules (quoted from an employee's handbook distributed in 1857) were imposed on the employees of a Chicago department store in the years preceding the Civil War:

—Store must be open from 6 a.m. to 9 p.m. the year around.

—Each employee must not pay less than five dollars per year to the church and must attend Sunday school regularly.

—Men employees are given one evening a week for courting and two if they go to the prayer meeting.

—The employee who is in the habit of smoking Spanish cigars, being shaved at barbers, going to dances and other places of amusement will surely give his employer reasons to be suspicious of his integrity and honesty.

Throughout most of this nation's history, both business and government opposed labor unions—sometimes using the police, National Guard and armies of "private detectives" to break up strikes and prevent efforts to organize unions. The individualist outlook of the American people was another factor that prevented unions from being formed. For many years, public sentiment was definitely not in favor of labor unions. As a result, union membership was small.

Figure 2.3 shows total union membership in the United States from 1900 to 1968. In the latter year, there were almost 19 million members, not counting 1.3 million additional members in Canada. Notice the sharp increase in members during the 1930s and 1940s. How is this to be explained?

Figure 2.3

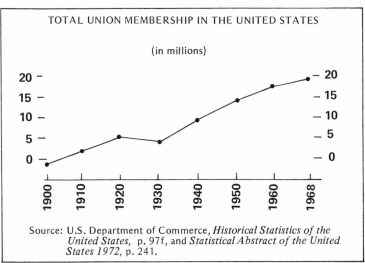

TOTAL UNION MEMBERSHIP IN THE UNITED STATES

(in millions)

Source: U.S. Department of Commerce, *Historical Statistics of the United States,* p. 97f, and *Statistical Abstract of the United States 1972,* p. 241.

Two factors explain most of the growth in union membership after 1930. First, the economic system suffered its most severe breakdown in history. The Great Depression caused millions of workers to be unemployed. From 1931 to 1940, the unemployment rate never fell below 14%. In the worst year, 1933, 1 worker out of every 4 was jobless. The American people lost confidence in the business system and looked for new ways, including unionism, to improve the economy.

The second factor was a change in the attitude of government. President Franklin D. Roosevelt publicly stated, "If I were a worker in a factory, the first thing I would do would be to join a union." In 1935, Congress passed the National Labor Relations Act (Wagner Act), guaranteeing workers the right to organize unions and bargain collectively with employers without interference from management. Employers now were legally required to bargain in good faith with any union certified as a bargaining agent.

There have been many changes in the law dealing with unions since 1935. Some of these new laws, such as the Labor-Management Relations Act (Taft-Hartley Act) of 1947, have been designed to limit the power of unions. They also were intended to make unions more responsible to their members and to the public. The Labor-Management Reporting and Disclosure Act (Landrum-Griffin Act) of 1959 is another example. Unions today are a solid fixture in the U.S. economic world. As President Dwight Eisenhower said in the 1950s, "Only a fool would try to deprive working men and working women of the right to join the union of their choice."

Even today, however, only 19 million men and women—less than one-fourth of all workers in the United States—belong to unions. But totals can be misleading. In certain industries unions are very strong, and almost all workers are union members. More than three-fourths of all workers in the transportation and construction industries are union members. At the other extreme, only about one-tenth of the workers in service industries, state and local government, finance and insurance, and retail and wholesale trade belong to unions.

Some national unions are very large. The Teamsters union, which includes truck drivers and others, has nearly 2 million members. The Auto Workers and the Steelworkers each have more than a million members. The Machinists, the Electrical Workers and the Carpenters are not far behind. The size and influence of some of these unions can be compared with the giant corporations they bargain with in labor negotiations, such as General Motors, Ford, U.S. Steel and General Electric.

What is the structure of organized labor in the United States? The first level includes the *local* unions that exist within particular factories or office buildings. Above the local is the national or international union. (Those that include Canadian workers are called international.) It is the *national union* that has much of the collective bargaining power, especially in an industry like steel or automobile production. In some unions there are *districts* or *conferences* interposed between the local and national levels. National unions are completely independent and self-governing, but for certain purposes they find it useful to affiliate with other independent unions in a *federation,* such as the AFL-CIO (American Federation of Labor and Congress of Industrial Organizations). As its name indicates, the AFL-CIO with head-quarters in Washington, D.C. is not a union but a federation of more than 100 unions with 16 million members. It does not engage in collective bargaining with employers but serves as the chief spokesman for organized labor on such national issues as federal taxes, the war on poverty, occupational safety standards and elections. Not all unions are affiliated with the AFL-CIO. In 1968 there were 63 national unions outside of the AFL-CIO family, including the giant Teamsters union and the United Auto Workers.

At the state and local levels, there are labor councils or "central bodies" that represent organized labor in political activities, educational programs and a variety of other areas.

In the early 1900s attitudes regarding workers and unions were quite different than they are today. In 1903 when railroad workers were trying to build a strong union and bargain with management over wages and working hours, George F. Baer, President of the Philadelphia & Reading Railroad, made the following statement:

> The rights and interests of the laboring man will be protected and cared for, not by the labor agitators, but by the Christian men to whom God in His infinite wisdom has given control of the property interests of the country. Pray earnestly that the right may triumph, always remembering that the Lord God Omnipotent still reigns and that His reign is one of law and order and not of violence and crime.

What is the future of labor unions in America? Some people say that unions played their most important role in the 1940s and 1950s and now there is less need for them. With the spread of automation, however, many workers have turned to unions to help protect their jobs and incomes. They feel that unions will play an important role in helping them achieve the goals of distributive justice and economic security. There are many who predict that unions will continue to be a major force in determining wages and working conditions and will assume great importance in new fields, particularly with white-collar workers. Unions of public school teachers and other government employees, for example, have grown up in recent years and attracted national attention.

Lesson in Brief

Labor unions have been a solid fixture in the U. S. economy since the 1930s. Their chief purpose is to give workers a stronger voice in dealing with employers over such matters as wages, working conditions, job security and fringe benefits. Today 19 million men and women, nearly one-fourth of all American workers, belong to unions. Workers are represented by local unions, national unions and by the AFL-CIO which is a national federation of unions.

There are more than 60 million consumer households in the United States. Together they spend two-thirds of a trillion dollars a year for the purchase of goods and services to satisfy the needs and desires of over 200 million Americans. Consumer spending plays an important role in the circular flow of economic activity by influencing the overall level of market demand and by sending "dollar messages" to business firms telling them which particular goods and services to produce for sale in the market. Patterns of consumer spending, in turn, are influenced by the way income is distributed among households.

The American people have been called the consumers of abundance. In the late 1950s, Professor John Kenneth Galbraith (who later became President of the American Economic Association) wrote a best-selling book entitled *The Affluent Society*. Most people agree that the title is a pretty apt description of the economy in the United States.

The economy produces food, housing, clothing, cars, cigarettes, liquor and other goods literally by the tons and megatons. Millions of automobiles, TV sets, household appliances and gadgets are manufactured. And transportation services, entertainment and many other services valued at billions of dollars are produced each year.

Today, 98% of all households in the United States wired for electricity have a TV set. Not quite as many have flush toilets and bathtubs or showers. Four out of every 5 households own a car and have telephone service. Nearly all of the wired homes have a refrigerator, and 95% have a washing machine. In most of the countries of the world only the richest 2% or 3% of all households are able to own a car and refrigerator and TV set.

The United States, with only 6% of the world's population, produces and consumes between 30% and 40% of the world's output of goods and services. By almost any standard—physiological needs or comparisons with the past or with other countries today—the United States is truly an affluent society.

The abundance of consumer goods and services is considered by many people to be conclusive proof that the American economic system is the most successful the world has ever known. This judgment is based on the assumption, which many economists make, that the chief purpose of all economic activity is consumption. Therefore, the quantity and quality of consumer goods produced is the best standard by which to judge the performance of the economy. While this is a powerful argument, human values and the general quality of life also must be taken into consideration.

In any case, consumption is a very important part of economic life. Everyone must consume in order to live. (It has been said that some people live in order to consume!) Some people live "higher on the hog" than other people. The rich have vastly more consumer goods than the 20 to 30 million Americans who live in poverty or severe deprivation.

As mentioned earlier, there are about 60 million consumer households in the American economy. A *household* includes all persons who occupy a house, apartment, room or group of rooms as separate living quarters. A household can consist of 1 person or a whole family. Since the population is roughly 200 million, the average size of each household is 3-1/3 persons.

How do the 60-odd million consumer households behave in the economy? What do they do? What economic functions do the households perform?

The circular flow model (Figure 2.4) shows that consumers spend money (indicated by the broken line) and obtain goods and services (indicated by the solid line) which they use to satisfy their needs and desires. Let's look at each of these functions in turn.

In 1971, consumers spent $665 billion to buy goods and services, an average of more than $10,000 of consumer spending per household. They spent 42% on *services* such as household operations, transportation and medical care. They spent another 42% on *nondurable goods* including food, clothing and tobacco. The remaining 16% of consumer spending was for *durable goods* such as automobiles, furniture and household equipment.

Figure 2.4

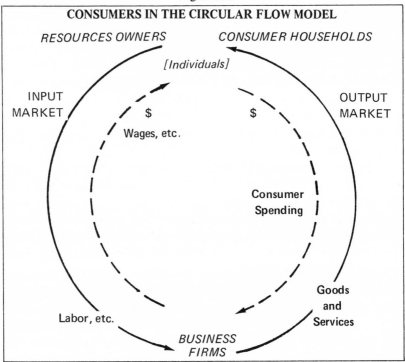

CONSUMERS IN THE CIRCULAR FLOW MODEL

RESOURCES OWNERS   *CONSUMER HOUSEHOLDS*

[Individuals]

INPUT
MARKET $ $ OUTPUT
MARKET

Wages, etc.

Consumer
Spending

Goods
and
Services

Labor, etc.

*BUSINESS
FIRMS*

Where did the households get the money needed to purchase all these goods and services? Although some of their purchasing power came from past savings, most of it was current income. Total *personal income* in 1971 for all persons in the nation amounted to $861 billion. Two-thirds of this personal income came from wages and salaries received for work that was done during the year.

As the circular flow model indicates, employed workers earn wages and salaries. Then in their capacity as consumers, they spend much of it for the purchase of goods and services. They also pay taxes, save a little and make other minor outlays. There is an important connection between earning and spending. One cannot spend money in the consumer goods market unless one has money to spend. The most important source of purchasing power is current income from wages and salaries.

What are the consequences of consumer spending? When consumer households spend money in the market, they create what economists call an *effective demand* for goods and services. They exchange money for goods, and this stimulates business firms to produce more goods. (Note: The term goods is used to include both commodities and services.) Spending in the market lubricates the wheels of commerce and industry—that is, when businessmen sell their merchandise, they continue to produce more goods. Thus, manpower and other productive resources continue to be employed.

Consumer spending creates a demand for goods, which stimulates production, which in turn creates a larger total of employment opportunities. But spending is always for particular goods and services. Therefore, consumer spending in the market also provides a system of signals or messages telling business firms to produce more of the particular goods and services that consumers say they want and less of the goods that are piling up on the shelves and in the warehouses. When a consumer spends $5.00 to buy a blue, size medium, short-sleeve shirt, in effect he is voting in favor of continuing the production of blue, medium, short-sleeve shirts. His dollar votes will influence not only the overall level of resource use in the economy but also the particular pattern of resource use.

The second major function of consumer households is to obtain goods and services for use in satisfying wants. People must consume in order to live. How people live is greatly influenced by the quantity and the quality of the goods and services consumed. Consider this paraphrase of the food faddist's motto: "We are what we eat." If people spend their consumer dollars for candy, cars, coke, cosmetics, liquor, cigarettes, guns, thrill magazines, drugs, gadgets and pills, they create a certain kind of world for themselves and their neighbors. Do they pollute the environment or improve it? Do they contribute to the quality of life for themselves and their fellow men or detract from it? What are the private and the social consequences of consumer behavior?

In another lesson, the concepts of social costs and social benefits will be discussed in some detail. Basically, *private costs* are those burdens or sacrifices associated with production or consumption that are borne exclusively by the business firm or individual responsible for making a particular economic decision. *Social costs* are those burdens or losses that "spill over" to third parties or the public at large. When John Jones pays 35¢ for a hamburger, he bears the cost and derives exclusive benefit from eating the sandwich. When Peter Polluter burns chicken feathers in his back yard, he enjoys the benefit of being rid of the feathers. His neighbors, however, bear much of the real cost by having to smell the foul odor.

In an affluent society, citizens have the economic power to produce and consume almost anything they choose. They have the freedom, within broad limits, to choose whatever they like. The kind of world they live in will depend to a very great extent on how wisely they choose and how well they use their freedom. For this reason, the subjects of economic interdependence and consumer values become 2 of today's most significant issues.

Lesson in Brief

The 60 million consumer households that function in the American economy exert a great deal of influence through their annual expenditures of two-thirds of a trillion dollars. Consumers perform 2 major functions—they spend money in the market, and they obtain goods and services for use in satisfying human wants. The total amount of spending, and the particular pattern of spending, influence the overall level of output and employment and influence the way the economy's resources are allocated in the production of particular goods and services.

Wages, Earnings and Family Income

Wages are the money payments that people receive for work. Three-fourths of the total national income is paid each year to workers as compensation of employees. These wage earnings are the most important source of income for most families. Hourly wages, weekly earnings and annual income vary greatly among workers and families. These wage and income differences are significant because there are strong linkages in the economy among jobs, earnings, consumer buying power and levels of living.

One reason people work is to "make a living." In the input market, workers exchange their manpower for wages which provide them with money to spend in their role as consumers for the purchase of goods and services in the output market. *Wages* is a general term that includes all forms of labor income—hourly wages, salaries, sales commissions, bonuses, personal fees, etc.

Three-fourths of total *national income* consistently is paid to the millions of people who contribute manpower in the productive process. In 1971, compensation of employees amounted to $644 billion, or about $8,000 per worker. If the labor incomes of self-employed businessmen, farmers and professionals are counted, the total would be even higher.

People who do different kinds of work get different rates of pay. This should not be surprising. Jobs differ in level of difficulty, in amount of education required and in many other ways. There are also differences in the relative supply and demand for workers with particular qualifications. If the supply of farm workers, for example, is relatively high while the demand for such workers is quite low, one would predict that farm wages will be low.

On the other hand, people who seem to be doing the same kinds of work sometimes get different rates of pay. Why? Many factors are involved, but one partial explanation is discrimination in the job market. In 1970, the median income for men working year-round full-time was $9,180. (That means half the men earned more than $9,180 and half earned less.) For women working year-round full-time, the median income was $5,440. White males had median incomes of $9,400 for full-time year-round work, while Negro males earned $6,400. Sex and race discrimination are certainly not the only explanation of these differences, but they are part of the story.

In 1972, the average production worker in manufacturing earned $3.80 per hour and approximately $150 per week. The average construction worker earned $6.00 per hour and $230 a week. The average employee working in retail trade (such as a department store sales clerk or checker in a supermarket) earned $2.70 per hour and about $90 per week.

Averages, however, can be misleading. Behind every average lies a distribution. Many construction workers make a lot less than $6 per hour, especially the young, the nonwhite and the unskilled (regardless of age or race). There are millions of employees, especially women, who are paid less than $2.70 per hour for the work they do in retail trade. Furthermore, there is a big difference between high *hourly* earnings and high *annual* income. Some workers are unable to obtain full-time, year-round jobs and are forced to live all year on what they can earn during the limited hours and weeks they are actually employed. Many workers employed in hotels, restaurants, textile mills and laundries earn $1.60 per hour or less. At that rate of pay, even with a full-time year-round job, they would earn less than $3,500 a year, which is below the poverty level for a 4-person family.

Professional, business and technical workers generally receive the highest pay, while laborers, farmers and service workers get the lowest. Except in agriculture, workers in the goods-producing industries generally are better paid than employees in those industries that produce services. On the average, workers with more schooling get higher pay than the less educated.

Wages and earnings have increased a great deal for American workers in the past 20 or 30 years. Back in 1929, 60¢ an hour was considered a pretty good wage. Average weekly earnings for employees in manufacturing was $24.76. In the depression of the

1930s, average earnings fell to $16.65 a week. Coal miners earned even less.

But during the wartime 1940s, wages rose sharply. By the mid 1950s, average earnings in manufacturing reached $70 per week. However, since prices rose during World War II and afterward, part of the increase in money wages was eaten up by inflation. Nevertheless, *real wages*—wages measured in dollars having a fixed buying power after adjusting for inflation—more than doubled between 1940 and 1970. On the average an hour of labor today earns twice as much real buying power as it did 25 years ago.

For most families, wage earnings are the most important source of income. Some families receive income from other sources such as dividends on shares of stock they own, interest on savings bonds and government transfer payments. Examples of the latter are Old Age, Survivors, Disability and Health Insurance (OASDHI) and Aid to Families with Dependent Children (AFDC). Also note that since many families have more than one wage earner average family income is greater than average earnings per worker.

In 1971, the *median family income* in the United States was $10,300. Half of the 53 million families in the country had incomes above $10,300 and half had incomes below $10,300. It is interesting to note that 5 million families (including 20 million persons) had incomes below the poverty income levels (approximately $4,000 per year for a 4-person family) set by the federal government. An additional 5 million unrelated individuals (not living in family units) had poverty incomes of less than $2,000 for the year.

In earlier lessons, 3 major questions to be answered by every economic system were listed:

1. What should be the *overall level* of economic activity? (How much to produce)
2. What *kinds* of goods and services should be produced? (What to produce)
3. How should the nation's income be *distributed*? (For whom to produce)

155

The third question asks, How should the income that is produced by the economy be shared among the families and individuals that make up the economic society? How should the money income be divided? Since distribution of money income determines the distribution of buying power, it also determines the quantities of goods and services that various consumers can purchase.

If the total personal income in the United States were divided equally among all consumer households (including 1-person units), the income per household would be over $12,000 a year. If income were distributed equally to each person, every 4-person family would get more than $16,000. But income is not equally divided in the United States. Only one-fourth of the families in 1970 had incomes as high as $15,000 a year (see Table 2.6).

Table 2.6
SHARE OF INCOME RECEIVED BY
EACH FIFTH OF U.S. FAMILIES, 1970

Family Ranking	Approximate Income Range	Percentage of Total U.S. Income
Lowest Fifth	(under $5,000)	5.5%
Second Fifth	($5,000–8,000)	12.0
Middle Fifth	($8,000–11,000)	17.4
Fourth Fifth	($11,000–15,000)	23.5
Highest Fifth	(over $15,000)	41.6
TOTAL		100.0%

Source: U.S. Bureau of the Census, *Current Population Reports,* "Income in 1970 of Families and Persons in the United States," Series P-60, No. 80, October 4, 1971.

Table 2.6 shows that, when all families in the United States are divided into 5 groups according to the amount of income they received in 1970, the lowest group—made up of 10 million families with approximately 40 million people—received only one-eighteenth (5½%) of the nation's income. The highest group—the 10 million families at the top of the income scale—received 42% of all the income. So the top group got almost 8 times as much income as the bottom group. The top 1% of families received almost as much total income as the lowest 20%, which means the richest families had 20 times as much income as the poorest families!

Families in the top income group are frequently headed by professional or technical workers or by business managers. Families in the lowest group are often headed by unskilled workers, farmers, or men and women who are not employed at all.

Many Americans are surprised by statistics on wages, earnings and family income. Some feel that the distribution of income in the United States is too unequal, while others consider that the total economic pie is divided just about the way it ought to be. One thing is clear, however; it would be very difficult to make an intelligent judgment about income distribution without the aid of economic statistics.

Lesson in Brief

Workers receive three-fourths of total national income every year as their payment for contributing manpower to the production process. There are great differences among workers and families in terms of hourly wages, weekly earnings and annual incomes. The average production worker in manufacturing earns about $3.80 per hour and $150 per week. Median family income in the United States is over $10,000 a year. Ranking all families according to the size of their incomes, the top one-fifth get 42% of total income, while the lowest one-fifth get 5% of total income.

When workers are employed, they are helping produce goods and services, earning income and doing something that may provide personal satisfaction and contribute to human development. In contrast, jobless workers are a waste of manpower. Their earnings stop. Their skills grow dull. They suffer the indignity of being judged "worthless" (at least temporarily) by the manpower market. What forces determine the total number of jobs available in the economy at any given time? In a market economy like that in the United States where jobs and incomes are linked, the question posed in the title of this lesson is of great importance to all potential workers and their families.

During the late 1960s the American economy was close to full employment. In 1969, 78 million men and women were employed in civilian jobs (plus 3½ million in the armed forces), and only 2.8 million workers—3.5% of the labor force—were jobless. Because so many of the available resources (both human and nonhuman) were employed, the economy was said to be operating virtually at full production.

By contrast, in the recession years of 1958 and 1971, there were 5 million unemployed workers in the U. S. economy. The unemployment rate climbed to 6.8% in 1958 and, with a larger labor force base, to 5.9% in 1971. Newspapers and magazines were filled with pictures and stories describing problems of the unemployed. The situation reminded older workers of the Great Depression of the 1930s when 13 million workers (25% of the labor force!) were jobless.

It has been noted that unemployment causes economic waste. Idle manpower contributes nothing to the GNP. Moreover, families are deprived of food, clothing and other necessities when the breadwinner has lost his job and earnings. Many workers also suffer feelings of personal frustration, humiliation and failure when they cannot find jobs.

What does economic theory have to say about the causes of unemployment? In an economy where wants are virtually unlimited and productive resources are considered scarce, why is it that workers go without jobs?

Let's begin by reviewing a modified form of the circular flow of economic activity (Figure 2.5).

Figure 2.5

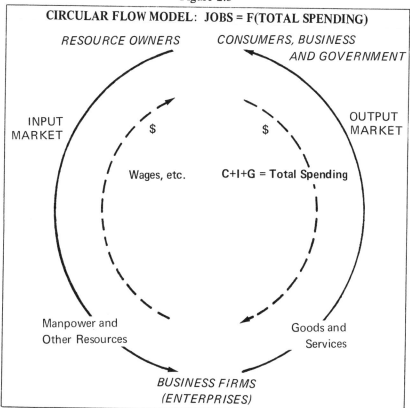

CIRCULAR FLOW MODEL: JOBS = F(TOTAL SPENDING)

RESOURCE OWNERS   *CONSUMERS, BUSINESS*
                                AND GOVERNMENT

INPUT   OUTPUT
MARKET   MARKET

                    $ $

        Wages, etc.   C+I+G = Total Spending

Manpower and   Goods and
Other Resources   Services

BUSINESS FIRMS
(ENTERPRISES)

The circular flow diagram shows that goods and services are produced for sale to consumers, business firms and government. When total spending (effective demand in the market) goes up, firms are able to sell more goods and services. But they cannot sell more unless they produce more. Since there is no such thing as a free lunch—that is, it takes input to get more output—firms must employ more manpower, capital and natural resources. Thus, increased spending in the output market leads to increased employment in the input market and to increased production.

Note, however, that there is a limit to this power of spending to create jobs and output. When all or nearly all the manpower and other resources are employed, additional spending cannot create additional jobs and output. The upper limit to a country's gross national product is reached in the short run when "full employment" of available resources has been achieved, generally indicated by an unemployment rate of around 3% of the labor force.

There is a very simple way to summarize this theory of total employment. $E = f(C+I+G)$ means that Employment (total number of jobs in the economy) is a function of (depends on) total spending (effective market demand) for Consumer goods plus Investment goods plus Government purchases of goods and services. Since spending is the same thing as GNP—the sum of consumption, investment and government purchases (plus net exports, which are ignored here)—total employment is determined by the level of GNP spending! The more total spending by consumers, investors and government, the more job opportunities there will be in the economy. Recalling the question that was posed in the title of this lesson, one may conclude that (except for seasonal, frictional and structural employment explained in Unit Four):

—there *will* be enough jobs for everyone if total spending is *high enough* to justify using all the available resources in production.
—there will *not* be enough jobs for everyone if total spending in the market is *too low*.
—there *will* be serious disruptions in the manpower market and the entire economy because of *inflation* if total spending is *too high*.

The subject of employment is a very broad one indeed. Many books have been written to try to explain the causes of employment and unemployment. Though we cannot deal here with all of the important ideas about employment, there is one additional issue to consider—the prediction that automation might cause mass unemployment. Will machines gobble up all the jobs and force tens of million of workers into the ranks of the unemployed? If so, when? If not, why not?

In 1964, a small group of Americans formed a committee and sent the President of the United States a document called the "Memorandum on the Triple Revolution." The memorandum called attention to the fact that important changes were taking place in the fields of *weaponry* (atomic and nuclear weapons), *human rights* (the civil rights movement, mainly by Negroes) and *cybernation* (technology, automation and economic life).

Writers of the memorandum claimed that America was entering a new period of economic life in which machines will do most of the work and tens of millions of men and women will be unable to find jobs—perhaps as early as the 1970s! The committee urged the American people to begin planning for the revolutionary changes brought on by cybernation so they could learn to accept a world where most people do not have jobs. Among other things, a new system of income distribution that did not rely on employment and earnings to determine how much each person and family would receive would have to be devised.

Public reaction to the message of the Triple Revolution Memorandum has been varied. Many people agree with the writers that machines are causing revolutionary changes in the economy and that automation is destroying millions of jobs. Other people feel this might happen a hundred years or so in the future but not now. They point out that total civilian employment in the United States is at an all-time high. Unemployment rates by the end of the 1960s were at the lowest level in 15 years, just at the time when cybernation supposedly was destroying so many millions of jobs. Why? Where did the jobs come from? Mainly, many of the new employment opportunities came from the continuing growth of the economy, especially in the service fields such as teaching, medical care, recreation and trade.

Indeed, as economists point out, the U. S. economy has become a "service" economy, with employment and production structured quite differently from the previous "goods" economy.

Rising incomes in an affluent society typically are spent to purchase services, both through the private sector and through government. Since the methods of producing services are not as highly automated as automobile assembly plants, food-processing establishments and similar goods-producing enterprises, service jobs are not eliminated as quickly as jobs in the goods-producing industries.

With poverty still a fact of life in the United States and so many human wants still unsatisfied even for middle income families, it is difficult to imagine a world of mass unemployment. Still, the fundamental message of the Triple Revolution Memorandum remains—people must look to the future and continuously re-examine the values and institutions upon which they have relied for organizing their economic life. As technology advances and income grows, new and better ways must be found to pursue the goals of full production, stable growth, freedom of choice, equality of opportunity, security, distributive justice and international balance as well as to define and pursue new goals desired by Americans.

Lesson in Brief

Employed workers are able to contribute to production, earn an income and participate in useful activity. But jobs are not always available to everyone able and willing to work. In general, the total number of job opportunities that exist in the economy will depend on the total level of spending by consumers, business firms and government. If total spending is too low, there will not be enough jobs for all persons actively participating in the labor force.

Money and the Trade-off between Unemployment and Inflation

A recurring problem in the U. S. economy is *inflation* defined as a rise in the general level of prices. The effect of inflation is to reduce the purchasing power of *money*. Recent experience suggests that it will be hard to achieve the goals of full employment and reasonable price stability at the same time.

Just about everyone in the United States knows the importance of money, even if he has never read a book on the subject or taken a course in economics. But not everyone understands the nature and functions of money. Nor do people always understand what is meant by inflation. In this lesson we shall consider very briefly the topics of money and inflation. We also will try to clarify a public policy issue that became very important in the late 1960s—the trade-off dilemma involving unemployment and inflation.

Money is defined as anything that is widely accepted in payment for goods and debts. The most familiar form of money is *currency* which includes coins issued by the United States Treasury and paper dollars circulated by Federal Reserve banks. But the most important form of money is *demand deposits* or checkbook money. About three-fourths of the total money supply (which exceeded $230 billion in 1972) consists of demand deposits. What makes it money is the fact that checks are widely accepted in payment for goods and debts.

Money performs several functions in the economic process. As noted in the circular flow model, money serves as a *medium of exchange.* Consumers trade money for the goods and services they buy in the market. Business firms exchange money for the resources they employ in production. Money is the principal medium of the economic communication system, the form in which income is typically received and what is spent to purchase goods and services. Money is what citizens "vote" with to express preferences and demands in the marketplace. Money also serves as

163

a *store of value*, as a *unit of account* and as a *standard for deferred payments* (i.e., a form in which the promise to pay in the future is expressed).

The *value of money* is determined by what can be purchased with it. The dollar is not "worth a dollar" because gold is stored at Fort Knox, Kentucky, or in Federal Reserve Bank vaults or even because the federal government says it is worth a dollar. The value of the dollar is determined by the quantity of goods and services that can be obtained in exchange for a dollar, and this depends on the prices at which goods and services are sold.

As explained in the earlier discussion of economic statistics when the general level of prices goes up, the purchasing power or value of money goes down. There is an inverse relationship between prices and the value of money. When the consumer price index (CPI) rises by, say, 5 points, the power of a dollar to buy food, clothing, housing and transportation goes down. Between the base year 1967 and June 1972, the CPI actually went up from 100 to 125. This means that in 1972 it took $1.25 to buy the same "package" of goods and services that could have been bought in 1967 for $1.00. The value of the dollar declined over this 5-year period from a full 100¢ to 80¢ (i.e., the 1967 index of 100 divided by the June 1972 index of 125 equals 80).

Because of inflation, a worker who earned $102 per week in 1967 and who managed to get a raise to $130 per week in 1972 nevertheless would find that his real income (actual purchasing power) had risen not by $28 but by only $2.00! Why? Because while the number of dollars the worker earned went up by 27%, inflation had reduced the purchasing power of the dollar by 20%.

When inflation occurs, it is necessary to *deflate* or adjust economic data such as GNP and average weekly earnings to reflect changes in the value of money. It would be very misleading to compare income data expressed simply in terms of current prices (note the case of the worker above) because the size of the measuring stick itself (the real value of a dollar) changes during periods of inflation. How can these important price level adjustments be made? This simple formula can be used:

$$\frac{\text{Price Index in Base Year}}{\text{Price Index In Current Year}} \times \frac{\text{Income Data In Current Year}}{1} = \begin{array}{c}\text{Current Year Data} \\ \text{Expressed in Base} \\ \text{Year Prices}\end{array}$$

Thus, if the price index in the base year (say, 1967) is set at 100 and the price index rises to 200 by the year 1980, and if GNP in current prices was $300 billion in 1967 and $450 billion in 1980, then real GNP would have *declined* by $75 billion between 1967 and 1980, expressed in constant 1967 prices.

$$\frac{100}{200} \times \frac{\$450b}{1} = \$225 \quad \text{and} \quad \$300b - \$225 = \$75b$$

Why is inflation considered to be a problem? The answer lies in understanding the *consequences* of inflation. Only 3 consequences will be mentioned in the present discussion. *First,* inflation has the effect of changing the distribution of real income because, during inflation, not everyone's current money income changes at the same rate. Yet, the prices consumers have to pay in the market do change at the same rate (roughly speaking) for all. People with fixed incomes suffer because the purchasing power of their dollars is declining while the quantity of their dollars remains unchanged. *Second,* inflation has the effect of distorting decision-making and economic activity in certain ways, many of which are harmful in terms of the goals society sets for the economy. *Third,* when inflation does occur, the federal government is compelled to follow certain policies to halt the rise in prices. Some of these government policies have the effect of creating unemployment.

Let's consider why this is so. What causes inflation?

In the simplest terms, inflation results from too much spending relative to the economy's ability to produce goods and services. (Two other kinds of inflation, cost-push and structural, will not be discussed here.) One solution to this situation is restrictive action—raising taxes, reducing government expenditure, "tightening" money and credit—taken by the government to force a cutback in total market spending. But a reduction (or insufficiency) in market demand is exactly what has been identified as a major cause of unemployment. And here lies the dilemma. Should the goal of full employment be sacrificed in order to stop inflation (that is, to pursue the goal of reasonable price stability)? If so, then how much unemployment should be traded for how much stability? What specific policy action should be taken to bring about the desired results? And what should be done to ease the burden on people who suffer from the consequences of these policy actions—the unemployed and the ones who are injured by inflation?

Although the complexities of money and inflation go beyond the scope of this introduction to economics, it is important to recognize that a variety of policy instruments are available. They include tax and spending charges, monetary policy, wage and price guideposts, wage and price controls, and incomes policy. It is a continuing challenge to the American people and their representatives in government to decide which combination of policy actions is in their best interest, both in the short run and in the long run.

Lesson in Brief

Inflation means a rise in the general level of prices, which reduces the purchasing power of the dollar. In the late 1960s and early 1970s, inflation was a major problem of the U.S. economy. Because certain policies aimed at assuring full employment run the risk of causing inflation, the nation may have to trade higher levels of unemployment in order to achieve reasonable price stability.

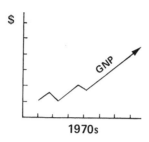

1970s

Economic growth is the steady increase of gross national product per person, year after year. It means a greater output of goods and services and, therefore, an increase in real income available. If the recent growth rate of 2½% a year (increased GNP per person) continues, incomes will double every 28 years. Will this growth of production and income solve all U. S. economic problems?

As noted in previous lessons, every economic system must answer 3 basic questions:

1. *How much* will be produced? (What will be the *overall level* of economic activity and GNP?)
2. *What* will be produced? (What specific kinds of goods and services will be produced? What will be the *composition* of the GNP?)
3. *For whom* will the income be produced? (How will production be shared among the various members of society? What will be the *distribution* of the nation's income?)

The specific goals established for the economy serve as targets to aim for when solving the basic problems. These specific goals include full production, stable economic growth, freedom of choice, economic security and distributive justice. In addition, because the American economy is part of the world economy,

167

there are certain problems and goals concerning relations with other countries which are acknowledged with the goal of international balance.

Between 1929 and 1959, the gross national product of the United States grew from $204 billion to $476 billion (in constant 1958 prices). During the 12-year period from 1959 to 1971, total GNP increased from $476 billion to $742 billion (again in constant 1958 prices). Real GNP per person rose from $2,700 in 1959 to $3,600—an average increase of about 2½% a year. By 1980, total GNP (in current prices) will approach two trillion dollars! Economic growth enlarges the income pie and makes it possible for every American to have more dollars, more goods and services, more savings. A few years ago, it was estimated that GNP per person in the United States (then $3,000) was 30 times as high as GNP per person in the underdeveloped countries of Africa and Asia ($100 per year) and nearly 10 times as high as the average income in Latin America ($330 income per person per year).

The central question to be raised in this discussion is, If economic growth is maintained successfully (at full employment, without inflation), will this mean that the other economic goals automatically will be achieved? Will growth solve all problems? Before answering, let's consider some of the problems currently facing the United States:

poverty	concentration of wealth
war	underemployment
racial discrimination	civil disorder
inadequate education	quality of employment
overpopulation	high taxes
concentration of power (government)	plight of older Americans
	crime
energy and materials shortages	public welfare system
	government controls
pollution of the environment	urban decay
physical and mental illness	rural decay
monopoly power (business)	gold losses

unemployment	disadvantaged groups
monopoly power	communism
(labor unions)	plight of handicapped
inflation	persons
automation	poor housing
drugs	high cost of medical care

Identify the problems which seem most serious. Then consider the sense in which they may be economic problems. Consider also how economic growth might, on the one hand, be part of the solution but, on the other hand, be part of the problem!

As previously stated, growth means more goods and services are available to satisfy consumer wants, more resources are available for investment, and more wherewithal exists for government to provide social services (such as education, highways, military defense, conserving natural resources). Economic growth increases both power and range of choice. For example, one reason why both the United States and the Soviet Union assign priority to economic growth is because growth allows a country to strengthen its military defense (and meet or beat the competition in the space race) as well as to provide a better standard of living for its people. A rich country has more control over its present and its future well-being than a poor country, just as a rich man has more control over the world he lives in than a poor man.

But does economic growth solve all problems? The record shows that the economy has grown in the past; yet many problems remain, such as poverty, inflation and war. Economic growth in the future may very well help Americans solve some of the remaining problems, but evidently growth alone does not automatically cure all ills. Indeed, the very opposite may be true.

Examine again, the 3 basic problems every economy must solve:

1.   The *overall level* of economic activity.

In spite of the fact that rapid growth was enjoyed in the U. S. economy in the late 1960s, the problems of inflation and unemployment were not solved. The general level of prices (consumer price index) rose more than 4% annually (on the average between 1965 and 1969) which meant that the purchasing power of the dollar went down because of inflation. And even as the economy approached full employment, millions of women, young workers, the unskilled, displaced older workers and those with limited schooling were jobless.

2. The *composition* of production.

In 1970, when GNP was nearly a trillion dollars, almost one-twelfth of total production was for national defense and unavailable for personal consumption, investment or peaceful government uses. (More money and resources were used for war and defense in 1970 than for the education of all 60 million students enrolled in American schools and colleges that year.)

3. The *distribution* of income.

Although in 1970 enough goods and services were produced to provide $15,000 of income for each family in the United States, the fact is that 25 million Americans were living in poverty. More than 10 million American children under the age of 18 were growing up in these low-income families. While the 10 million families at the low end of the American income scale had to subsist on only 5% of the nation's income, the 10 million families at the high end of the scale were receiving more than 40% of the country's income, after taxes.

And to add a final dismal note, despite the rapid economic growth and record-breaking prosperity of the sixties, in the seventies Americans were threatened by nuclear war, environmental pollution, population explosion and growing resentment over the widening gap between the rich nations and the poor nations.

The economic outlook for the future may seem dismal or bright depending on one's world-view. Two facts stand out, however. First, knowledge is expanding rapidly. Men and women are acquiring skills and tools that make them the most productive human resources in history. Second, knowledge is power. History shows that the growing productive power of man can be used wisely or foolishly, constructively or destructively. To paraphrase an 18th century Irish statesman, Edmund Burke, the effect of affluence on individuals is that they may do what they please. Society ought to see what it pleases them to do with their growing amounts of tools and wealth and power before risking congratulations. In other words, "more" is not necessarily "better." To improve the quality of life, U.S. society must define useful and worthy *ends* as well as develop efficient *means* to achieve these ends.

It may be true, as many have argued, that economic abundance is a necessary condition for the well-being and happiness of people. Current experience suggests, however, that affluence is not the sufficient condition for a high and improving quality of life. It seems clear that, to solve the socioeconomic problems of poverty, pollution, power, population and the rest, large doses of individual concern, compassion, courage, creativity, wisdom and institutional renewal will be required.

Lesson in Brief

Economic growth results in the increased production of goods and services available for consumers, business firms and government. In spite of steady growth, many economic and social problems remain to be solved in the United States. These include poverty, inflation, monopoly power, unemployment, pollution of the environment, war, increasing population, crime, and others. Whether these problems will be solved depends on the decision-making ability and the determination that Americans demonstrate in the 1970s and beyond.

UNIT THREE
The Manpower Market

One of the most important institutions of the U.S. economy and the world of work is the *manpower market*—an established arrangement for bringing workers and jobs together in a pattern of exchange relations. Employers hire men and women to provide the manpower services needed to help produce the nation's output. In return for their time, effort, skill and productivity, employed workers receive money payments called compensation of employees or wages. Forces of supply and demand interact in the manpower market to determine the total number of employment opportunities in the economy, the particular kinds of jobs and the wages that workers receive. These 3 outcomes, in turn, influence the total level of production, the kinds of goods and services produced and the way income is distributed. The manpower market also sends out signals that encourage men and women to develop certain skills that are in short supply; to move to occupations, industries and locations where more workers are needed; and to choose careers that offer higher levels of personal satisfaction. Lessons in this unit deal with the structure, dimensions and processes of the manpower market, describe some realities of the world of work, and indicate what employers expect of men and women who want to obtain and hold good jobs.

Understanding the manpower market requires a study of labor force statistics, historical changes that have taken place and the basic theory of employment. In order to measure the changes that are taking place in the world of work, governmental agencies and other groups make careful estimates of the number of men and women who are employed, unemployed and not in the labor force. Detailed statistics are reported on the sex, race, age, occupation, industry, education and earnings of the nation's work force. Data are also gathered to show how local manpower markets are operating in the 50 states, in large cities and in special geographic areas.

When workers and their families suffer from such problems as unemployment, low incomes, job discrimination, inadequate training, dead-end jobs and unsatisfying careers, it is a sign that the manpower market is not functioning properly. A few of the attempts to improve the manpower market through private and public programs, including collective bargaining and unemployment insurance, are described in this unit. The causes of unemployment are explained as well as some effects of joblessness on individual workers, their families and the nation as a whole.

Learning about the manpower market increases the individual's understanding of the economic environment and acquaints him with an institution that serves as the doorway to personal career opportunities.

The Manpower Market: Workers and Jobs

The manpower market is the meeting of workers and jobs. It takes in the institutions, processes and policies that make it possible for employers to obtain human resources needed to produce the economy's goods and services. Men and women find opportunities for employment in the manpower market. By participating in the manpower market, workers have an opportunity to help produce the nation's output, to earn an income and to satisfy other human needs. A worker's chances of successful participation in the manpower market depend on the factors of supply and demand.

The manpower market brings together the suppliers of labor (workers) and the users of labor (employers who comprise the demand side of the market). It is the means by which people obtain jobs and productive enterprises obtain human resources.

It is no simple matter for workers and jobs to be matched satisfactorily and efficiently in the manpower market. Information, communications and movement are necessary to help put the right people in the right jobs. This lesson contains information that should be useful to people who want to achieve success in the manpower market.

The term *manpower market* is used to refer to the common features of the many different job markets. Actually, there is no such thing as a single manpower market that brings together all the nation's workers and all the employers in one large pattern of exchange transactions. Figure 3.1 is merely a simplified model that is used to represent the workings of various manpower markets in the economy. It is a summary of the factors at work in manpower markets. There are thousands of job markets in the United States. The boundaries of some job markets are primarily geographical—that is, there are job markets in and around cities such as Columbus, Ohio, and Fort Smith, Arkansas. Job markets are also limited by occupational considerations. Unemployed coal miners, for example, are not in the same job market as surgeons because they do not have the necessary skills to be licensed for the practice of medicine.

Just as there are markets for products like fresh eggs where the forces of supply and demand influence price, there are also markets for productive resources such as labor, natural resources and capital. In these input markets, supply and demand factors determine the price of the input and, therefore, influence the amount of income that each resource will receive. What is known about these market forces?

Figure 3.1

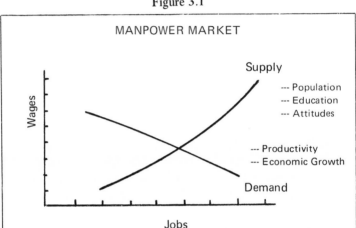

First, the demand for labor is a *derived demand* that depends upon the demand for the goods or services in whose production it is utilized. Employers are willing to hire workers because the workers help produce goods and services that are in demand. Changes in consumer demand for products in the output market will have effects in the manpower market. The demand for labor differs among the various manpower markets because particular types of labor make different contributions to output. Some types of workers are more in demand than others because their skills are needed by employers and they are more productive workers.

The demand for labor in the manpower market is affected by the economy's growth in production—both the overall level and the composition or pattern of growth—because as the gross

176

national product grows, the demand for labor also increases. It takes additional resources to produce more goods and services. (Remember the relationship between inputs and output explained in Unit Two and the derived nature of the demand for labor mentioned above.) Since recent growth in the output of the economy is accounted for largely by the greater production of services, do not be surprised to find that service-producing rather than goods-producing workers are more in demand.

Second, the *supply of labor* differs among the various manpower markets because of the different characteristics of jobs, where people live and the degree to which particular jobs are attractive to labor. Time and expense required for men and women to obtain the education and skills needed for certain jobs also affect the supply of labor. The topic of education and its relationship to employment and earnings will be explored in Unit Six.

Another factor affecting the number and kinds of workers in the manpower market is the attitudes and values of men and women who participate in the labor force. Certain attitudes, values and behaviors seem to make workers more acceptable to employers or more productive or both. These may be called *functional work attitudes.*

Some examples of functional attitudes that might increase a young person's chances of success in the manpower market include courtesy and cooperativeness with fellow workers; taking pride in his work; and a sense of responsibility to be on the job regularly, on time and with a desire to do high quality work.

In addition to the market forces labeled demand and supply, there is a third area of understanding about the manpower market that is important. This is the *structure* of the market and how it functions. The level of employment and unemployment, wage rates, job satisfaction, opportunities for better jobs and pay are all influenced by the structure and processes that prevail in manpower markets. For example: Is the market "organized"? (Do workers belong to labor unions?) Is there a good flow of information about job vacancies and available workers? Do employers discriminate against certain workers on the basis of race, sex, age, ethnic or religious background? Are there agencies that provide such manpower services as training, relocation assistance and personal help after a worker is placed on a job?

In summary, the manpower market is made up of the institutions, processes and policies which bring together the workers (who are the suppliers of labor) and the employers (who are the users of labor). This input market, like all markets, is influenced by supply factors (such as population, education, attitudes and values) and demand factors (productivity, economic growth and needs of particular employers based on the demand for the products they sell). These supply and demand factors interact within a framework of manpower market structures and processes to accomplish several purposes. First, workers obtain jobs and employers obtain human resources. Second, wages and earnings are determined. Third, manpower is allocated among competing employers. Fourth, certain adjustments take place over time such as the development of new jobs and new skills.

Lesson in Brief

Manpower markets bring workers and jobs together. Supply and demand factors determine employment opportunities in the economy. Effective participation on the supply side of the manpower market depends upon the skills that workers have acquired as well as their values and functional work attitudes. The manpower requirements of employers on the demand side of the manpower market are influenced by the growth of the economy and the needs of their particular enterprise.

In order to understand the manpower market, it is necessary to use concepts corresponding to facts which can be measured. The labor force is a concept economists have developed to measure the manpower potential of the economy. Two additional concepts, employment and unemployment, are used to measure the status of the labor force and evaluate the performance of the manpower market. An understanding of labor force, employment and unemployment facts can help in evaluating manpower market opportunities.

In Unit Two the need for statistics to evaluate the performance of the economy was discussed. Labor force statistics are valuable because they make it possible to measure changes in the status of the most important economic resource—manpower.

The labor force is a dominant factor in the economy, as the nation's economic accounts show. In 1971, American workers received three-fourths of the total national income as compensation for their contribution to production. Consumer expenditures for goods and services—paid for mainly out of current earnings from employment—were 63% of GNP. Thus, on both the expenditure and income sides of the nation's economic accounts, labor accounted for most of the activity. Furthermore, of all the resource owners in the economy, the overwhelming majority possess no productive resources other than their own manpower.

Information on the characteristics and use of the nation's human resources is gathered by state and federal government agencies and reported to the public in great detail. For example, separate figures are published for agricultural and nonagricultural workers by sex, color, marital status, age and hours worked. The occupational and industrial make-up of the labor force is described. And information about persons who are not in the labor force is also published. These figures are the most important data that economists, governmental officials, businessmen, labor unionists and other interested parties have for checking on the manpower market. To understand and use labor force data, it is necessary to know the definitions of the terms used by the governmental agencies and the methods they use in compiling these statistics.

Let's begin an examination of labor force statistics by describing the concepts and methods used by the federal government and cooperating state agencies in measuring the status of the labor force. Agencies that provide most of the data on labor force, employment and unemployment are the Bureau of Labor Statistics (in the U.S. Department of Labor) and the Bureau of the Census (in the U.S. Department of Commerce).

In monthly surveys that are made of a sample number of households and businesses throughout the United States, each individual 16 years of age and over is classified as "employed," "unemployed" or "not in the labor force" according to his activity during the week of the survey. The sum of the employed and unemployed comprise the *civilian labor force* (LF = E + U). (An estimate of the *total labor force* is obtained by adding the number of persons in the Armed Forces regardless of where they are stationed.) Men and women 16 years of age and over who are not classified as employed, unemployed or in the Armed Forces are defined as *not in the labor force*. These people are students, housewives, retired or disabled persons, institutionalized persons, those doing less than 15 hours of unpaid family work and the voluntarily idle.

To be counted as *employed* in the survey, the person must put in at least 1 hour a week on a job for pay as a wage or salary worker or for profit as an owner of a business. Also counted as employed are the "unpaid family workers" (examples: sons, daughters or wives working in a family business such as a store or farm) who work at least 15 hours a week without pay. Persons not working or looking for work but who had jobs or businesses from which they were only temporarily absent because of illness, bad weather, vacation, labor-management dispute or various personal reasons are also counted as employed. In 1971, the average number of employed civilian workers in the U.S. economy was almost 80 million, or 94% of the civilian labor force.

Unemployed persons include those who are not employed for as much as 1 hour a week, but who have been actively seeking employment and are currently available for work if employment can be found. The general test of "seeking employment" is that a person must have actively looked for a job (by going to the State Employment Service, applying to an employer, answering a job want ad, etc.) within the last 4 weeks. In 1971, 5 million workers were unemployed on the average, which amounted to almost 6% of the civilian labor force.

An easy rule to remember for deciding whether people should be considered in the labor force or not in the labor force is to note their activity. Activity involving work classifies one as employed. Activity involving looking for work identifies one as unemployed. Activity or nonactivity that does not involve work or searching for a job describes people who are not in the labor force.

The following list of different labor force situations provides an opportunity to assess one's understanding of the Bureau of Labor Statistics (BLS) classification system. What is the labor force status of each person?

1. A full-time housewife.
2. A truck driver who is visiting his state employment service looking for employment and who is ready to go to work as soon as he can find a job.
3. A 16-year-old girl who is employed as a carhop at a drive-in restaurant 12 hours a week.
4. A high school senior who applies in April for a job he wants to begin in June after he graduates.
5. A woman who was fired from her job 2 months ago and has been sitting around the house brooding over her bad luck ever since.
6. An inmate of one of the state prisons who works in the metal shop stamping out license plates and is paid 75¢ an hour.
7. A 17-year-old boy who spends 20 hours a week doing chores on his family's farm.
8. A factory worker who is on strike against his employer.

9. A 13-year-old boy who delivers newspapers 15 hours a week.

10. A man working 10 hours a week as an unpaid stock clerk in his wife's hobby and craft shop.*

In order to know the dimensions of activity in the manpower market, the number of people working at jobs or seeking jobs must be counted. In other words, some manpower concepts must be given numerical values. The concepts of labor force, employment and unemployment are used by the U.S. Department of Labor, U.S. Bureau of the Census and other federal and state governmental agencies to gather statistics on the boundaries and operation of the manpower market. These governmental agencies make estimates of the status of the labor force by surveying a sample of the nation's households and nonagricultural business establishments. Detailed reports are published for use by employers and other people interested in the manpower market.

Lesson in Brief

The dimensions and performance of the manpower market can be measured and evaluated by using the concepts of the labor force, employment and unemployment. Data are gathered and published by governmental agencies such as the U. S. Bureau of Labor Statistics (BLS) to describe the functioning of the manpower market. Labor force and employment data are essential for those who want to understand how the nation's human resources are being used.

*Answers: 1 (Not in the Labor Force—NLF); 2 (Unemployed—U); 3 (Employed—E); 4 (NLF); 5 (NLF); 6 (NLF); 7 (E); 8 (E); 9 (NLF); 10 (NLF).

The labor force (or manpower supply) is made up of workers who already have jobs plus those who are able and willing to accept employment. It is from this group that employers choose their workers. The supply of manpower keeps changing, in number and in composition. Knowledge of the changing labor force can prove valuable to men and women who are planning careers. Among other things, this knowledge helps identify the amount and type of competition to be faced in tomorrow's manpower market.

In this lesson, changes that are taking place in the size and composition of the American labor force are considered and the significance of some of these changes from the viewpoint of the individual worker and the economic system as a whole are explored.

The overall size of the labor force has been growing steadily. In 1870 there were about 13 million workers in the economy. By 1970 the total labor force had grown to 86 million, amounting to a sixfold increase (up 560%). By 1980 it is expected that 100 million men and women will be active in the U.S. labor force.

What factors influence the size of the labor force? Population is one major determinant. Another is the *labor force participation rate* (percentage of the working-age population actually in the labor force). Between 1940 and 1970, the population grew from 132 million people to 203 million, an increase of 54%. Without a dramatic shift in the age composition of the population or a big change in the labor force participation rate, one would expect the labor force to grow by about the same percentage. It did. The number of workers increased from 56 million to 86 million, or 54%. Actually, the identical percentage figures hide 2 facts. The population became younger (fewer working-age people as a fraction of the total population), but this was offset by a higher aggregate labor force participation rate (caused mainly by entry of more women into the job market).

Now let's consider the sex and age composition of the labor force. Figure 3.2 shows the structure of the civilian labor force in

March 1971. (Note: Civilian Labor Force equals Total Labor Force minus Armed Forces.)

Figure 3.2

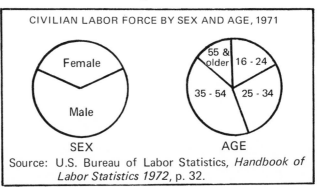

CIVILIAN LABOR FORCE BY SEX AND AGE, 1971

SEX   AGE

Source: U.S. Bureau of Labor Statistics, *Handbook of Labor Statistics 1972*, p. 32.

Figure 3.2 shows that, in 1971, 38% of all workers in the civilian labor force were women, while 62% were men. Young workers (age 16-24) made up 22% of the force. Workers in the 25-34 age class accounted for 21% of the total. Mature workers 35-54 years of age comprised 40% of the U.S. labor force. Older workers (55 years and over) accounted for 17%.

The sex and age composition of the labor force has been changing. Women increasingly play a more important role as workers in the economy. At present, 3 out of 8 workers in the labor force are women. During the 1960s, they entered the labor force at twice the rate of men. Middle-aged women, especially, are participating in the job market in increased numbers. During a 25-year period (1947-1972), the number of female workers in the labor force increased by 17 million, while the number of male workers grew by only 10 million! In the 1970s, however, the difference in growth rates between male and female workers will narrow.

In the sixties, the labor force became younger. Data show that between 1960 and 1970 the number of young workers grew by 54% while the labor force as a whole expanded by only 19%.

184

During the 1970s, growth rates of the various age groups will be more nearly equal than in the 1960s.

Another way to examine age and sex trends in the manpower market is to note *particular* labor force participation rates—the percentage of workers who are in the labor force out of the total number of people in a certain group of the population. For example, about 96% of all males 25-54 years of age are currently in the labor force. This is the same rate projected for 1980. For women (all ages combined), the participation rate rose from 33% in 1950 to over 40% in 1970. By 1980, nearly half of all women 25-54 years of age are expected to be in the labor force. The growing participation of women in the labor force creates both opportunities and problems for many individuals, families and society as a whole.

Significant changes in the composition of the labor force are taking place not only in regard to sex and age but also in terms of such factors as level of education, occupation and industries in which people are employed. These subjects are discussed in Unit Four.

To summarize, the labor force is growing rapidly. From 73 million in 1960, the labor force is expected to expand to 100 million by 1980. During the 1960s, women and young men entered the labor force in increasing numbers. In the 1970s the relative growth in numbers of young workers will be about one-third of that in the 1960s. The growth rate of women joining the labor force will also slow down during the 1970s. However, the participation rate of women is still creeping upward and is projected to be above 40% by 1980.

The significance of this growth in the labor force is that the economy will have to create an average of about 1½ million additional jobs every year between now and 1980 in order to employ all the new labor force entrants. These jobs are above and beyond the more than 2 million jobs a year needed to offset the productivity gains of American industry. In other words, the economy will need a growth rate (real GNP) of 4% to 5% every year between now and 1980 to supply the additional 3½ million jobs per year needed to provide employment opportunities for all the men and women in the American work force.

In terms of age and sex composition of the labor force, it is evident that more women will be competing with men for jobs. Middle-aged women re-entering the labor force after rearing their families will be especially tough competition for younger girls and for men seeking employment opportunities. The growing youthfulness of the labor force means that competition among young people for jobs will be keen. The economy must generate an average of 300,000 entry-type jobs every year to take care of young people who are entering the labor force.

Employers in the 1970s and 1980s will have a large number of workers to choose from and will undoubtedly prefer to employ those having the best education and training. Young men and women entering the labor force in the 1970s will face stiff employment competition from their peers as well as from workers who are a few years older and have greater work experience.

Lesson in Brief

Because of population growth and the increasing number of women entering the labor force, the U.S. labor force has been growing rapidly. By 1980 the U.S. economy will have 100 million workers. A high rate of economic growth will be needed to provide employment opportunities for present and new members of the labor force. Since competition for jobs will be keen during the 1970s and 1980s, employers will tend to hire those who have the best education and training.

Collective bargaining, an important institution in manpower markets that are "organized," is a process used by labor unions and employers to arrange the terms and conditions of employment for workers in such markets. Collective bargaining typically involves the negotiation of contracts listing such details as rates of pay for workers and grievance procedures for carrying out and enforcing the contract. Knowing how labor and management work together in a system of "industrial law and justice" will provide a better understanding of the modern manpower market.

Collective bargaining is a process of determining the terms and conditions of work by means of formal agreements between employers and labor unions. (For a review of the structure and purposes of unions, see Unit Two.) The results of discussions and negotiations—and sometimes strikes, picketing and lockouts—are written out in a collective bargaining agreement, or contract, that is legally binding on the employer and the union. This contract spells out in detail the terms and conditions under which employees are to work.

While the provisions of collective bargaining contracts vary widely among different industries and even among different firms, there are certain elements found in nearly all collective bargaining agreements. These include wage rates and other forms of compensation, security provisions for workers and unions, hours of work, and work loads or production standards. Collective bargaining agreements typically contain a clause that maintains there will be no strike or lockout during the terms of the contract. The agreement may specify that certain decisions are exclusively the right of management, such as deciding on plant locations and supervising the work force. Other work rules, such as those relating to discipline and layoff, may be subject to determination by both the labor union and management.

The contract also includes a procedure for dealing with grievances. A *grievance* is a complaint, usually by an individual worker or management representative (but sometimes by the union or company), concerning interpretation of the terms of the collective bargaining contract. Disagreements sometimes arise over what the collective bargaining agreement actually provides. The grievance procedure is a method of resolving these differences by determining whether the disputed action of the employer, his representative, worker or union official was in accordance with the contract. It is especially helpful to the worker as a means of protecting his rights and promoting justice in the work place. From the viewpoint of management, the grievance procedure can serve as a key element in the company's communication system.

The grievance procedure may involve as many as 3 separate steps, though most grievances are settled at the first stage.

1. A meeting of the grievance committee is held to consider the disagreement and to determine if a solution can be found. This committee often includes the shop foreman (and/or department head representing management), the shop steward—a worker in the firm who also is a union official—and/or a local union representative.

2. If these people cannot settle the disagreement among themselves, they turn the dispute over to management and union representatives who have higher positions in their respective organizations, such as the plant manager and the president of the union local. They, in turn, sometimes use a mediator in their attempt to find a solution to the disagreement. The *mediator*, who is a third party agreeable to both union and management, may be called upon to suggest ways of settling the grievance. The mediator's recommendations are usually in the form of a compromise solution to which both parties can agree.

3. If the first 2 steps fail to settle a grievance, the third and final step involves submitting the grievance to final and binding arbitration. In *arbitration*, a third party—the arbitrator—is selected to settle the dispute. The arbitrator, agreed on by both parties, hears both labor's and

management's arguments about the grievance and then makes a final decision that resolves the grievance.

The institution of collective bargaining is sometimes described as a system of industrial law for setting the detailed rules of the work place and for administering these rules.

Collective bargaining is also seen as a procedure for setting wage rates and the details of compensation. Compensation consists not only of wages but also of a variety of benefits, such as health and welfare plans, vacations-with-pay, holidays-with-pay and pensions. The income received by union members is a central concern because members rely on their union to secure higher wages or salaries. The compensation of employees is important to management because it may affect their competitive position in the output market. A modern factory, for example, employs hundreds of different kinds of workers. Wage-rates for these jobs are important to employees because wages determine their income. The higher, the better! Management, however, looks at wages mainly as a cost of production. The lower, the better!

Finally, collective bargaining is a system for settling disputes centering on the content of an agreement and how the contract is interpreted and carried out. Collective bargaining does not eliminate labor-management conflict, but it does establish rules and procedures for settling disputes in a more responsible way.

Sometimes the talking phase of collective bargaining breaks down and work stoppages result. The company may order a *lockout*, thus shutting down the plant and keeping workers from performing their jobs and getting paid. Or the union may call a *strike* during which workers temporarily walk off their jobs, thus forcing production to stop. More will be said about work stoppages and their impact on the economy later in this lesson.

How well does collective bargaining work in the United States? Let's try to anwer this question by examining a list of advantages and disadvantages claimed for collective bargaining:

Benefits

1. Reduces the power of the employer to play one worker against another in order to cut wages. (Employers prefer lower wages in order to reduce the company's labor costs.)
2. Leads to higher wages that provide additional purchasing power for consumers. (This helps keep market demand high and prevents recession.)
3. Increases the voice and power of workers through their union. (This protects their rights and assures them of justice and fair treatment on the job.)

Criticisms

1. Leads to numerous and costly work stoppages (strikes and lockouts).
2. Results in inefficient work rules, e.g., "featherbedding" (requiring more workers for a job than really are necessary).
3. Causes inflation by increasing wages faster than productivity.
4. Gives too much power to unions and management which they may use to promote their own selfish interests at the expense of consumers and the public. (This concentration of power will eliminate the competition necessary for maximum efficiency and output of the economy.)

The criticism that collective bargaining leads to many costly work stoppages can be evaluated by looking at the data to see how often negotiations have broken down and resulted in strikes or lockouts. Table 3.1, concerned with work stoppages lasting more than 1 day, shows that in 1970 the 5,716 work stoppages that took place resulted in a loss of less than 1% of the total amount of time worked by all employed workers. Work stoppages involved 3.3 million workers, 5% of all those employed, and averaged 25 days duration. Figures for 1970 were unusually high compared with averages for the past decade.

Table 3.1
WORK STOPPAGES IN THE UNITED STATES,
SELECTED YEARS 1940 to 1970

Year	Work Stoppages Beginning in Year		Workers Involved		Man-days Idle During Year	
	Number	Average Duration (calendar days)	Number (thousands)	Percentage of Total Employed	Number (thousands)	Percentage of Estimated Working Time
1940	2,508	21	577	2%	6,700	0.10%
1945	4,750	10	3,470	12	38,000	0.47
1950	4,843	19	2,410	7	38,800	0.33
1955	4,320	18	2,650	6	28,200	0.22
1960	3,333	23	1,320	3	19,100	0.14
1965	3,963	25	1,550	3	23,300	0.15
1970	5,716	25	3,305	5	66,400	0.37

Source: U.S. Department of Commerce, *Statistical Abstracts of the United States, 1966 and 1972*, p. 247 and p. 244.

Working time lost through strikes and lockouts typically is only a small fraction of the time lost each year through illness and absenteeism.

Lesson in Brief

Collective bargaining is used by labor unions and employers to set the terms and conditions of employment for workers. It involves agreement on a contract covering such matters as wage rates, working conditions and grievance procedures. This provides workers with a system of industrial law and justice. Collective bargaining is sometimes criticized on grounds that it interferes with the free operation of the manpower market. Data on work stoppages show that collective bargaining works smoothly in most cases and that strikes and lockouts typically affect only a small fraction of workers and total working time.

There are many different ways of finding a job. Job seekers can read newspaper want ads; check with private employment agencies, labor unions, the public employment service; go directly to employers; or simply depend on luck and let jobs come to them. Often friends and relatives will provide information and help. The Public Employment Service—a government agency operated by the state with help from the federal government—offers many valuable services to young workers in addition to actual job placement. Knowledge of the various sources of information and assistance in finding employment can be very useful when entering the manpower market.

Let's investigate how to find a job by seeing how workers actually get their jobs. The job-seeking activity of the typical worker is largely a product of his environment. He often obtains information about employment opportunities from relatives and friends. Alertness and luck are of prime importance in finding a job. A worker hears that a certain firm is hiring or he knows of a company that is accepting employment applications. Labor market analysts estimate that 75% of all workers get their first job through relatives, friends or chance encounters. Other common methods through which workers find employment are newspaper want ads, direct application to an employer, labor unions, and public and private employment agencies. Public and private agencies fill about 1 of every 5 job vacancies, with most of these filled by the various state affiliates of the United States Employment Service, a division of the U.S. Department of Labor.

Let's take a brief look at the *private* employment agencies. In a recent year, there were about 4,000 business firms engaged full time—and 2,500 part-time—in the private placement of workers in employment. They are profit-seeking businesses that "produce" and sell job placement services. These firms tend to be concentrated in the larger cities. The private agencies concentrate their placement efforts in clerical, sales, professional and managerial occupations; but some of them do business in occupations such as baby-sitting, domestic service and jobs involving unskilled labor. The private agencies usually charge a fee often based on a percentage of the salary earned by the worker they place. In some cases, the fee for placement is paid by the employer. Some of these private employment agencies offer job counseling and testing as well as actual job placement.

In addition to these privately owned and operated employment agencies, there are *public* employment agencies. Local offices of the federal-state Public Employment Service—the United States Employment Service and the 50 state affiliates such as the Colorado Division of Employment—serve about 4,000 communities in the United States through approximately 2,000 full-time and 2,000 part-time offices. These local offices are administered by state agencies and financed by federal funds raised through a tax paid by employers. The public agencies place a large percentage of farm, service, semiskilled and unskilled workers. In addition, they also place hundreds of thousands of professional and managerial workers, craftsmen and foremen, clerical and sales, and other white-collar workers.

Let's look at a typical State Employment Service (SES) whose services are available to workers in most urban and some rural areas. The SES helps people choose, prepare for and obtain suitable employment. Its local offices provide free employment counseling and testing. They offer occupational information that includes local, state and national manpower market trends. They make referrals for training opportunities in such programs as apprenticeship, Manpower Development and Training Act institutional and on-the-job training, Job Corps and Neighborhood Youth Corps. Local SES offices help with job placement both locally and outside of the local area. In larger cities SES agencies have established Youth Opportunity Centers designed especially to help young people get skill training, gain work experience and obtain jobs when they become employable.

To illustrate how SES interviewers and counselors actually help young workers, consider 2 actual case studies of young workers who came to a Youth Opportunity Center (YOC) in the 1960s for help. These cases give some insight into the policies and procedures of the State Employment Service.

SALLY GREEN

Sally Green, age 19, first came to the office seeking some sort of factory work. She followed the usual procedure; she filled out an application and then was interviewed.

During Sally's visit to the office, the interviewer noted the following information: Sally was an above-average student at a small northeastern Ohio high school. She tended to do best in courses like shorthand (she earned an A), typing (B), general math (B), history (2 Bs) and English (C and 2 Bs). Her weakest areas were science (2 Cs) and languages (D and 2 Cs) with the exception of French 1 (A—summer school). In the beginning of her junior year at the age of 16, Sally quit school and got married. She now has 2 children. Her husband left school in the sixth grade and can neither read nor write. He works at a plastics factory and earns $240 a month. The family recently acquired extra financial burdens, and Sally felt that she must work to supplement their income. She took a job as a clerk at a dairy store where she tripled as a waitress, cashier and cleaning woman — all for $1.00 an hour. This job lasted only 3 months when she quit because of difficulties with her baby sitter.

On her first visit, YOC found nothing suitable for Sally in factory work. She left the office thinking that perhaps she would find a job on her own.

Two months after the initial interview, she returned for her second visit. This time the interviewer felt that Sally could benefit from some guidance from an employment service counselor since she expressed an interest in training but was uncertain about the choice of training. Sally spent almost an hour with the counselor exploring areas of interest, school and work experiences, and occupational information. She was pleased to find someone who would take time to help her think through what she wanted from work and life and assist her in planning a way to obtain her goals. Results of an interest check list inventory which Sally's counselor gave her indicated that Sally's chief occupational interests were in the areas of bookkeeping and clerical work. She also expressed interest in writing, sketching and baking. The areas she seemed to dislike most were sales, laboratory and mechanical work. At this point, the counselor gave Sally some occupational information concerning the areas in which she had shown interest. Sally discovered that the counselor was able to provide some facts about the work she was interested in, including job opportunities, pay, working conditions and requirements for entry. (The counselor used the *Occupational Outlook Handbook* and the *Employment Information Series* which contain specific job descriptions.)

On the basis of school achievement, interests and occupational information, Sally decided to apply for a clerk-typist training course. Since she and her husband lacked funds, she was happy to learn she could receive free training under the Manpower Development and Training Act (MDTA).

The YOC helped her to find stopgap jobs until the clerk-typist course was scheduled to begin. She worked as a waitress for 1 month then as a toy demonstrator (2 nights a week) for a month.

In November, Sally had a final interview for clerk-typist training. She began training 2 weeks later at the local Manpower Development and Training Center. In April, the Ohio State Employment Service testing department administered some of the standard typing tests to her and she achieved a score of 50 words per minute.

At the end of the training course, Sally came into the office again to look for general office work. She had received a good rating from the training center and had also passed the city, state and federal tests for a clerk-typist. She had also received a high school equivalency certificate. Sally was referred to a local university and was hired as a clerk-typist at $260 a month.

CARL STANLEY

Carl Stanley came to the Youth Opportunity Center after having spent more than 2 years in juvenile institutions in Ohio. He had been involved in petty theft and was finally sent to the Boys Industrial School (BIS) for incorrigibility. From there he was sent to the Training Institute of Central Ohio (TICO), where he received training in cooking and auto mechanics. It was not until 6 months after his release on parole that he came to the Ohio State Employment Service's Youth Opportunity Center for help.

Carl's work history indicated that after his release from the correctional institution he had quickly gotten a job as a banquet waiter at a local hotel and had worked for 1 month. He had left the job because of "too little pay"—he had been getting 91¢ an hour. He next worked for 3 days at a drive-in restaurant as a dishwasher for $1.00 an hour and left that job because of a "misunderstanding." His last job had been that of laborer in a foundry where he worked as a shake-out man cleaning dirt off molds by shaking and brushing them. He made $2.04 an hour but he was "laid off" this job.

Further exploration by the interviewer revealed additional background information. Carl was 19 years old, one of 2 children. He had an older sister, and his father had seldom lived in the home. His mother had raised both children with the help of relatives and welfare assistance. Carl had been in his junior year of high school when he was sent to BIS. He finished his junior year in the BIS and TICO. He had married since his release but was not living with or supporting his wife. He stated he was interested in getting a job as a service station attendant.

When no appropriate job was discovered in YOC files, Carl was referred to an auto wash but was not hired. Subsequently, he was referred to a uniform rental agency as a laborer but was not hired. Later he was called in to take a test for a company that was looking for machine operator trainees. However, he did not report for the test.

About a month later he was back in the office; because the interviewer felt he did not make a good impression and was unsure of his choice of work, he was referred to the counseling department. Initially, the counselor and Carl talked about his interests. The youth stated he wanted a chance to be a grill cook. The counselor set the stage by calling an employer, telling him of Carl's juvenile record and arranging an interview. Because Carl was dressed in dirty trousers and was not clean-shaven, the counselor advised him to go home to clean up before going to the interview, particularly to cut and clean his long fingernails. Carl ignored the counselor's advice and was not hired.

When Carl returned to the YOC office a few days later, he said he felt he had been refused the job because of his race. The counselor suggested this reasoning was the easy way out, that had Carl made sure his appearance was unobjectionable this might be the case, but he could not be sure. The importance of a person's appearance and the first impression a person makes were discussed. Subsequent counseling of this youth directed toward changing a negative attitude—reflected in his dress, appearance and behavior—was largely without results. Although Carl acknowledged the need for him to make changes in his approach to employment, he never put these things into practice. Later in the counseling process, Carl expressed an interest in a local Manpower Development Training Act instructional program (courses for Building Maintenance and Stock Clerk were scheduled at the time); as a result, he was given the General Aptitude Test Battery. However, he refused training upon learning he would get only a small allowance instead of wages during the training. Out-of-town training in the Job Corps was also discussed but rejected by Carl since he did not want to leave the city. He asked again to be referred to a job.

Carl obtained a job at a pancake house, but the job lasted only 3 days before he was fired. He told his counselor that he "did not fry the bacon crisp enough." After this job experience, the counselor talked with Carl about the possibility that he might be better suited for some other type of work. Carl agreed to try a different type of job, and he was referred to a factory as a trainee in a motor repair shop. He was not hired. Carl returned to his counselor discouraged and ready to quit trying to work at all. "I don't really have to work," he stated. The counselor spent some time talking with Carl, and apparently he left with his spirits lifted. Later that same day, Carl returned. He announced that he had gotten a job on his own as a bus boy at a restaurant. He was very proud that he had gotten the job himself.

It turned out that Carl worked only a day as a bus boy before being fired for picking up a waitress's tip. He told the counselor later that he had not meant to keep the tip but only to save it for the waitress. After this experience, the counselor again tried to get Carl to realize how his actions were defeating his stated purpose of getting and keeping a job. Not long afterward, Carl quit coming to the OSES. A notice sent to him by his counselor came back with the notation "Moved—Left No Forwarding Address."

These 2 real-life cases suggest that local offices of the State Employment Service are able and willing to offer help to young workers. But, as one manpower official put it, "They can never promise roses."

Lesson in Brief

Public and private employment agencies, labor unions, direct application to employers, friends, relatives, newspaper want ads and chance contacts are sources of help when seeking employment. One or all of these aids can be used to find a job. Some of these forms of assistance, such as those offered by local offices of the State Employment Service, are more valuable than others since they provide counseling services and information on training opportunities as well as job placement.

To get and hold a job, a worker has to meet certain requirements set by his employer. These include not only particular skills but also personal qualities that the employer believes the worker must have to be successful on the job. A worker who knows what employers expect and require can develop skills and attitudes that will help him obtain employment by being prepared for the all-important job interview.

There are several different ways of finding out what employers expect from their workers. One approach is to examine the procedures employers use for hiring new employees. Usually, a prospective worker is asked to fill out a job application form to provide personal information about himself. The employer learns several valuable things about the worker from the information on the application form. For example, he learns something about the communication skills of the potential employee. Can he read and follow directions? Does he write or type neatly? Can he complete a simple task? Information on the worker's education, training and prior work experience is also obtained.

If the worker's completed application suggests that he is qualified for the job, he may then be given a personal interview. This interview will involve the prospective employee and either the employer himself or one of his representatives, such as a job interviewer or personnel manager. The interview may also include the supervisor with whom the applicant would work if hired.

The employer or his representative will usually begin an interview by asking questions about information given on the job application form which he finds interesting or about which he may want more details. The interviewer will listen very closely to the answers that are given, paying attention not only to what the applicant says but how he says it. The prospective employee, in turn, is given an opportunity to ask questions about the work he is expected to do if hired. For some kinds of jobs, the interviewer will evaluate the prospective employee on the basis of what type of questions he asks. Is the worker interested primarily in opportunities for promotions, high starting pay, fringe benefits, short hours, special working conditions?

To summarize, employers expect their employees to be able to follow directions and fill out simple forms neatly, clearly and thoroughly. Since application forms almost always ask about education, training and work experience, one may assume that employers are interested in the type and amount of skills an applicant has. The fact that employers sometimes insist on an interview with the prospective employee points out the importance of communication and human relations skills. Most workers are expected not only to be able to express themselves but also to have skill in listening to others and following instructions.

Another way of finding out what employers expect from their workers is to consider the particular questions they ask prospective employees when they actually interview them. The primary purpose of the interview is to get information from the worker which will help the employer decide whether to hire him. This information may very well include the potential employee's attitudes and values. The following questions illustrate some of the concerns that employers have as they consider whether to hire a particular job applicant:

— What are your future career plans?
— What qualifications do you have that will make you successful in this job?
— Can you follow the directions of a supervisor without getting upset and angry?
— What do you want from this job?
— Do you understand the importance of the work you would be doing?

Although workers must have specialized knowledge, particular skills and work experience to qualify for some jobs, many employers place 75% to 85% of the emphasis in their hiring practices on personality and character qualifications. This attention to personal attitudes and characteristics is especially prevalent when hiring young workers.

Reports published by business firms and by the U.S. Department of Labor indicate that employers want their workers to be productive, dependable, cooperative, industrious, loyal to the enterprise. Some additional personal characteristics and functional work attitudes that employers have mentioned are initiative, cheerfulness and taking pride in one's work.

Industrial sociologists point out that the expectations of workers and employers often differ regarding what will happen in the work place and on the job because people have differences in attitudes and values and because people have different ways of defining and expressing the same attitudes and values. ("Value conflicts" are discussed in Unit One and in Unit Five.)

These differences in expectations give rise to job adjustment problems. The nature of these problems gives another insight into what employers expect from their workers. A study made a few years ago found that the following were the most frequently mentioned job adjustment problems of young white-collar workers:

— Willingness to start at the bottom, regardless of education; realization that personal advancement requires hard work, often on routine and seemingly unimportant tasks.
— Learning to get along well with supervisors and fellow workers; adjusting to the personalities of others; working cooperatively with persons who have less schooling and more experience.
— Learning to live on a lower salary than was expected and accepting the fact that advancement may be slow.
— Developing efficient work habits and the abilities to work independently and to plan time carefully, not trying to do everything at once.

Another insight into what employers expect from their employees can be obtained from the research that has been done on the reasons why workers are fired. In most cases (60% to 90%), the chief reason for dismissal is a shortcoming in personal traits, not technical skills. Emotional and social weaknesses rather than technical incompetence is the reason most workers are fired. Industrial relations studies reveal that workers are fired in many cases because of inability or refusal to follow instructions, laziness, unexplained or frequent absences or tardiness, and carelessness on the job.

One final point—it seems to make little difference whether the employer is a private business firm, a government agency or a nonprofit organization. All managers have responsibilities to carry out. They need certain kinds of workers to help get the job accomplished. Their preference generally is for employees who have the training, experience and technical skills needed to be productive. In addition, they require some measure of cooperation, dependability, loyalty and initiative.

Lessons in Brief

Employers expect their workers to have both the skills and the personal characteristics needed to perform their jobs in an efficient manner. This includes both productive ability and functional work attitudes. Knowing what employers expect from their employees is an important part of realistic world-of-work understanding.

Supply and demand are never in perfect balance in the manpower market. In the giant U.S. economy, there have always been some unemployed workers. What are the causes of unemployment? What are the consequences? Is unemployment a serious socioeconomic problem? Answers to these questions will help clarify some dimensions of the unemployment problem and provide a basis for understanding the policies and programs designed to deal with unemployment.

Is unemployment a problem in the United States? Let's examine unemployment data for the 25-year period 1947-1972, for the Great Depression of the 1930s and for the "boom" period of World War II.

The total number of people in the civilian labor force (16 years and over) who were unemployed in recent years has ranged from a low of under 2 million in 1953 to a high of 5 million in 1971. Unemployment rates (annual averages) varied from 2.9% in 1953 to 6.8% in 1958. On the average, more than 3 million men and women in the labor force were unemployed in over half the years between 1947-1972. During these 25 years, the unemployment rate was below 4% in only 9 years; it was above 5% in 11 of those years. In the remaining 5 years, unemployment was between 4% and 5%.

In 1933, the worst year of the Great Depression, the number of unemployed workers reached 13 million or 25% of the labor force. During the height of World War II, in 1944, only 670,000 workers were jobless; the unemployment rate dropped to an all-time low of 1.2%.

What are the *causes* of unemployment? Why are some men and women jobless, even though they are able and willing to work? Note what a recent survey of unemployed workers revealed.

— A 47-year-old electrical engineer, with more than 20 years of work experience, was *laid off* (involuntary separation from employment through no fault of worker for an indefinite period of time) by a West Coast plant since orders from the U.S. Defense Department had declined.

—A coal miner in his early thirties is unemployed as a result of the closing of one of the few remaining mines in his area.

—A teen-age Negro, just arrived in a large northern city from a rural area, signed up with the local office of the State Employment Service looking for unskilled work.

—A single woman in her fifties has been out of a job for 2 months because the company she worked for merged with another firm.

—The former owner of a small retail business that failed is looking for work as a salesman in his field.

—A 54-year-old family man, given a layoff notice a month earlier by a medium-sized machine-tool plant, is hopeful of being called back to work any day.

There are several different ways to classify the causes of unemployment. The classification system most frequently used includes 4 types of unemployment—frictional, seasonal, structural and cyclical unemployment. Consider the following definitions of these types of unemployment and the importance of each in the total unemployment picture.

The term *frictional* unemployment describes the joblessness caused by the imperfect working of the manpower market itself. Even if the total demand for labor is high, it takes a while before workers show up at the right time, in the right places and with the right skills needed to fill the available jobs. This type of short-term unemployment is caused by the normal "frictions" that exist in a free manpower market. In the typical case of this kind of unemployment, some time lag is bound to occur before the worker and the job get together. Part of this unemployment is unavoidable in a big and complicated economy.

Let's examine some statistical evidence of the presence of frictional unemployment. Even during the height of World War II there was an unemployment rate of 1.2%. Since 1929, there has been only one other year — the Korean War year of 1953 — when the unemployment rate was below 3%. Thus, something in the range of 1% to 3% of the unemployment rate appears to be frictional in nature since it is the lower limit even during times when there is the greatest demand for workers.

A second type of joblessness is *seasonal* unemployment. High unemployment rates for farm and construction workers occur in the winter, while low rates occur in the summer. Unemployment rates in retail trade are low before Christmas and Easter. In the automobile industry, unemployment rises during the late summer and early fall during model changeover time. Unemployment affected by seasonal forces usually tends to be for short periods of time. However, where the seasonal period is long and adult males make up the bulk of the work force (as in the construction industry), seasonal unemployment can account for a large part of the unemployment picture in the industry and is no trivial matter. For the labor force as a whole, seasonal unemployment probably accounts for ½% to 1% of total unemployment.

Structural unemployment is joblessness brought about by fundamental changes that alter the patterns of demand for and supply of workers. The impact of automation and technological change, the changing geographical location of American industry, the exhaustion of natural resources, major changes in the size and composition of the population, and changes in the types of workers needed and the industries needing them — all these are examples of structural changes in the economy that can cause unemployment, especially long-term joblessness. Because of the fundamental and drastic nature of many of the changes, structural unemployment is one of the most difficult types to deal with.

Technological advance and automation provide a dramatic illustration of what is happening to jobs in a changing economy. It is estimated that every year some 2 million jobs are affected by technological change. During the 1970s, more than 20 million jobs will be either altered or eliminated by technology. (Meanwhile, of course, new jobs will be created.)

Examples of structural changes that have created unemployment problems are well-known. The decline in the mining of bituminous and anthracite coal in Pennsylvania, West Virginia and

Kentucky along with a change to labor-saving methods resulted in thousands of miners losing their jobs. The shift from steam to diesel locomotives put thousands of railroad men out of work. The exhaustion of high-grade iron ore deposits in the Mesabi Range in Minnesota created widespread unemployment. The geographical shift of much of the cotton textile manufacturing industry from New England to the southeastern part of the United States hurt northern workers. Increasing productivity in agriculture (fewer farmers producing greater output of farm products) cost millions of farmers their jobs. Installation of automated equipment in the automobile industry, reduced demand for unskilled labor and the shift from being predominately a nation of goods-producers to basically a nation of service-producers are further examples of structural changes leading to unemployment. About 1% to 2% of the unemployment rate is caused by structural unemployment.

As the name implies, *cyclical* unemployment is caused by periodic cycles (changes or fluctuations) in the total level of economic activity. When the total demand for the economy's goods and services declines, as noted in Unit Two, the demand for workers to produce those goods and services also declines. As a result, the amount of unemployment increases when the business cycle is on the downswing or in a slump. A "business cycle" is a way of picturing total business activity over a period of time. A cycle has 5 phases of business activity—expansion or prosperity; peak or "boom"; recession or contraction; trough or low point; and recovery leading once again to prosperity. When the peak of business activity is passed and the cycle is on its downward path, the unemployment rate rises quite sharply. Unemployment reaches its highest level near the low point of the business cycle and stays high for several months after business activity begins to increase again.

What can be done about the cyclical type of unemployment? Essentially, the solution is implied by the analysis of the cause. If unemployment is caused by insufficient spending for goods and services in the market — not enough consumer expenditure, business investment spending and government purchases of goods and services — then the logical solution is to increase some combination of consumption, investment and government spending. To carry out its stabilization function (discussed in Unit Two), government can cut taxes leaving more spendable money in the hands of consumers and business. Or government can increase its own spending, obtaining the necessary money by borrowing. In both cases, total market demand goes up and unemployment goes down. Whenever the unemployment rate goes above 4%, much of the excess can be explained as cyclical unemployment.

The questions of how much unemployment and what kinds of unemployment American workers have experienced have been discussed. But what are the *results* of unemployment?

Strictly from an economic point of view, there are 2 major consequences of unemployment. One is lost output. The other is lost earnings.

When productive resources are not used, the economy loses the potential output that the resources could be producing. When workers are unemployed, the loss to the economy can be measured in opportunity cost terms as the goods and services that might have been produced but were not. During the high-unemployment years 1970-71-72, approximately $150 billion of potential GNP was lost. Because manpower's contribution to production is highly perishable (hours of labor cannot be stored), the potential contribution is lost forever. Every $50 billion of lost GNP can be translated into something like 2 million middle-income houses that are not available to American families; or 12 million new automobiles; or thousands of new schools, parks and other facilities that could improve the quality of life for millions of people.

Unemployment also results in lost earnings. True, some unemployed workers draw unemployment insurance payments. But many workers are not eligible for such benefits. Those who do receive unemployment compensation still must live on less than their regular wages. Loss of earnings because of unemployment deprives families of adequate income for consumption and for maintaining their economic security.

Going beyond the narrow income effects of unemployment, bitter experience has taught that more is lost through unemployment than just production and earnings. There are many human problems such as social and psychological frustration, feelings of rejection and uselessness, a sense of personal failure. Idleness also results in the erosion of human capital or productive ability. When a worker is denied an opportunity to apply his skills and functional work attitudes, he may actually lose them (like the high school senior who has forgotten all of the vocabulary and rules of grammar learned in his ninth grade Spanish class because he did not have the opportunity to put them to use in the years immediately afterward).

Many of the social tragedies of unemployment arise from the fact that the burden of joblessness falls disproportionately on particular workers and their families. This is true whether the unemployment is caused by insufficient aggregate demand or by structural factors (let's ignore frictional and seasonal unemployment for now). For example, a 4% unemployment rate may not seem terribly serious for the American economy as a whole; but for the particular workers who have no jobs and no earnings, the situation is painful. ("The unemployment problem is nothing but a vicious rumor circulated by a group of malcontents who have no jobs or incomes.") The fact remains that people with certain characteristics are singled out time after time to bear the burden of unemployment.

The unemployment rate (UR) for Negro workers in recent years has been consistently double the rate for white workers. For young workers, regardless of race, the UR is about triple the rate for the labor force overall. Women consistently have higher unemployment rates than men. Workers lacking a high school diploma have unemployment rates double those of high school graduates. Workers in the lower-skilled occupations have higher rates of unemployment. In 1969, for example — the best employment year in recent history — at a time when the UR for craftsmen and foremen was 2.2% and for professional and technical workers 1.3%, unemployment of unskilled, nonfarm laborers was much higher at 6.7%.

A profile of the unemployed reveals that the risks of unemployment and underemployment (working less than full time, below one's skill level or at substandard wages) are highest for the nonwhite, the unskilled, the young, the school dropouts, women and the people who live in rural areas. Their plight is discussed in the next lesson.

Lesson in Brief

Unemployment is a waste of the productive capacity of part of the labor force and results in a loss of income to jobless workers. Frictional and seasonal factors account for about 3% of the unemployment in the economy. Structural unemployment is caused by technological progress and other changes in the economy that affect supply and demand in the manpower market. Cyclical unemployment is caused by insufficient spending in the output market. Risks of unemployment and the human costs of joblessness fall most heavily on workers having certain characteristics.

Labor force statistics show that there are millions of unemployed workers in the U.S. economy. But what are the personal character-istics of these jobless workers? Are they men or women? Young or old? White or nonwhite? Skilled or unskilled? High school graduates or dropouts? Information about the unemployed may be of interest to the general citizen and also prove useful in making personal career decisions.

During the 1960s, the number of unemployed workers in the American economy averaged between 3 and 4 million men and women a year. In the early 1970s, unemployment was even higher. Even when the economy is working close to full capacity, about 2 million workers are unemployed. (This figure is accounted for by frictional unemployment described in the preceding lesson).

Who are these jobless workers? What particular characteristics seem to "select" these men and women for unemployment? What kinds of workers face the highest risks of unemployment?

For answers to these questions, let's examine the manpower statistics compiled by the U.S. Department of Labor and the cooperating state government agencies responsible for employ-ment security. There are data, for example, showing the per-sonal characteristics of the unemployed and rates of unemploy-ment for men and women in various occupations. Figure 3.3 shows that about 13% of young workers (age 18-24) with 8 years of schooling or less were unemployed in March 1970, a time when the unemployment rate for the total labor force was a little above 4%. At the same time, the jobless rate for workers in the 25-54 age bracket having the same amount of schooling (8 years or less) was only 5%. In fact, for each different level of education, younger workers consistently had higher unemployment rates. But even for these young workers, unemployment was lower for high school graduates than for dropouts. Also, the unemployment rate was lower for young college graduates than for young high school graduates.

The data suggest that while youthfulness may be a handicap in the job market — for various reasons ranging from their more limited work experience to employer appraisals of their attitudes and reliability — *education is a definite advantage.* In terms of describing the unemployed, Figure 3.3 indicates that youthfulness and lack of education generally increase a worker's chances of unemployment.

Figure 3.3

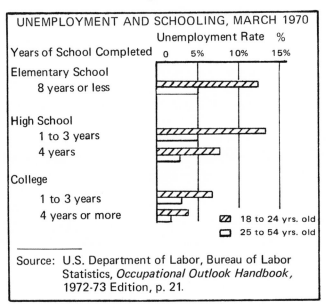

UNEMPLOYMENT AND SCHOOLING, MARCH 1970

Source: U.S. Department of Labor, Bureau of Labor Statistics, *Occupational Outlook Handbook,* 1972-73 Edition, p. 21.

Sex and color are additional characteristics that seem to mark workers for different unemployment rates. As Table 3.2 shows, unemployment rates are highest for female workers and for nonwhite workers. Before the mid 1960s, UR differences between men and women were not very large. But in recent years, rates for female workers have been about one-third higher than for male workers. In 1971, 2.2 million of the 5.0 million unemployed workers were women. This means that, while women made up 37% of the civilian labor force, they accounted for 44% of the unemployment.

212

Table 3.2
UNEMPLOYMENT RATES BY SEX AND COLOR,
SELECTED YEARS, 1958-1971
(Percentage Unemployed)

Year	Total[a]	Male[b]	Female[b]	White[c]	Negro and Other Nonwhite Races[c]
1958	6.8%	6.8%	6.8%	6.1%	12.6%
1961	6.7	6.4	7.2	6.0	12.4
1966	3.8	3.2	4.8	3.3	7.3
1967	3.8	3.1	5.2	3.4	7.4
1968	3.6	2.9	4.8	3.2	6.7
1969	3.5	2.8	4.7	3.1	6.4
1970	4.9	4.4	5.9	4.5	8.2
1971	5.9	5.3	6.9	5.4	9.9

Source: *Manpower Report of the President 1972*, p. 175.
[a]Unemployment rate for total labor force, including both sexes and all races.
[b]Includes all races.
[c]Includes both sexes.

Negro and other nonwhite workers consistently suffer higher unemployment rates than white workers. In 1971, as Table 3.2 shows, the UR for Negro and other nonwhite races was 9.9%, while for white workers the UR was 5.4%. Throughout the 1960s, the ratio of nonwhite to white unemployment rates was approximately 2 to 1. That meant "double trouble" for black workers in the manpower market.

These data indicate that if a worker is female or nonwhite the chances of being unemployed are increased. When a worker combines the 2 characteristics, female and nonwhite, the risk of joblessness is even greater. And when youthfulness is added to sex and race, the unemployment statistics begin to tell a tragic story. In 1971, the unemployment rate for nonwhite, female workers in the 18-19 age group was 34%, nearly 6 times the rate for the civilian labor force as a whole!

Another characteristic of workers that is linked to unemployment rates is skill level. One way to study this factor is to look at unemployment statistics of different occupational groups. Table 3.3 indicates, for example, that in 1971 only 3 out of every 100 professional and technical workers were unemployed (2.9%). But the jobless rate for nonfarm laborers was 11 out of every 100 (10.8%). Note how the unemployment rates of blue-collar workers (numbers 4, 5, 6 in the list of occupation groups) fluctuate more than the UR of white-collar workers (numbers 1-4). The unemployment rates reported for farmers and farm laborers hide a lot of "underemployment" in the form of part-time work and separation from mainstream manpower markets.

The portrait of the unemployed sketched by these statistics suggests that certain types of workers are more likely to be found among the ranks of the unemployed. The risk of unemployment is highest for the school dropout, the young, women workers, Negroes and other nonwhites, and workers with lower skill levels.

Unemployment rates for Negroes, youth, school dropouts and unskilled workers on the average have been twice as high as those of their counterparts. The employment needs of these groups are not being met by the manpower policy, as it now operates. This situation presents a special challenge to America's manpower policy.

Table 3.3
UNEMPLOYMENT RATES OF EXPERIENCED WORKERS BY MAJOR OCCUPATIONAL GROUPS, SELECTED YEARS, 1958-1971
(Percentage Unemployed)

Major Occupational Groups	1958	1960	1966	1969	1971
TOTAL, All Groups[a]	6.8%	5.5%	3.8%	3.5%	5.9%
1) Professional & technical workers	2.0	1.7	1.3	1.3	2.9
2) Managers, officials & owners (except farm)	1.7	1.4	1.0	0.9	1.6
3) Clerical workers	4.4	3.8	2.9	3.0	4.8
4) Sales workers	4.1	3.8	2.8	2.9	4.3
5) Craftsmen & foremen	6.8	5.3	2.8	2.2	4.7
6) Operatives	11.0	8.0	4.4	4.4	8.3
7) Laborers (except farm & mine)	15.0	12.6	7.4	6.7	10.8
8a) Private household workers	5.6	5.3	4.1	3.6	4.5
8b) Service workers (except private household)	7.4	6.0	4.8	4.3	6.6
9) Farmers & farm laborers	3.2	2.7	2.2	1.9	2.6

Source: *Manpower Report of the President 1972*, p. 179.
[a]Total includes persons with no previous work experience; other data are for experienced workers only.

Lesson in Brief

The unemployed tend to be the undereducated, the unskilled and workers who are discriminated against because of their age, color or sex. More equal opportunities in the manpower market along with increased investment in human resources can help improve the employability, productivity and earnings of men and women having these "high-risk" characteristics.

In the early 1970s, the number of unemployed workers in the American economy averaged between 4 and 5 million per year. What policies and programs have been adopted to deal with the problem of unemployment? Knowing what federal-state-local governments, business firms and labor unions are doing to assist unemployed workers can help citizens evaluate these programs and also acquaint workers with the types of help they might someday need if they become unemployed.

Public policies designed to deal with unemployment include programs that create jobs, provide manpower training, help workers locate jobs and provide income for workers who are temporarily unemployed.

First, let's review some tools that the federal government can use to deal with unemployment, especially cyclical unemployment. The use of government taxing and spending powers to influence the total demand for goods and services in the economy is called *fiscal policy*. An increase in market demand (total spending) for additional output will bring about some increase in the total demand for workers to produce the additional goods and services. In Unit Two we introduced a formula for counting the nation's total output of goods and services: $C + I + X_n + G = GNP$. The letters on the left side of the equation represent the 4 groups of buyers of the nation's output. Spending by consumers, business firms, foreigners and government determines the total amount of GNP demanded and produced by the economy. This formula will be helpful in understanding how the tools of fiscal policy are used to combat unemployment.

The purchasing power of 3 of the groups of buyers in the GNP formula (excluding foreigners) can be greatly influenced by the spending and taxing policies of the federal government. For example, the government can reduce corporate taxes in order to stimulate investment purchases of capital equipment by business firms. It can also reduce the rate of the personal income tax to put more purchasing power into the hands of consumers. The federal government can also increase the size of its own expenditures as well as the funds it gives to state and local governments under revenue sharing and other programs.

All of these policies have the effect of making more income available to consumers, businesses and government. With higher incomes, their spending will go up. Purchases of additional goods and services will increase the demand on business firms to supply the additional output. Business firms, in turn, will hire additional workers to help produce the extra output that is demanded. The total number of jobs in the economy is increased, and this reduces the amount of unemployment.

Of course there are limitations in using fiscal policy to combat unemployment. Increased spending, for example, can cause inflation. But the fact remains that expansionary fiscal policy along with appropriate *monetary policy* (regulating the supply of money and bank credit) are the biggest guns in the war against unemployment.

The federal and state governments have also developed special programs to help unemployed workers obtain jobs. Some programs operate on the *demand* side of the manpower market, such as creation of particular jobs for disadvantaged workers. The JOBS program (Job Opportunities in the Business Sector) was established in the late 1960s to create more than half a million jobs in private industry. The National Alliance of Businessmen (NAB) was organized to work in partnership with the U.S. Department of Labor and, in some cases, with labor unions. The plan called for private employers to hire disadvantaged workers, provide them with training on the job and help them deal with various kinds of personal problems so they could retain their jobs. In addition, the federal government has provided funds for state and local government agencies themselves to hire more workers. One example is the Public Employment Program (PEP) set up in 1971. Many people who favor job creation as a solution to unemployment feel that the government ought to become the "employer of last resort." This means that some agency of federal, state or local government would guarantee jobs to workers who are unable to find any other regular employment.

218

There are also programs for the unemployed that operate on the *supply* side of the manpower market. Examples are skill training for eligible workers under the Manpower Development and Training Act (MDTA) and employability training under the Concentrated Employment Program. Local offices of the State Employment Service assist unemployed workers with counseling, testing and job placement. Some workers have been helped with money and services so they could relocate to manpower markets where jobs are more plentiful.

Finally, there are programs to help improve the way the manpower market itself operates. This includes better information on jobs that may be available for unemployed workers in a local area. It also refers to efforts aimed at reducing job discrimination against minority workers, women and other groups.

To summarize, there are government policies and programs designed to increase the total number of jobs in the economy as a whole (through fiscal and monetary policy); to provide extra jobs in particular areas; to train workers so they can qualify for job opportunities; and to provide information to help workers find existing jobs.

Now let's consider another side of the unemployment problem. What happens when jobs cannot be found? What do workers live on when they are unemployed? The vast majority of wage and salary workers in the United States are covered by *unemployment insurance* (sometimes called unemployment compensation). Established in 1935 under the Social Security Act, this joint federal-state program provides payments to eligible persons for specified periods of time. State-administered funds, obtained through payroll taxes paid by employers, provide money for these programs. The amount of money that workers get, how long they can draw payments and the tax rates paid by employers vary among the states.

Unemployment insurance (UI) plays a key role in aiding the unemployed. It provides more income to more unemployed persons than all other programs of aid combined. Total benefits averaged about $3 billion a year for the nation as a whole in the 1960s. Weekly benefits average about $50 for each eligible worker.

UI supplies the unemployed with purchasing power to carry them over while they are seeking new employment. This extra purchasing power also increases total demand in the economy, which helps keep unemployment from rising even higher.

Private (nongovernmental) programs created by management and labor for dealing with unemployment are characterized by fitting the benefits to particular situations and pioneering in new directions rather than along established lines of public programs. Three of these programs are supplementary unemployment benefits, severance pay and early pensions.

A *supplementary unemployment benefit* plan (SUB) is one that supplements or adds to the benefits paid by public unemployment insurance programs. These SUB programs came into being as a result of negotiations between labor unions and management. Leading unions such as the United Auto Workers and the United Steelworkers felt that the amounts and duration of benefits under public UI programs were not adequate. They wanted their members to receive additional compensation when they are unemployed and persuaded the companies to set up a SUB program. In the 1960s about 2 million workers were covered by SUB plans, in some cases paying benefits of $50 or more per week in addition to regular unemployment insurance benefits.

Severance pay consists of one lump-sum payment made by an employer to an employee when his job is terminated by the company. Because the worker is considered to have a kind of "property right" in his job, the benefit is paid to compensate him for the loss of that right. Nearly half of all workers under union collective bargaining agreements are covered by severance pay plans. Payments vary greatly from firm to firm, ranging from $50 or $100 up to $1,000 or more, depending on years of service to the company.

Some private business firms, often with prodding from labor unions, have established private pension plans which allow workers to retire earlier than the usual retirement age of 65. This provision for *early retirement* is especially helpful to older workers who are laid off or lose their jobs, because they often have trouble finding another job. Usually, the early retiree is paid less than the full pension he would get if he retired at age 65. But when early retirement is not completely voluntary, some plans pay the full amount until the retiree becomes eligible for Social Security benefits.

Lesson in Brief

There are several different types of governmental and private programs for dealing with unemployment problems. Governmental programs have been developed to increase the total number of jobs available throughout the economy, create new job opportunities in particular areas, train or retrain the unemployed, supply information on job openings and provide unemployed workers with temporary income through unemployment insurance benefits while they look for a new job. Private programs designed to deal with unemployment include such plans as supplementary unemployment benefits (SUB), severance pay and early pensions.

UNIT FOUR
Career Opportunities in the American Economy

The present and projected structure of employment — by occupation, industry and geographic location — will largely determine the pattern of career opportunities facing young men and women who enter the world of work in the 1970s. Information of this type has implications for career planning and public understanding of manpower policy as it evolves in local communities and across the nation.

How do manpower economists and vocational counselors deal systematically with the great number and variety of jobs waiting for workers who have the necessary qualifications? Lessons in this unit describe the day-to-day realities of the manpower market and describe employment trends by occupational and industrial groups. Data compiled by the U.S. Bureau of Labor Statistics are presented on white-collar, blue-collar, service and farm occupations and on the changing importance of goods-producing and service-producing industries in terms of the jobs they offer.

A special lesson is devoted to the growing role that women play in the labor force and to some of the myths and practices that hinder the progress of female workers. Another lesson provides information on the changing geography of employment opportunities in the United States and the personal characteristics of mobile workers. The fact that some states and geographical areas have faster rates of employment growth than others is important to career planning.

223

Projections into the future are examined to help determine which occupations and industries will offer the most job openings based on economic growth and replacement needs. The last lesson in the unit provides a historical perspective on the vast changes that have occurred in the occupational and industrial sources of employment in the United States since the Roaring '20s.

I am the people—the mob—the crowd—the mass.
Do you know that all the great work of the world
is done through me?

Carl Sandburg

The division of labor is carried so far in the American economy that workers today are employed on 36,000 different jobs in 479 separate occupations. Reviewing this panorama of jobs will help an individual discover the various opportunities there are for employment. The more a person knows about jobs, the better he will be able to understand the manpower market and the career opportunities that exist there.

As noted in Unit Two, specialization and the division of labor help increase the productive powers of labor. But how is the work divided in the U.S. economy? What specific kinds of jobs do men and women have?

There is a great variety of jobs in the American economy. According to the federal government's job classification system, there are 479 individual occupations which have 23,000 definitions and 36,000 titles. These jobs differ in many ways—hours of work, pay, working conditions, employment requirements, location and size of employing enterprise.

Consider the following job announcements which are typical of want ads printed in American newspapers each day. Which of these jobs seems interesting? Why? What types of education and training are required for each? What are the similarities and differences among the jobs?

The information in the ads suggest certain things about jobs in the economy and the way they are advertised. For example, many of the job advertisements seem to make a direct appeal to a certain type of personality. What other characteristics of jobs and their advertisements can be identified?

GRAPHIC DESIGNERS: ARE YOU TIRED OF THE CITY?

Let us offer you the opportunity to design high style collateral material and the facilities to work from beginning to end under one modern roof.

Send us 6 of your best pieces along with a brief resume. If suitable, we'll fly you to our place in the country. You'll find national accounts for your ego and a pastoral atmosphere for your peace of mind. (Check us in D & B if you just can't believe it.)

HOUSEWIVES

Part-time work in sales evenings and Saturdays. Some daytime hours. Immediate discount on purchases. Apply in person.

ASSISTANT TREASURER

Educational service organization man with accounting background needed to assist department head and oversee accounting department. Must be good correspondent and able to communicate with contacts in financial community. Accounting degree required, experience in college fund accounting desirable but not necessary. Generous fringe benefits. Salary open. Send detailed resume.

DISPATCH CLERK

Opening on evening shift for young man, 19 to 35, interested in future with transportation. Apply in person.

MACHINE REPAIR SPECIALISTS

Full-time, 2nd shift, must know Lathe, Shaper and Miller, must have own tools. Shift premium, good fringes, no age limit.

TRADEMARK LAWYER

Responsible opportunity in New York law firm for lawyer with 1-4 years trademark background.

DANCING INSTRUCTORS

Full- or part-time trainees. No experience necessary. Are you over 19 years old, well-groomed and neat in appearance? Here's an opportunity to meet and be with a wonderful group of people, attend dances and parties, become an outstanding dancer and teacher. Top salaries. Frequent increases. Apply in person.

DINNER HOSTESS

Short evening hours. We will train you. Prefer eastside resident. Apply in person to Mr. Tonetti, between 11 a.m. and 2 p.m.

FURNITURE DECORATOR and SALES PERSON

A progressive furniture store needs the services of an outstanding sales person. Store has over 40,000 sq. ft. all on one floor. 10 yr. retirement pension plan, plus other added incentives. Store sells nationally known medium-priced furniture. Replies will be held in strict confidence.

DISH MACHINE OPERATOR

Day shift and night shift. Better than average starting pay.

LABORERS

wanted to assist brick mason. 50 hrs. per week, total pay approximately $140. Call between 9-5.

JANITORIAL WORK Part Time

Applicants desired for steady work. Late eves. 12 p.m. to 6 a.m. Sun. through Thurs. Must be in good health, between 21 and 50. No police record, must drive and have own car.

BEHAVIORAL SCIENTISTS
For Management Development

The Challenge: Developing managerial resources in one of several multi-divisional complexes. The Program: Independent responsibility in an all-out, close-working group operation that involves Managerial Performance Evaluation, Executive Selection and Assessment, Early Identification of Potential, Organizational Analysis and Planning. The Goal: Transformation of management potential into a dynamic and productive management force. The Requirements: An advanced degree in psychology, 5 or more years combined clinical, industrial or consulting experience. Ability to use sophisticated personnel assessment techniques and behavioral principles for genuine contributions to the very highest levels of management. The Atmosphere: Rewarding, with full recognition for this important function in a progressively expanding billion-dollar corporation.

Positions exist at several attractive locations. Please send resume, salary progress and current requirements.

SOLENOID VALVE SALES

Due to expansion of present line of solenoid valves, large midwest manufacturer has openings for additional sales engineers. Three or 4 years experience is required with a preferred background in pneumatics and hydraulics. There will be some nationwide travel from the base operation. Company car, excellent salary and liberal employee benefits programs will be available to the right men. Submit resume and salary requirement.

GO-GO DANCERS

wanted for afternoon cocktail hour. Apply in person.

PHARMACOLOGIST

A major effort is now being made by our company in the field of pharmaceuticals. Opportunities are now available at the BS, MS, and PhD levels with plans to continue staffing throughout next year. Areas of interest include: Biochemical Pharmacology, Cardiovascular Pharmacology, Neuropharmacology. Enjoy the benefits of an industrial research affiliation in an academic environment. Your inquiry will receive prompt and confidential consideration.

ACTUARIAL ASSISTANT

Nationally known company offers excellent opportunity to college graduate with major or minor in mathematics. Intent to study actuarial science and prepare for Society of Actuaries examinations necessary. Applicant will assist actuary in rate computations, statistical studies and mathematical analysis. This is a tremendous opportunity to assume professional responsibility immediately and increase your stature based upon your own capabilities. Send complete resume including salary requirements.

MEDICAL TECHNOLOGIST, A.S.C.P.

Full-time position available, salary commensurate with experience. Excellent fringe benefits. Apply to personnel office.

YOUR OWN COSMETICS BUSINESS

We have the MAGIC MIST line. Less than $25.00 starts business. Unlimited earnings. No door-to-door selling. For free samples and color brochures, send $1.00 for postage and handling.

227

Lesson in Brief

There are many different types of jobs in America. All workers in these jobs make a contribution to producing the economy's goods and services. These jobs differ a great deal in terms of employment qualifications, pay, hours, working conditions, etc. Some of these jobs may offer young people employment opportunities when they enter the manpower market.

The current operation of the American manpower market involves the activities of more than 80 million workers employed in thousands of occupations. To start planning and preparing for employment, an individual should examine the many different types of jobs that exist in the economy and seek answers to the following questions: In what types of occupations are U.S. workers employed? How are jobs classified according to particular occupational groups? How many workers are employed in each of the occupational groups? How are workers classified according to industrial groups? How many workers of various types are employed in each industrial group?

Let's begin an examination of the multitude of jobs in the economy by organizing the jobs (putting them into meaningful groupings) and by determining the number of people employed in the various occupational groups.

One way to classify jobs and workers is by occupational group—white-collar, blue-collar, service and farm. An occupational group contains a number of different jobs which have similar broad characteristics such as entrance requirements, potential earnings, or a way of life and labor.

White-collar workers are distinguished not only because they often wear "white-collar" clothes but because they work in occupations that are centered in offices, laboratories, classrooms, stores and salesrooms. In general, these workers normally do not depend on their manual or physically manipulative skills to perform their work. Rather, their work involves a relatively high degree of mental and communication skill and is characterized by dealing directly with people, their property or their records. They teach, practice medicine, manage enterprises, handle legal problems, design bridges, create knowledge and look after accounts.

In 1970, of the total civilian work force of almost 79 million, about 38 million men and women (48% of total employment) were employed in the white-collar occupations. More than half of all women employed in 1970 were working in white-collar occupations. For men, the comparable figure was 41%.

What is the breakdown (subgrouping) of these white-collar jobs? *Professional and technical* workers accounted for 11 million of the white-collar jobs in 1970; there were almost 14 million *clerical* workers; there were 8 million *managerial* workers (*managers, officials and owners*); and there were nearly 5 million *sales* workers.

Blue-collar or manual workers include *craftsmen and foremen* (sometimes termed "skilled workers"); *operatives* such as machine operators, assemblers, drivers and inspectors (sometimes referred to as "semiskilled workers"); and *laborers* (sometimes termed "unskilled workers"). Blue-collar workers, who often wear "blue-collar" clothes to work, use physical or manipulative skills, work primarily with their hands and work more with things than with people. These workers help transform the ideas of scientists, engineers, managers and administrators into goods and services. They operate equipment, build, control, repair, move, wrap, pack and unload. They provide most of the manpower muscle. In 1970, 35% of all employed workers were working in blue-collar occupations. Of the nearly 28 million blue-collar workers in 1970, 14 million were craftsmen and foremen, 10 million were operatives and 4 million were laborers.

Service occupations employed about 10 million workers in 1970—almost 13% of total employment. Service jobs provide protective, personal, building maintenance and private household services to individuals, organizations and communities. Service workers serve food, cut hair, baby-sit, fight fires and clean buildings. More than one-fifth of all women workers in 1970 were employed in this occupational group. On the other hand, only about 7% of the total number of men employed in 1970 held service jobs. Subgroups include *private household* workers and *other service* workers.

Farm workers include *farmers and farm managers* and *farm laborers and foremen*. These workers are employed to produce food and fiber. In 1970, 3.1 million farm workers (mostly men) were employed, only 4% of total employment. This total is more than 2 million less than in 1960 and only one-third the number of farm workers employed in 1940.

One quick way to grasp the relative importance of employment in each of these occupational groups is to note their respective share of the total number of workers employed. Consider the breakdown in 1970:

White-collar	48%	(38 million workers)
Blue-collar	35%	(28 million workers)
Service	13%	(10 million workers)
Farm	4%	(3 million workers)
TOTAL	100%	(79 million workers)

Knowledge about employment should also include information about the work place and setting where the job is performed. Almost every occupation can be practiced in a number of different industries and enterprises. Industries are classified into 9 major divisions. These industrial divisions represent roughly similar lines of economic activity. The 9 industrial groups can be divided into 2 general categories—those that produce goods and those that produce services. The 4 *goods-producing* industries—agriculture, contract construction, mining, manufacturing—harvest food and fiber, build houses and office buildings, extract minerals and manufacture merchandise.

The 5 *service-producing* industries—government; transportation and public utilities; trade; finance, insurance and real estate; service and miscellaneous—are involved in selling, governing, transporting, insuring, financing, repairing, and providing energy, communication services and personal care.

In 1970 the goods-producing industries employed 27 million workers (36% of the total number of employed workers). The service-producing industries employed more than 47 million workers (64% of total employment). An additional 5 million workers employed in 1970 were self-employed or unpaid family workers. It is clear that in the 1970s the U.S. labor force is occupied more with the production of services than with the production of goods.

The occupational and industrial classification systems used in this book were established by the U.S. Department of Labor for presenting manpower data. The categories are the means of summarizing a great variety of occupations and industries. For example, the ninefold occupational classification system (sometimes 11 categories when service workers and farm workers are each subdivided into 2 additional categories) summarizes a total of 30,000 occupations. There are approximately 250 industries in the economy, according to 1 classification system. These are summarized under 9 industrial categories in the lessons of this book.

The dynamic nature of the manpower market is illustrated by the number of changes that take place in the listing of jobs done by the U.S. Department of Labor in the *Dictionary of Occupational Titles* (DOT), a standard reference volume that lists and defines various occupations in the economy and groups these jobs according to basic occupational, industrial or worker characteristics. For example, the 1965 edition of the DOT included 6,432 new jobs not listed in the 1949 edition and dropped many obsolete jobs.

Figure 4.1, which outlines and summarizes the occupational and the industrial classification systems introduced in this lesson, will be useful when studying career opportunities in the American economy.

Lesson in Brief

Jobs and workers can be classified according to occupations and the industries in which work is performed. These classification systems can be used to investigate and explore the thousands of different occupations in which more than 80 million American workers are employed. Currently, more Americans are employed in white-collar occupations (48%) than in any other occupational group; 35% of the employed civilian labor force works in blue-collar occupations; about 13% are service workers; and 4% are farm workers. Based on industrial classification, 64% of the workers are employed in the service-producing industries, while 36% are producing goods.

Figure 4.1

SUMMARY OF OCCUPATIONAL AND INDUSTRIAL CLASSIFICATIONS

Occupational Groups

WHITE-COLLAR
Professional and technical workers
Managers, officials and owners (nonfarm)—sometimes termed "Managerial"
Clerical workers
Sales workers

BLUE-COLLAR or Manual
Craftsmen and foremen (includes mechanics and repairmen)—also termed "Skilled"
Operatives (includes assemblers, drivers and inspectors)—also termed "Semiskilled"
Laborers (nonfarm and nonmining)—also termed "Unskilled"

SERVICE
Service workers (includes private household workers)

FARM
Farmers and farm managers (includes farm laborers and foremen)

Industrial Groups

GOODS-PRODUCING or Production Industries (sometimes excludes Agriculture)
Agriculture
Manufacturing (includes durable and nondurable goods)
Contract Construction—also termed "Construction"
Mining (includes forestry and fishing)

SERVICE-PRODUCING or Service Industries
Government (includes local, state and federal governments and public schools)—also termed "Public Administration"
Transportation and Public Utilities (includes communications)
Trade (includes wholesale and retail)
Finance, Insurance and Real Estate
Service and Miscellaneous (includes nonpublic education, medical and repairs)

The United States is becoming a nation of white-collar workers. The time is approaching when more than half of the labor force will be employed in white-collar occupations. It is helpful in career planning to look at the various types of jobs these white-collar workers have, to note how many men and women are employed in particular white-collar occupations and to see the types of enterprises they work for.

The last lesson revealed that 38 million men and women were employed in white-collar occupations in 1970. The white-collar group is the largest of the 4 occupational groups—bigger than the blue-collar, service or farm occupations—and accounts for 48% of total employment in the U.S. economy. What kinds of jobs do these white-collar workers perform?

In 1970, 11 million white-collar workers (which is more than 14% of total civilian employment) were employed in *professional and technical* occupations. These workers held jobs in such professional occupations as physician, lawyer, teacher and scientist. They also held technical jobs in such occupations as draftsman, x-ray technician and engineering aid.

One of the chief characteristics of professional work is that it generally requires either college graduation—often with an advanced degree such as M.D., D.D.S., LL.B.—or experience of such kind and amount as to provide comparable knowledge. Most professional occupations require theoretical knowledge of a specific field such as law, medicine or engineering. However, there are some occupations—such as newspaper or magazine editor, musician and actress—that do not require as much specialized or theoretical knowledge. These professional jobs require a great deal of creative talent and certain skills that are acquired chiefly through experience.

The technical occupations are closely related to the professions. People in these jobs work closely with engineers, scientists, physicians and other professional personnel. Employment in these technical occupations usually requires a combination of basic scientific knowledge and specialized education or training in some particular aspect of technology or science. Such training is usually acquired by the worker through attendance at a technical institute, junior college or other schools or through on-the-job training from a supervisor or a fellow worker who has already mastered the required information and skills.

Figure 4.2 lists the major professional and technical occupations. It shows, for example, that in 1970 there were 4

Figure 4.2

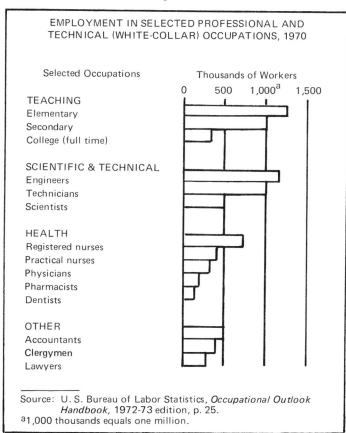

EMPLOYMENT IN SELECTED PROFESSIONAL AND TECHNICAL (WHITE-COLLAR) OCCUPATIONS, 1970

Source: U. S. Bureau of Labor Statistics, *Occupational Outlook Handbook,* 1972-73 edition, p. 25.
[a]1,000 thousands equals one million.

professional occupations—elementary school teachers, secondary school teachers, engineers and technicians—in which a million or more men and women were employed.

The data in Figure 4.2 yield a number of interesting facts about employment in professional and technical occupations. For example, in 1970 more than twice as many registered nurses as physicians were employed and more technicians than scientists were employed.

In 1970, about 7 million men and 1.3 million women were *managers, officials* or *owners* of the nation's business, governmental or private nonbusiness enterprises. More than 10% of the employed labor force is busy administrating the affairs of society's various public and private organizations. These men and women, whether working in large or small organizations or for themselves or others, make decisions and see that they are carried out. The soundness of their decisions and how well they are carried out has a great deal to do with the success or failure of the enterprises.

Managers and salaried officials account for about three-fourths of all workers employed in this administrative occupational group. Executives and other managerial personnel in business firms account for the largest part of this salaried manager group. However, there are also several hundred thousand people in this group who are officials of federal, state and local government agencies and such nonprofit organizations as the Red Cross, private foundations, and Boy Scouts and Girl Scouts.

About 14 million people were employed in *clerical* or closely related kinds of work in 1970. In other words, more than 17% of total civilian employment is concerned with such activities as record-keeping, paperwork and other office activity. Clerical workers perform such tasks as handling communication through mail, telephone, telegraph and messenger services; attending to the shipping and receiving of merchandise; and ringing up sales on the cash registers of stores and restaurants. Their work involves jobs that vary widely in skill and experience requirements. For example, executive secretaries usually are highly skilled and have a great deal of experience and responsibility. On the other hand, the jobs of messengers and file clerks usually require little skill and experience.

Clerical occupations are dominated by women—7 of every 10 clerical workers are women. In fact, more than half of all women who go to work after completing high school find work in clerical occupations. Figure 4.3 indicates the major types of occupations in which clerical workers are employed, by sex. It shows, for example, that in 1970 more than 2.7 million men and women were employed as secretaries and stenographers.

Figure 4.3

EMPLOYMENT IN SELECTED CLERICAL OCCUPATIONS, 1970, BY SEX

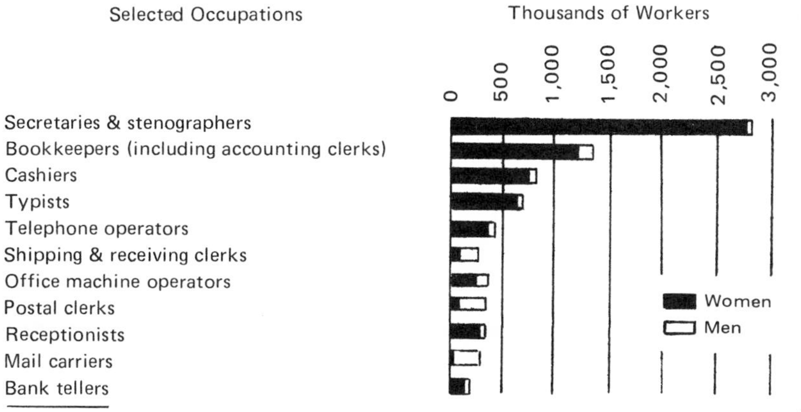

Source: U.S. Bureau of Labor Statistics, *Occupational Outlook Handbook*, 1972-73 edition, p. 283.

The data in Figure 4.3 indicate that in 1970 over a million bookkeepers and accounting clerks were employed in the United States and that most of these workers were women. Women are employed more frequently than men in most of the clerical occupations shown in Figure 4.3.

In 1970, about 4.9 million men and women—6.2% of the employed labor force—were in *sales* and marketing work. Workers in this occupational group sell goods and services for manufac-

237

turers, insurance companies and other producers. They work for wholesalers who stock large quantities of goods that are sold in smaller lots to retail stores. They also sell for drugstores, dress shops and other retailers who deal directly with the public. A list of the items that sales workers sell would be practically endless and would include the entire range of goods and services produced by the economy.

Sales work varies a great deal. It includes people who have less than a high school education as well as those who are college graduates; workers who travel in their jobs and those who do not; salaried employees and those who are self-employed; persons who sell to business men and those who sell to consumers. Over half of all sales workers are employed in retail selling. One-fourth of the sales workers are employed part-time—working less than 35 hours a week. Forty percent of those employed in sales work in 1970 were women who worked primarily in retail stores. Men provide the greatest share of the sales force in wholesale, manufacturing, real estate, securities, insurance and other nonretail sales.

Let's summarize what has been observed about employment in the white-collar occupations. Forty-eight workers out of every 100 in the United States have white-collar jobs. Increasingly, these workers are on top of the employment pyramid—with expanding job opportunities, higher pay and greater demands for their skills. Growing emphasis on the production of services as opposed to goods will further strengthen the position of white-collar workers in the manpower market. Eleven million of these white-collar workers are employed in professional and technical occupations. Many of them need some type of post-high school education or training to perform their jobs. More than 8 million workers—about 1 employee in every 10 in the economy—have jobs as managers, owners or officials in the nation's enterprises. Another 13.7 million men and women—17% of the work force—are employed with record keeping and other paperwork. These 14 million clerical workers are predominantly women—7 of every 10. Secretaries and stenographers account for about 1 of every 5 jobs in this group. Finally, almost 5 million men and women are employed in sales work, mainly in retail sales. One of every 4 sales workers is employed part-time. Forty percent of all sales workers are women.

Lesson in Brief

There are more white-collar workers than any other occupational group employed in the U.S. economy. These white-collar workers are employed in professional and technical, managerial, clerical, and sales occupations. White-collar workers play a key role in today's service-producing era. Professional and technical occupations and clerical occupations have the greatest number of white-collar workers. In some white-collar occupations, such as office work and retail selling, women occupy the majority of the jobs.

Farm, Blue-Collar and Service Workers

Farm workers provide food and fiber necessary for the nation's health and comfort, indeed, for it's very survival. However, blue-collar and service workers also provide essential goods and services. These 3 groups of workers—farm, blue-collar and service— comprise more than half of the total employed labor force; their skills are vital to the operation of the economy.

Let's begin an exploration of the employment of farm, blue-collar and service workers in the economy by taking a detailed look at the largest group of the three—the blue-collar occupations. In 1970, 27.8 million workers were employed in blue-collar occupations. Roughly 1 of every 3 workers in the entire economy in 1970 was employed in a blue-collar occupation (craftsmen and foremen, operatives, or laborers).

Blue Collar

More than one-third of all blue-collar workers are classed as *craftsmen and foremen* or skilled workers. In 1970, there were 10.2 million of these skilled workers employed in the American economy. They include craftsmen and foremen working in the building trades, printers, bakers, those who operate and maintain equipment, repairmen, and workers responsible for making the patterns, models, tools, dies, machines and equipment without which the industrial process could not be carried on. Twenty-eight percent of the skilled workers are employed repairing the equipment used in industry and the mechanical equipment and appliances used by consumers. More than one-quarter of the craftsmen and foremen are employed constructing homes, commercial and industrial buildings, and highways. In 1970, there were at least 18 different skilled-workers occupations in which 100,000 or more workers were employed. However, many skilled occupations are small in number. For example, there are fewer than 20,000 workers employed as photoengravers, blacksmiths and glazers.

Although craftsmen and foremen are employed in almost every branch of industry, more than 60% are in manufacturing and construction. In the building trades, a large percentage of craftsmen are self-employed. Only a small proportion (about 3%) of the craftsmen and foremen in the economy are women.

Figure 4.4 shows 18 skilled workers occupations, each of which employed more than 100,000 workers in 1970. For example, it indicates that more than 800,000 automotive mechanics were employed—making it the largest of the craftsmen and

Figure 4.4

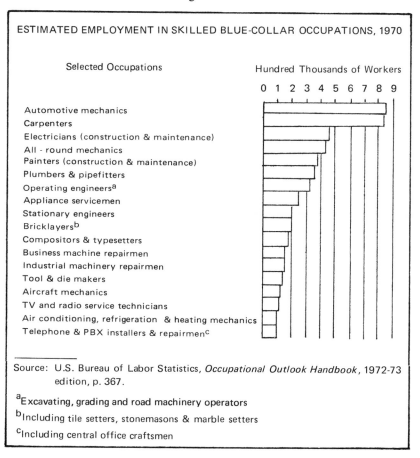

ESTIMATED EMPLOYMENT IN SKILLED BLUE-COLLAR OCCUPATIONS, 1970

Selected Occupations   Hundred Thousands of Workers

0 1 2 3 4 5 6 7 8 9

Automotive mechanics
Carpenters
Electricians (construction & maintenance)
All - round mechanics
Painters (construction & maintenance)
Plumbers & pipefitters
Operating engineers[a]
Appliance servicemen
Stationary engineers
Bricklayers[b]
Compositors & typesetters
Business machine repairmen
Industrial machinery repairmen
Tool & die makers
Aircraft mechanics
TV and radio service technicians
Air conditioning, refrigeration & heating mechanics
Telephone & PBX installers & repairmen[c]

Source: U.S. Bureau of Labor Statistics, *Occupational Outlook Handbook*, 1972-73 edition, p. 367.

[a] Excavating, grading and road machinery operators

[b] Including tile setters, stonemasons & marble setters

[c] Including central office craftsmen

241

foremen occupations. There were more than twice as many plumbers and pipe fitters employed than aircraft mechanics.

Now let's look at another category of blue-collar employment—the *operatives* or semiskilled workers. With almost 14 million workers in 1970, this was the largest occupational subgroup in the nation's labor force. One of every 6 workers employed in the U.S. economy in 1970 was in an operative occupation.

In general, operatives rely primarily on their hands to do their work. Many of these workers use a variety of hand tools such as screwdrivers, pliers, files, soldering irons, measuring devices and cutting tools. They also make simple adjustments and do minor maintenance work on the machines they operate. Some operatives are required to keep simple records of their work. Millions of operatives run power-driven machines in factories. Many use sewing machines for making clothing, awnings and other items. Others operate machines to stamp out metal parts; still others use machine tools, such as lathes and milling machines, to shape metal to precise sizes.

A considerable number of operatives operate equipment that is used in handling and moving materials, such as power forklift trucks to move raw materials and manufactured products from place to place in factories. Large numbers of operatives are employed as assemblers and inspectors. Assemblers install components into finished products, such as radio and television sets. Inspectors examine and test products to see if their quality meets specific standards. Many operatives in factories are employed as helpers to assist workers who are more highly skilled (for example, firemen who help the skilled stationary engineers operate and maintain steam boilers and heating plants).

About 9 million operatives are employed in manufacturing industries principally as machine operators, material movers, assemblers and inspectors. They help produce such things as clothing, automobiles, food, machinery, and electrical and electronic equipment. Outside of manufacturing, half of all operatives are drivers.

About 30% of all operatives are women. Female workers hold a large portion of the semiskilled jobs in the apparel, textile and food industries—they are sewing machine operators, packers and wrappers, assemblers, and laundry and dry cleaning machine operators. On the other hand, the iron, steel and petroleum industries employ relatively few women in operative jobs.

In 1970 there were 3.7 million unskilled *laborers* working in industries other than farming and mining. (Laborers or unskilled workers is the third and last subgroup of blue-collar workers.) What sort of work do they do? They load, unload, dig, haul, hoist, wrap and mix. Some jobs involve very heavy physical work but do not require much education or specialized training. Almost half of the unskilled manual workers are employed in manufacturing and construction work. A large proportion of the remainder are employed in the trade, transportation and public utilities, and service industries.

There are relatively few jobs for laborers in today's economy. Technological changes have decreased the demand for unskilled workers.

Service

Another major occupational group is service workers. In 1970 more than 9.7 million service workers were busy policing streets, serving food, putting out fires, and helping clean houses and buildings. They are employed as baby sitters, elevator operators, golf caddies, barbers and theater ushers. About 1.5 million *private household* workers (as the name indicates) are employed in private homes preparing and serving meals, making beds, doing cleaning and laundering, and taking care of children. Ninety-eight of every 100 workers in this type of service work are women. Most private household workers are employed part-time (less than 35 hours a week).

About 1 million *protective service* workers protect lives and property from harm or damage. The great majority of these are policemen, guards and firemen employed by local, state and federal governments.

The *other service* workers—about 7.2 million in all—comprise a group primarily dealing in personal and building services. More than 2.7 million of these workers prepare or serve food in restaurants, hotels and institutions. Another 2 million clean and service buildings. More than 1 million service workers (for example, hospital attendants and nurses aides) are employed in health services occupations. Over 800,000 service workers (such as barbers and cosmetologists) provide grooming and personal services.

Farm

The last of the 3 major occupational groups to be examined in this lesson are farm workers. Farmers and farm managers, laborers, and foremen are among the most productive and essential workers in the economy. In the last 20 years, farm productivity has increased at double the rate of the rest of the economy. In fact, the farmer has been so efficient that he has been working himself out of a job. In 1970, there were 3.1 million farm workers—1.7 million farmers and farm managers and 1.4 million farm laborers and foremen. These workers produce the food and fiber which provide raw materials for many American industries and which are so essential to the consumer's well-being.

Most of the workers on farms are either self-employed farmers or are members of farm families. The number of hired workers on farms (including family members who are paid wages) is subject to seasonal fluctuations. For example, in the month of January about 800,000 hired farm workers are employed, while at the peak of the harvest in September the number is about 2 million.

Lesson in Brief

More than one-half of American workers are employed in farm, blue-collar or service occupations. These workers play important roles in the economy—they provide food, produce manufactured goods and service the nation's personal and protective needs.

This lesson summarizes some of the data and concepts that have been used to explore the occupational and industrial sources of employment in the U.S. economy and presents additional data in a somewhat different format. Employment in 9 occupational and 9 industrial groups will be examined to compare the number of jobs in each. Knowledge of contemporary employment patterns can be useful in identifying sources of jobs in the economy and in planning a career.

One way to study occupational and industrial sources of jobs is to examine the *Occupational Outlook Handbook*. Available in many classrooms, counseling offices and libraries, this book describes jobs and provides a wealth of data on employment by occupation and industry in the U.S. economy.

Another way to identify various job sources is to review and reorganize the data presented in the last few lessons. Let's examine some charts which show occupational and industrial employment in the United States in recent years.

Figure 4.5 shows total employment, by sex, in the United States in 1970 in each of 9 occupational groups. Operatives, the largest occupational group in the economy, included 9.6 million men and 4.3 million women. (In 1971, clerical workers moved ahead of operatives to become the largest occupational group in the labor force.)

The data in Figure 4.5 also indicate that in 3 occupational groups women represented about 50% or more of all employed workers; that all types of service workers combined accounted for almost as much employment in 1970 as did craftsmen and foremen; and that in 4 occupational groups there were more than 6 million men employed.

Figure 4.5

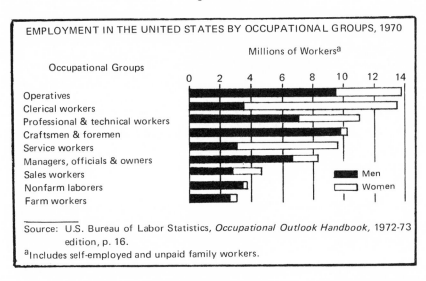

EMPLOYMENT IN THE UNITED STATES BY OCCUPATIONAL GROUPS, 1970

Source: U.S. Bureau of Labor Statistics, *Occupational Outlook Handbook,* 1972-73 edition, p. 16.
[a]Includes self-employed and unpaid family workers.

Figure 4.6

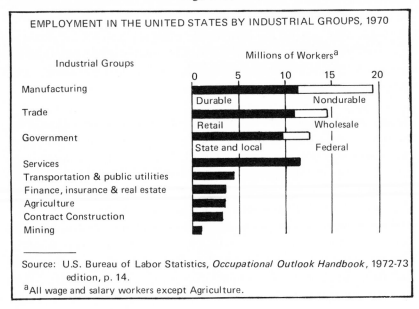

EMPLOYMENT IN THE UNITED STATES BY INDUSTRIAL GROUPS, 1970

Source: U.S. Bureau of Labor Statistics, *Occupational Outlook Handbook*, 1972-73 edition, p. 14.
[a]All wage and salary workers except Agriculture.

Figure 4.6 shows the total amount of employment in 1970 for each of the 9 major industrial groups in the economy. It also provides more detailed information on employment in 3 of the industrial groups. For example, it shows that there were about 15 million workers employed in the trade industry—about 11 million in retail trade and 4 million in wholesale trade. This means that there were 3 times as many workers employed in trade in 1970 as there were in transportation and public utilities.

The data in Figure 4.6 also show that 4 industrial groups employed about three-quarters of all workers in 1970. It also is clear that in 1970 many more workers were employed by state and local governments than by the federal government.

Figure 4.7 presents the industrial sources of white-collar, blue-collar and service employment and shows the percentage of employees that each of the 3 occupational groups accounts for in nonagricultural industries. For example, more than 67% of all workers employed in manufacturing were blue-collar employees. However, the proportion of blue-collar employment varies a great deal among particular nonagricultural industries. In services, blue-collar workers account for about 12% of the total employment in that industry. However, in contract construction 78% of the work force consists of blue-collar employees.

The data in Figure 4.7 also indicate that, in 1970, 4 industrial groups employed 50% or more white-collar workers. Note, too, that blue-collar workers make up the majority of employees in 4 industrial groups. The data suggest there is a relationship between occupational and industrial employment opportunities. For example, opportunities for service workers look better in some industries than others.

To summarize, the thousands of different jobs that workers have in the economy can be analyzed by using occupational and industrial classification systems. These 2 classification systems make use of categories of occupations and categories of industries. All the occupations in the "white-collar" occupational category, for example, share certain common characteristics, just as all the industries in the "goods-producing" industrial category do. "Professional and technical" occupations have a number of important similarities as do the industries in the "manufacturing" industrial classification.

Figure 4.7

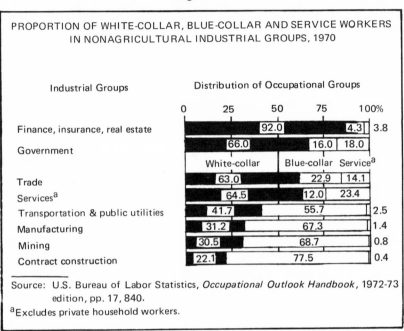

Source: U.S. Bureau of Labor Statistics, *Occupational Outlook Handbook*, 1972-73 edition, pp. 17, 840.

[a] Excludes private household workers.

Data on broad occupational groups show that 48% of U.S. workers in 1970 were employed in white-collar occupations. The remainder were employed as follows: blue-collar, 35%; service, 13%; farm, 4%. A more detailed examination of occupational employment in 1970 shows the following distribution; operatives, 18%; clerical, 17%; professional and technical, 14%; craftsmen and foremen, 13%; service, 12%; managers, owners and officials, 11%; sales, 6%; laborers, 5%; farmers and farm managers, laborers, and foremen, 4%.

With respect to industry grouping, employment data for the year 1970 show the service industries provided 64% of the total employment while the remaining 36% is accounted for by the goods-producing industries. A more detailed analysis of the industrial sources of employment disclosed that manufacturing provided the most jobs. The other industries, ranked from highest to lowest as sources of employment, were as follows: trade; government; services; transportation and public utilities; finance, insurance and real estate; agriculture; construction; mining. In 1970, blue-collar workers dominated the employment picture in the nonagricultural goods-producing industries. The white-collar occupations were prominent in the service-producing industries.

Lesson in Brief

The millions of workers in the U.S. economy are employed in several thousand occupations and many different types of industries. Occupational and industrial concepts have been developed by the U.S. Department of Labor to identify workers' jobs. These concepts can be used to classify and record the changing employment situation in the manpower market.

Women do much of the work in today's society. Not only are they responsible for day-to-day management and care of the majority of American homes and families, but millions of women are also entering the manpower market and accepting employment outside the home. Almost every American woman is employed at some time in her life. There are a number of myths about women workers which make it difficult for them to achieve equality with male workers. A brief overview of the changes taking place in the working lives of women and the myths about women workers will help young women and young men understand how the work role of women is changing and how these changes are influencing personal, social and economic lifestyles.

What kinds of work do women perform in the United States? In the nation's 50-odd million families, women do most of the housework. In some 30 million families, women also are responsible for taking care of 1 or more children. In about 5.5 million families, women are the heads of the households.

The average value of work done by American housewives has been estimated to range from $4,000 to $14,000 per year. These figures are based on wages paid to persons employed as private household workers for housecleaning, cooking, child-care and related services.

But this is not the only work women do in America. Table 4.1 shows that in 1971 nearly 30 million women were "gainfully employed" for pay outside their homes. Over 10 million women held jobs as clerical workers, which represented 34% of all the women employed in 1971. Seventy-five percent of all clerical workers employed in 1971 were women.

The data in Table 4.1 also indicate there were 3 occupational groups in which women represented over 50% of the total employment in 1971. It is also clear that the proportion of women employed was higher in 1971 than in 1960. The data show too that 4 occupational groups accounted for almost 80% of all the women employed in 1971. Why are so many women workers employed in these 4 occupational groups? What trends in the employment of women from 1960 and 1971 can be identified from the data in Table 4.1?

Table 4.1
MAJOR OCCUPATIONAL GROUPS OF
EMPLOYED WOMEN, 1960 AND 1971

Major Occupational Groups	Numbers (in thousands)		% Distribution of All Women Employed		Women as % of Total Employment[a]	
	1971	1960	1971	1960	1971	1960
Professional & technical workers	4,334	2,703	15%	12%	39%	36%
Managers, officials & owners (except farm)	1,493	1,099	5	5	17	16
Clerical workers	10,132	6,617	34	30	75	68
Sales workers	2,155	1,680	7	8	42	40
Craftsmen & foremen	387	222	1	1	4	3
Operatives	3,968	3,333	13	15	31	28
Laborers (except farm & mine)	250	82	1	1	6	2
Private-household workers	1,449	1,943	5	9	98	99
Service-workers (except private-household)	5,192	3,236	17	15	57	54
Farmers & farm managers	86	109	1	1	5	4
Farm laborers & foremen	428	848	1	3	32	35
TOTALS	29,875	21,874	100%	100%	38%	33%

Source: U.S. President and U.S. Department of Labor, *Manpower Report of the President 1972*, pp. 171-172.

[a]Both men and women, 16 years and over.

Let's examine data published by the Women's Bureau of the U.S. Department of Labor concerning the life and employment patterns of tomorrow's women.

Unless they go to college, the majority of unmarried young women will go to work at age 17 or 18 after leaving high school. Within 3 or 4 years, a large number of these young women will marry. Some of them will stop working for pay in order to get a new home organized, but a majority will continue to work to make it possible for a husband to complete post-secondary schooling or training or to permit purchase of such things as a car, a home or labor-saving equipment. Then when the first baby arrives, the vast majority of young mothers will give up their jobs and remain out of the manpower market until the youngest child is old enough to go to school. (About 1 in 5 women with pre-school children will continue to work—because of economic need among other reasons—but generally the 25-34 age group will provide the smallest share of women workers.)

When the youngest child no longer needs constant care, many mothers will choose to return to paid employment. Most of these women will be approaching their middle 30s and will have been out of the work force for 8 to 10 years. Once back, they will remain in the labor force (though perhaps not continuously) until age 65. By 1975 nearly half of all women between 35 and 65 will probably be either working or looking for work. Unless things change radically and unexpectedly in the years ahead, more women age 45 to 54 will be active in the labor force than any other age group.

For the 1 young woman in 20 who remains single, the length of her working life will differ little from that of a man. Since most single women must support themselves, and often parents or other relatives as well, they must continue to hold a job.

To summarize, the "work-life expectancy" (as it is often called) for the women of tomorrow will be about 40 years for single women; about 30 years for childless married women; and about 15 to 25 years for married women with children, depending on the number of children.

This portrait of the life pattern of American women poses questions that young women and men should consider. For example, what are the educational, social and economic implications of the role of women for the individual? What is good or bad about the changing employment patterns of women?

According to the Women's Bureau of the U.S. Department of Labor, there are a number of myths about women workers in America that make it difficult for them to achieve equality with men in the world of work. The Women's Bureau offers some examples of the myths and provides data and information which represent the reality of the situation:

Myth: A woman's place is in the home.

Reality: Homemaking no longer has to be a full-time job. Goods and services formerly produced in the home are now commercially available; labor-saving devices have lightened or eliminated much work around the home. Today, half of all women between 18 and 64 years of age are in the labor force where they are making an important contribution to the growth of the nation's economy. Studies show that 9 of 10 women will work outside the home at some time during their lives.

Myth: Women aren't seriously attached to the labor force. They work only for pin money.

Reality: Of the 31 million women in the labor force in March 1970, nearly half were working because of pressing economic need. They were either single, widowed, divorced, separated or had husbands whose incomes were less than $3,000 a year. Another 5.7 million were married and had husbands with incomes between $3,000 and $7,000—incomes which did not meet the criteria established by the Bureau of Labor Statistics for even a low standard of living for an urban family of 4.

Myth: Women should stick to "women's jobs" and shouldn't compete for "men's jobs."

Reality: Jobs with extremely rare exceptions are sexless. Women were found in all of the 479 occupations listed in the 1960 census. Tradition rather than job content has led to labeling certain jobs as women's and others as men's. For example, although few women work as engineers, studies show that two-thirds as many girls as boys have an aptitude for this kind of work.

Myth: The employment of mothers leads to juvenile delinquency for their children.

Reality: Studies show that many factors must be considered when seeking causes for juvenile delinquency. Whether a mother is employed does not appear to be a determining factor. These studies indicate that it is the quality of a mother's care rather than the time consumed in such care that is of major significance.

Myth: Women don't work as long as their male coworkers; their training is costly and largely wasted.

Reality: The average woman worker has a work-life expectancy of 25 years compared with 43 years for the average male worker. However, single women average 45 years of work. Statistics based on the 1960 census comparing men and women at age 35 show that the average single working woman can expect to be on the job another 31 years (about 2.5 years longer than the average man). The average married woman, including those with children, will be employed an additional 24 years.[1]

---

1. From U.S. Department of Labor, Women's Bureau, *The Myth: Male Workers Are More Equal than Female Workers, The Reality: All Workers Are Equal.*

Several conclusions about women and their role in the manpower market might be drawn from the realities that have been presented—for example, many women work because their families need additional income to maintain an adequate standard of living. As job barriers are removed, many women will enter occupations previously dominated by male workers.

Lesson in Brief

There is a great deal of truth in the saying "woman's work is never done." American women work in homes, factories, offices, laboratories and classrooms. Women provide an increasing share of the human resources that are the key to the nation's economic productiveness. In fact, 9 of every 10 young women today will be employed at some time during their lives. There are a number of myths about women workers which prevent them from achieving equality with men in the world of work. However, times are changing and career opportunities for women are increasing.

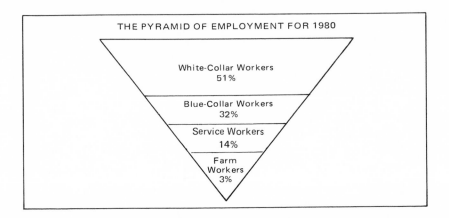

Previous lessons disclosed that the United States is becoming increasingly dependent on white-collar and service workers. Blue-collar employment is growing very slowly, and the number of farm jobs actually is declining. This shifting pattern of employment suggests that occupational opportunities in the future will be different from those of the past. Young people need to know the details of the manpower market they will be entering after they have finished school. Specifically, they need to know which occupations and which occupational groups will provide the most jobs and show the greatest increase in employment during the 1970s. The information can help greatly in career planning.

Detailed information about the changing manpower market can be obtained from the Bureau of Labor Statistics (BLS) which is part of the U.S. Department of Labor. This agency has prepared employment projections through 1980. These employment projections give some idea which occupations and which industries will offer the best career opportunities in the 1970s. The more an individual knows about the future of employment in the economy, the more likely he is to make intelligent decisions about his own career.

Table 4.2 shows recent and future employment by occupation in the United States.

Table 4.2
U.S. EMPLOYMENT BY OCCUPATION, 1970, AND PROJECTED 1980
(Numbers in thousands)

Occupational Groups	Actual 1970 Employment		Projected 1980 Employment		Percentage of Change 1970-80
	No.	%	No.	%	%
WHITE-COLLAR WORKERS	37,997	48.3%	48,300	50.8%	+ 27%
Professional & technical	11,140	14.2	15,500	16.3	+ 40
Managers, officials & owners	8,289	10.5	9,500	10.0	+ 15
Clerical	13,714	17.4	17,300	18.2	+ 26
Sales	4,854	6.2	6,000	6.3	+ 22
BLUE-COLLAR WORKERS	27,791	35.3%	31,100	32.7%	+ 12%
Craftsmen & foremen	10,158	12.9	12,200	12.8	+ 20
Operatives	13,909	17.7	15,400	16.2	+ 11
Nonfarm laborers	3,724	4.7	3,500	3.7	- 5
SERVICE WORKERS	9,712	12.4%	13,100	13.8%	+ 35%
FARM WORKERS	3,126	4.0%	2,600	2.7%	- 16%
TOTALS, All Groups	78,627	100.0%	95,100	100.0%	+ 21%

Source: U.S. President and U.S. Department of Labor, *Manpower Report of the President 1972*, p. 259.

For example 13.9 million operatives were employed in 1970 (17.7% of total employment for the year). The BLS estimates that by 1980 there will be 15.4 million operatives employed who will account for 16.2% of the total number of workers employed in that year. The number of operatives employed will increase 11% between 1970 and 1980. However, this increase of employment will be less than the predicted average—21%—for all groups in the 1970-80 period. Although the number of operatives employed will increase by 1,591,000 (the difference between 13,909,000 and 15,400,000) between 1970 and 1980, their share of total employment will decrease by 1.5% (the difference between 17.7% and 16.2%). Thus, while operative employment will be greater in numbers in 1980, it will be relatively less significant as a source of jobs.

The occupational groups represented in Table 4.2 are not projected to have the same rate of growth in employment between 1970-1980. Some of these groups will have more employment growth than others. For example, employment for service workers during the 1970s will grow at a rate much greater than the average for all workers.

Let's investigate where the job openings are going to be in the 1970s. When considering a possible career, an individual should not eliminate occupations just because his choices are not among the most rapidly growing. Although growth is a key indicator of future job outlook, more jobs will be created between 1970 and 1980 from *deaths, retirements* and *other labor force separations* than from employment growth. Replacement needs will be particularly significant in occupations that have a large proportion of older workers and women. Furthermore, slow-growing occupations with many workers may offer more openings than fast-growing occupations with few workers. For example, among the major occupational groups, openings for operatives resulting from growth and replacement combined will be greater than the number for craftsmen, although the rate of growth for craftsmen will be more than twice as rapid as the rate of growth for operatives.

Figure 4.8

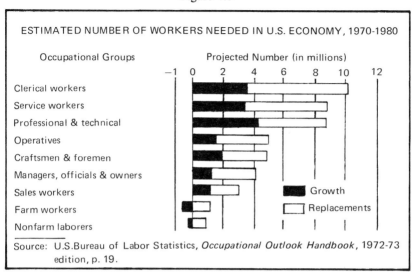

ESTIMATED NUMBER OF WORKERS NEEDED IN U.S. ECONOMY, 1970-1980

Occupational Groups   Projected Number (in millions)

Source: U.S.Bureau of Labor Statistics, *Occupational Outlook Handbook*, 1972-73 edition, p. 19.

Figure 4.8 shows the total number of workers that will be needed in various occupational groups during the 1970s. The chart indicates which part of the demand for workers is due to *growth* in employment and which is due to *replacement needs* caused by such events as death and retirement. More than 10 million clerical workers, for instance, will be needed during the 1970s. Growth of the economy will be responsible for less than half (about 3.6 million) of the total number of clerical workers needed during this period. Some 6 million clerical workers will be needed for replacement purposes.

Figure 4.8 projects that replacement needs will create more job openings in the 1970s than will employment growth. What other conclusions about occupational opportunities in the 1970s can be derived from the data?

A word of caution is needed regarding the employment picture in the 1970s. Reference has been made in this lesson to the employment projections for 1980 made by the U.S. Bureau of Labor Statistics. The"crystal ball"used to predict the future can get cloudy, even for BLS experts. They have prepared 4 different 1980 projections. We have chosen to use the services economy 3%

259

unemployment model which seems to be the BLS's favorite. Their estimate of what things will be like 10 years in the future depends on certain assumptions. One of the assumptions involved in all the projections mentioned in this lesson is that in 1980 the rate of unemployment in the labor force will be 3%. In view of the high unemployment rates for much of the 1950s, 1960s and early 1970s, this is a very optimistic assumption. Moreover, assumptions to be made about the rate and direction technological change will take between now and 1980 involve a certain amount of educated guesswork. The Bureau's experts provide the very best estimates possible, but they are still guesses as to what will happen in the future.

Lesson in Brief

The labor force of the 1970s increasingly wears a white collar. White-collar and service occupations will have the fastest rates of growth. Employment in blue-collar occupations, while growing in number, will nevertheless represent a smaller share of the total employment picture in 1980 than now. The number of farm workers will continue to decline. In thinking about a career, an individual should not eliminate occupations just because they are not growing. During the 1970s more jobs will be created by death, retirement and other labor force replacement activities than by employment growth. The continuing shift in the occupational basis of employment in the economy has important implications for career planning.

Job opportunities in the future will be different from those of the past, in part because the industrial composition of employment in the economy is changing. What are the details of these changes? In what industries will workers be employed and what kinds of goods and services will they be producing in the 1970s? How many workers will be employed in 1980 in each of the industrial groups? Which groups will show the greatest growth in employment? Just as it was useful to learn which occupational groups will show the most growth in the years ahead, knowledge of employment by industrial groups will also be helpful in planning a career.

Information on the industrial basis of employment, now and in the future, is provided by the Bureau of Labor Statistics (BLS), a division of the U.S. Department of Labor. BLS has prepared industrial as well as occupational employment projects for 1980. These projections provide some idea of which industries will offer the best job opportunities in the 1970s.

Let's take a look at some figures showing the industrial sources of jobs in the 1970s. Table 4.3 presents the actual employment by industrial groups for the United States in 1968 and projected employment by industry for 1980. For example, 4,154,000 workers were employed in agricultural industries in 1968. These agricultural workers represented 5.1% of total employment for 1968. By 1980 the Labor Department estimates that there will be only 3.2 million agricultural workers, accounting for only 3.2% of total employment in that year. Thus, Table 4.3 shows that between 1968 and 1980 employment will actually decrease 23% in agricultural industries.

Table 4.3 also projects that some industrial groups will have greater employment growth during the period 1968 to 1980 than others. For example, the number of workers in the agricultural and mining industries is projected to decline between 1968 and 1980.

Table 4.3
TOTAL U.S. CIVILIAN EMPLOYMENT BY INDUSTRIAL GROUPS, 1968, AND PROJECTED, 1980
(Numbers in thousands)

Industrial Groups	Actual 1968 Employment		Projected 1980 Employment		Percentage Change 1968-1980
	No.	%	No.	%	%
GOODS-PRODUCING	28,975	35.8%	31,618	31.7%	+ 9%
Agriculture	4,154	5.1	3,188	3.2	- 23
Mining	646	.8	590	.6	- 9
Contract construction	4,050	5.0	5,482	5.5	+ 35
Manufacturing	20,125	24.9	22,358	22.4	+ 11
Durable goods	(11,854)	(14.7)	(13,274)	(13.3)	(+ 12)
Nondurable goods	(8,271)	(10.2)	(9,084)	(9.1)	(+ 10)
SERVICE-PRODUCING	51,813	64.2%	67,982	68.4%	+ 31%
Transportation & public utilities	4,524	5.6	4,976	5.0	+ 10
Trade, wholesale & retail	16,604	20.6	20,487	20.6	+ 23
Finance, insurance, & real estate	3,726	4.6	4,639	4.7	+ 24
Services, including households	15,113	18.7	21,080	21.2	+ 40
Total government	11,846	14.7	16,800	16.9	+ 42
Federal government	(2,737)	(3.4)	(3,000)	(3.0)	(+ 10)
State & local government	(9,109)	(11.3)	(13,800)	(13.9)	(+ 52)
TOTALS, All Industries	80,788	100.0%	99,600	100.0%	+ 23%

Source: U.S. Bureau of Labor Statistics, *The U.S. Economy in 1980, A Summary of BLS Projections*, 1970, p. 49, U.S. Department of Labor, *U.S. Manpower in the 1970s, Opportunities and Challenge,* 1970.

Note: Includes wage and salary employees, self-employed and unpaid family workers. Percentage figures are rounded and may not add up to 100.

One way to picture the effect that the changing industrial sources of jobs will have on employment opportunities in the 1970s is to look at the relative rates of employment growth in each of the industry groups. Changes in the industrial basis of employment in the economy between 1968 and 1980 are pictured in Figure 4.9. The projected rates of change have been classified into 5 categories: No Change, Less-than-Average, Average, More-than-Average, and Decline. Table 4.3 shows the average rate of change in employment for all occupational groups between 1968 and 1980 to be 23%. This figure is used as the middle of the "Average" range in Figure 4.9 and shows, for instance, that 3 industrial groups—government, services and contract

Figure 4.9

PROJECTED CHANGE IN EMPLOYMENT BY INDUSTRY, 1968-1980					
		PROJECTED EMPLOYMENT GROWTH			
Decline	INDUSTRY	No Change	Less Than Average	Average	More Than Average
	Government (total)				→
	Services				→
	Contract construction				→
	Finance, insurance & real estate			→	
	Trade			→	
	Manufacturing		→		
	Transportation & public utilities		→		
←	Mining				
←	Agriculture				
Source: Table 4.3					

construction—are projected to have a rate of growth in employment between 1968 and 1980 greater than the average for that period. Because these 3 industrial groups show the greatest increase in employment, they will be good sources of job opportunities in the 1970s.

Figure 4.9 clearly shows that growth rates in employment will not be the same for all industries in the economy in the future. Mining and especially agriculture will have less employment. The government, services and construction industries will have above-average rates of employment growth during the period 1968-1980. Finance, insurance and real estate, and the wholesale and retail trade industries will have average increases in employment through 1980. Below-average increases in employment will occur in the manufacturing and the transportation and public utilities industries. Overall, the service-producing industries—with the exception of transportation and public utilities—will have average or above-average employment growth rates between 1968 and 1980. By 1980, 2 of every 3 workers will be employed in the service-producing industries. The goods-producing industries, with the exception of contract construction, will have below-average employment growth rates. However, by 1980, 1 of every 5 workers will still be employed in the manufacturing industries.

With the exception of agriculture and mining, additional employment opportunities will be available in the 1970s in all industrial groups. The *total* number of job opportunities—additional jobs plus replacement needs—will vary among industries just as they differ among occupations (see Figure 4.8).

Career planning based on manpower projections should include an examination of both occupational and industrial trends. For example, an individual who is interested in employment as a technical worker needs to know which industries employ large numbers of people with technical skills. An industry which already employs hundreds of thousands of technical workers will require a great many people in the 1970s simply to *replace* those who die, retire or otherwise leave their jobs. A *growing* industry needs additional employees to increase its total work force. Good job opportunities, therefore, will exist in both types of industries.

Lesson in Brief

The industrial sources of employment in the 1970s will be somewhat different from those in the late 1960s. The United States increasingly is becoming a nation of service-producers. By 1980, 2 of every 3 workers in the American economy will be employed in the service-producing industries. However, in 1980, 1 of every 5 workers will still be employed in manufacturing, which is a goods-producing industry. The changing nature of the industrial sources of employment in the 1970s has some important implications for career planning.

Individual workers must adjust not only to industrial and occupational changes in the employment situation but also to changes in the places where jobs are available. Information on the mobility or movement of Americans will be useful in understanding why so many workers are on the move. Knowing the geography of changes in employment opportunities is valuable in career planning because it suggests where the jobs of tomorrow are most likely to be located.

Each year, many Americans change their place of residence. Records kept by the federal government on the mobility of the population show that every year about 1 of every 5 people in the United States moves. However, only about 7% of the more than 40 million Americans who change their residence during the year move to a different county or state.

One might ask why all these people are moving. Many of the reasons are personal, such as health, but the most important reason why people move is economic opportunity—which includes the search for a job or for a better job.

Who are the people on the move? Do they share any special characteristics? One way to answer these questions is to check the records of people who actually changed their residence in a recent period and see if there are differences in characteristics between those who moved and those who did not. Table 4.4 shows 4 important factors—education, age, occupation and sex—that may account for differences in mobility. For example, the data reveal that 16% of all women who had some college education changed residence during the period March 1969 to March 1970, whereas 20% of college-educated men made a move.

The data in Table 4.4 show that mobility is not the same for people with different characteristics. Certain groups of Americans are more likely to move than others. Higher mobility rates may indicate more freedom of job choice for workers.

The geography of employment opportunities has shifted a great deal in the past and will continue to change in the future. Table 4.5 shows geographic employment trends from 1961 to

Table 4.4
MOBILITY OF U.S. POPULATION
BY SELECTED CHARACTERISTICS
March 1969 to March 1970

Personal Chacteristics	Percentage in Each Group that Moved	
	Women	Men
EDUCATIONAL LEVEL:		
8th grade or less	11%	13%
9th - 11th grades	14	15
High school: 4 years	13	15
College: 1 or more years	16	20
AGE:		
20-24 years	43	40
25-34	25	30
35-44	13	16
45-64	9	10
65 and older	8	8

OCCUPATIONAL GROUPS:	Women and Men
Professional & technical	22%
Managers, officials & owners	15
Clerical workers	18
Sales workers	20
Craftsmen & foremen	17
Operatives	20
Laborers	21
Service workers	16
Farm workers	10

Source: The Conference Board, "Geographic Mobility in the Sixties," *Road Maps of Industry*, May 15, 1971.

1968. These statistics show, for example, that the Middle Atlantic states had a 16% increase in the number of jobs during the period 1961-1968 (much less than the national average for that period). But New Jersey (which is a Middle Atlantic state) had a 22% increase in number of jobs—almost as great as the average for the nation.

The data in Table 4.5 also indicate that employment in 3 geographical areas was growing slower than the national average during the period 1961 through 1968, while 25 of the states had a growth in employment greater than the national average. What causes the differences in the growth of employment among the various states and regions?

After examining data on mobility and the location of new job opportunities, a number of conclusions may be reached. For example, the more schooling a person has, the more likely he is to move. Professional and technical workers, who usually have the most formal education, are highly mobile. In addition, job opportunities increased faster in the Far West and South during the period 1961-1968 than in other parts of the country.

Lesson in Brief

The United States is a nation on the move, with the better educated, younger, professional and technical, and male workers changing their residences more often than others. The location of jobs has shifted a great deal in the past few years and will probably continue to change.

Table 4.5
PERCENTAGE INCREASE IN NUMBER OF JOBS IN THE UNITED STATES BY GEOGRAPHICAL REGION, 1961-1968

Increase in Jobs for Total U.S.: +26%

New England	**+19%**		**East South Central**	**+31%**
Maine	17		Kentucky	32
New Hampshire	24		Tennessee	36
Vermont	30		Alabama	24
Massachusetts	15		Mississippi	34
Rhode Island	18			
Connecticut	26		**West South Central**	**+33%**
Middle Atlantic	**+16%**		Arkansas	35
New York	14		Louisiana	33
New Jersey	22		Oklahoma	24
Pennsylvania	17		Texas	34
South Atlantic	**+35%**		**Mountain**	**+26%**
Delaware	34		Montana	17
Maryland	35		Idaho	21
District of Columbia	23		Wyoming	6
Virginia	34		Colorado	27
West Virginia	13		New Mexico	17
North Carolina	36		Arizona	35
South Carolina	31		Utah	23
Georgia	37		Nevada	70
Florida	45			
East North Central	**+26%**		**Pacific**	**+33%**
Ohio	23		Washington	34
Indiana	29		Oregon	33
Illinois	23		California	33
Michigan	32		Alaska	39
Wisconsin	24		Hawaii	31
West North Central			**+24%**	
Minnesota	30		South Dakota	14
Iowa	26		Nebraska	18
Missouri	22		Kansas	21
North Dakota	22			

Source: U.S. Bureau of Labor Statistics, *Employment and Earnings for States and Areas 1939-1970*, 1971, p. XV.

Note: Nonagricultural wage and salary employment.

During the past 50 years, vast economic changes—including changes in the number of workers employed in various occupations and industries—have occurred in America. In 1920 the United States was mainly a nation of blue-collar and farm workers. Today a majority of workers are white-collar and service workers. These trends in employment reflect the technological change, growth and decline in different industries in the economy. Whereas the goods-producing industries provided most of the jobs in the 1920s, now the majority of workers produce services. These employment trends affect the opportunities available in the changing manpower market.

Let's begin this lesson by learning what life was like for a typical young American worker in 1920.

EARL SWANSON—THE WORKER AND THE MAN

Earl Swanson was employed as a semiskilled worker making Model T Fords in an automobile plant, one of the fastest growing industries in the United States. Earl worked 50 hours a week and was paid $.70 an hour. He did not belong to a labor union because employers generally were opposed to unions and often threatened to fire workers involved in union activities. Earl voted for James Cox (the Democratic Party's candidate) in the Presidential election that year because he thought that Cox's support of the Treaty of Versailles was right; but the Republican candidate, Warren Harding, won and became President of the United States. Silent movies (with Charlie Chaplin and Rudolph Valentino) were Earl's favorite leisure time activity, except on Sunday afternoons when he went to the ballpark to watch Ty Cobb play second base. Prohibition had just gone into effect, and Earl missed being able to drink beer with his friends. The current economic recession worried Earl because he might be laid off his job any day or find his wages cut.

That was 1920, more than half a century ago. Times have changed—the Model Ts, Hardings, Valentinos and Cobbs are

Table 4.6
INDUSTRIAL DISTRIBUTION OF NONAGRICULTURAL
EMPLOYMENT IN THE UNITED STATES IN 1920, 1940, 1970

(Numbers in millions)

Industrial Groups	1920 No.	%	1940 No.	%	1970 No.	%
Manufacturing	10.7	39%	11.0	34%	19.4	27%
Mining	1.2	5	0.9	3	0.6	1
Contract construction	0.8	3	1.3	4	3.4	5
Transportation & public utilities	4.0	15	3.0	9	4.5	6
Trade	4.5	17	6.8	22	14.9	21
Finance, insurance & real estate	1.2	4	1.5	4	3.7	5
Service & miscellaneous	2.4	8	3.7	11	11.6	17
Government	2.6	10	4.2	13	12.5	18
TOTALS	27.4	100%	32.4	100%	70.6	100%

Source: U.S. Bureau of Labor Statistics, *Employment and Earning Statistics for the United States, 1909-66,* October, 1966, p. xvi, U.S. President and U.S. Department of Labor, *Manpower Report of the President 1972,* p. 215.

Note: Wage and salary workers. Percentage figures are rounded and may not add up to 100.

gone—and sweeping changes have taken place in the way people live and work. The changes that have taken place in employment since 1920 can be seen in the data presented in 2 different tables. Table 4.6 shows the nonagricultural sources of employment by industrial groups for selected years since 1920. It indicates, for example, that 1.2 million people (about 5% of all wage and salary workers employed that year) were employed in mining in 1920. By 1970, there were only 600,000 workers employed in mining—less than 1% of the total number of wage and salary workers.

The data in Table 4.6 indicate that about 4 of every 10 nonagricultural workers in 1920 were employed in manufacturing industries. Two industrial groups showed an 80% or greater increase in employment from 1920 to 1970 as measured by their relative share of total employment. Three industrial groups had a percentage decrease in their relative share of total employment. What other trends in industrial employment may be identified from the data in Table 4.6?

Now let's consider the changes that have taken place in the occupational composition of jobs in the United States since 1920. Table 4.7 shows workers' occupations during the period between 1920 and 1970. For example, it indicates that, in 1920, 10.5 million workers (25% of all workers in the economy) were employed in white-collar occupations. By 1970 there were 38 million workers employed in white-collar occupations—almost a fourfold increase—bringing the white-collar worker's share of total employment up to 48%.

The data in Table 4.7 also show that the number of service workers employed almost tripled between 1920 and 1970. The percentage of farm workers and blue-collar workers declined during this 50-year period. What other occupational trends in employment since 1920 can be identified from the data in Table 4.7?

In the current human resources era, the most important factor of production (or input) for the economy is the brainpower of man. The muscle power that was so important to past economic development now plays a less significant role. Increasingly, the dominant output of the economy is not goods but human services.

Table 4.7
CIVILIAN EMPLOYMENT BY OCCUPATION IN THE
UNITED STATES, SELECTED YEARS 1920-1970
(Numbers in millions)

Occupational Groups	1920 No.	1920 %	1940 No.	1940 %	1950 No.	1950 %	1970 No.	1970 %
WHITE-COLLAR WORKERS	10.5	25%	16.1	31%	22.4	38%	38.0	48%
Professional & technical	2.3	5	3.9	8	4.5	8	11.1	14
Managers, officials & owners	2.8	7	3.8	7	6.4	11	8.3	11
Clerical	3.4	8	5.0	10	7.6	13	13.7	17
Sales	2.1	5	3.5	7	3.8	6	4.9	6
BLUE-COLLAR WORKERS	17.0	40%	20.6	40%	23.3	39%	27.8	35%
Craftsmen & foremen	5.5	13	6.2	12	7.7	13	10.2	13
Operatives	6.6	16	9.5	18	12.1	20	13.9	18
Laborers[a]	4.9	12	4.9	9	3.5	6	3.7	5
SERVICE WORKERS	3.3	8%	6.1	12%	6.5	11%	9.7	12%
FARM WORKERS	11.4	27%	9.0	17%	7.4	12%	3.1	4%
TOTALS, All Groups	42.2	100%	51.7	100%	59.6	100%	78.6	100%

Source: National Industrial Conference Board, *The Economic Almanac 1964*, pp. 44-45, U.S. President and U.S. Department of Labor, *Manpower Report of the President 1972*, p. 259.
Note: Percentage figures are rounded and may not add up to totals.
[a]Excluding farm and mine laborers.

This shift to the production of services influences employment opportunities (see Figure 4.10). By 1980, almost 7 of every 10 workers in America will be employed in the production of services rather than goods.

Figure 4.10

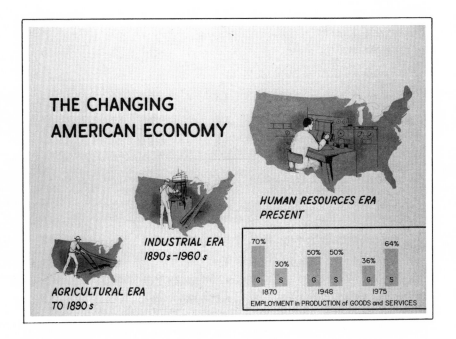

Let's summarize what has been observed about employment trends in the nation's economy during the last half century. Since 1920, more and more workers have been employed in service-producing industries; by 1950, the nation's workers were predominately service-producing. This trend also has been reflected in changes in the occupational structure of the economy. Since 1920, white-collar and service workers' occupations have become increasingly more important; by 1950, white-collar workers outnumbered blue-collar workers for the first time.

Lesson in Brief

The occupational and industrial basis of employment has changed in the last 50 years. Today, the United States is predominantly a nation of service-producers employed in white-collar and service occupations.

UNIT FIVE

Rational Decisionmaking, Values and Career Planning

The basic theme in Unit Five is that young people can benefit from using facts and systematic analysis to make important decisions about their lives. This unit contains lessons dealing with decisionmaking skills, career planning and personal growth. Special attention is given to the changing structure of opportunity for women in American life. Another lesson deals with the all-important subject of value judgments.

One very important lesson describes the 5 steps in economic decisionmaking (define the problem, identify goals, consider alternative solutions, study probable outcomes, then choose the best solution). Other lessons suggest how these steps can be applied to personal economic questions such as educational planning and career choice. Learning about rational decision-making is one thing. Applying the 5 steps in economic decision-making to a concrete problem is quite another. Only through experience does one actually acquire these performance skills. Opportunities to practice decisionmaking skills are provided in 2 of the lessons. People who have acquired skill in basing judgments on reason and fact are less likely to fall into the lazy person's trap of simply assuming conclusions.

A potential bonus in this unit is the discovery of a general approach to making value judgments that are personally beneficial and socially responsible.

Economic problems are like other kinds of problems. The ability to find good solutions is increased by organizing one's thinking and using a systematic, step-by-step approach which involves understanding the problem, thinking about goals, considering the various possible solutions and their consequences, then making a decision.

As noted in Unit Two, every economic system faces 3 basic problems. Often, people disagree with the way these problems are being solved. How does a person reason out a good solution to a basic economic problem or to any of the smaller, related problems? For economic as well as other kinds of problems, good solutions are reached through organized thinking and the use of a systematic, step-by-step approach. The following 5-step method of decisionmaking can prove useful in dealing with economic and career-related problems:

1. *Define the problem*. Determine which facts are the most important, and study the main issues and questions.
2. *Identify goals*. What are the things to be accomplished or achieved?
3. *Consider alternatives*. Usually, several options or methods of reaching goals are available. Think creatively.
4. *Analyze the consequences*. Study the probable outcomes for each of the alternative solutions. What are the costs? The benefits? Other consequences?
5. *Choose the best solution* in terms of stated goals.

These *5 steps in economic decisionmaking* can be used to solve general problems (for example, How can poverty in the United States be reduced?) and specific or individual problems (for example, What kind of career will be best for me? How do I prepare for my chosen career?). Lesson 60 in this unit provides an opportunity to apply the 5 steps in decisionmaking to personal career planning.

Lesson in Brief

The 5-step approach used by economists in economic decisionmaking may be used by groups and by individuals to seek solutions to many kinds of problems. First, define the problem. Second, identify goals. Third, consider alternatives. Fourth, analyze the consequences. Fifth, choose the best solution.

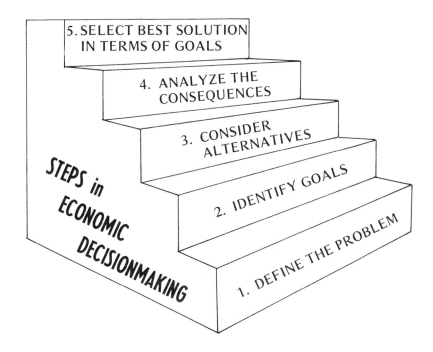

Education is not simply a matter of learning to market oneself, but of discovering oneself.

W. Wesley Tennyson

A person's education, work experiences and attitudes influence the formation of his identity and help determine the kind of individual he becomes and the place he makes for himself in society. Although each person's total experiences are unique, everyone progresses through similar stages of development relative to work and personal fulfillment.

Individuals change with time and experience. Let's explore how a person's identity is formed and consider some of the factors and experiences that promote change and growth. Finally, let's examine the role work plays in this process.

To know oneself is often inconvenient, always difficult, but vitally important. Family, travel and extracurricular activities are some of the factors that shape identity. In addition, other people and institutions—for example, friends, jobs, hobbies—are influential. Young people in their teens pursue many goals that have far-reaching effects on their adult lives. The young man who seeks new and better relationships with persons of both sexes is actually striving to fulfill the goal of social acceptance. The young woman who wants to earn her own money may be working to achieve independence. Through their activities and associations, young people can move closer to what they want to become.

The following developmental stages form a dynamic model reflecting the overall pattern of vocational development throughout a person's lifetime. Although the specific ages when attitudes and skills develop differ among individuals, the estimated ages generally are accurate. The 6 stages listed here are based on the literature of career development.

1. Identifying with workers. With the individual's parents and other adults serving as models, the idea of working becomes an important part of life. 5-10 years of age.

2.   Acquiring the basic habits of industry. The individual learns to organize time and energy to accomplish work, such as school assignments or chores in the home. 10-15 years.

3.   Acquiring identity as a worker in the occupational structure. The individual chooses and prepares for an occupation through education and training, and he acquires work experience as a basis for occupational choice and for economic independence. 15-25 years.

4.   Becoming a productive person. The individual masters the skills of an occupation and progresses within his occupation or career. 25-40 years.

5.   Helping maintain a productive society. The individual sees himself as a responsible citizen in a productive society and pays attention to the civic responsibility attached to his job. Since he is at the peak of his career and has time and energy to undertake broader activities, his emphasis now shifts toward society and away from preoccupation with himself as a worker. He also introduces younger people into the third and fourth stages. 40-65 years.

6.   Contemplating a productive and responsible life. The individual retires from his job or is in the process of withdrawing from the worker's role. He reviews his work life with satisfaction, recognizes his social contributions and is more or less pleased with himself. While he may not have achieved all his ambitions, he accepts his life and believes himself to be a productive person of dignity and worth. 65+ years.

Within these stages, of course, different individuals encounter different experiences. Will the person whose mother is employed full time outside the home have different attitudes toward work and household tasks than another person whose mother is a full-time housewife? Can adults other than one's parents influence one's career choice? Will the young person who organizes his time have different habits than the individual who goes from activity to activity without planning? Can a part-time job help a person decide whether he enjoys working with objects or data more than with people or whether he prefers using mental ability to physical strength? Where can the individual acquire skill in getting along with people, in taking responsibility, in following through with an assignment to its completion?

Whether a person is going to school or is employed at a job, he needs to feel he is striving toward goals, he is making progress or only temporarily marking time, he is doing something worthwhile.

Awareness of the stages of vocational development leads to the conclusion that work attitudes and habits change and develop *throughout* a person's lifetime. It is important for the individual to take time from everyday activities and hectic schedules to examine himself, to learn who he really is and what he is becoming.

Lesson in Brief

The individual will find it necessary to know himself and what he wants from life, both personally and vocationally. Because this process is lifelong and because new experiences constantly shape his identity, he must periodically re-examine himself and his goals.

Most people instinctively and actively try to achieve goals. But how does one go about achieving? What personal and social factors influence what one is able to achieve? Aspirations + Ability + Action = Achievement is a formula that offers some useful guidelines to help a person accomplish the goals he sets for himself.

Let's consider the following ideas in terms of the role they play in determining success:

> 4. ACHIEVEMENT: Reaching goals
>
> 3. ACTION: Effort with purpose and enthusiasm
>
> 2. ABILITIES: Talent of various kinds
>
> 1. ASPIRATIONS: Setting goals

Aspirations. What goals has the individual set for himself? What past achievements can he build upon? What are his interests, ambitions and needs? The answers to these questions will help the individual begin to define his aspirations.

Abilities. Different types of ability are required to achieve goals. The amount and kind of talent needed depend upon the goals selected. In Unit Six the basic manpower skills of communication, computation, manual dexterity and group organization will be discussed. This information will prove useful to the individual ready to develop specific abilities.

Action. Aspiration and ability alone will not guarantee achievement. *Action,* which is well-defined and continuing effort directed toward a specific goal, is needed for achievement. To take action sometimes is difficult for people; however, a plan that is not acted upon will never lead to achievement.

The following true story shows how one man overcame serious obstacles to achieve his goals.

HOW TO SUCCEED BY TRYING

Dr. Black, a cancer specialist, developed a tumor on the spinal cord of his neck. The tumor was noncancerous, but during its removal a nerve was cut and he lost the power to raise his right hand and to bend his elbow.

Although he could still use the fingers and forearm muscles of his right arm, Dr. Black's career as a surgeon appeared to be over. However, with the help of experts in appliances together with his own determination, Dr. Black created a steel and leather harness equipped with springs to do what his useless muscle could not do.

Dr. Black also developed certain skills using his left hand. No special adjustments other than a higher operating table were necessary. Dr. Black successfully performed very difficult and delicate operations despite his handicap.

Dr. Black had certain career aspirations, and he developed special abilities to fulfill them. He took action to achieve his goal. Dr. Black followed the formula for achievement.

Consider how society can influence achievement on the job. There are basically 2 kinds of societies—the ascribed society and the achievement society. In an *ascribed* society, jobs are distributed on the basis of who the person is rather than what he can do. As can be imagined, when jobs are assigned or ascribed on the basis of status, caste or heredity, workers find little opportunity for upward mobility. The ascribed society usually does not change very rapidly.

In an *achievement* society, jobs are distributed mainly on the basis of the person's ability to perform the required tasks and, perhaps, to meet certain standards such as passing a test or completing a certain type and amount of education or training.

No society is completely ascribed or achievement-oriented. For example, inheritance of property and relatives or friends with "connections" may influence the opportunities of a worker even in an achievement society. Also, certain factors set limits on how much people are able to achieve. Thus, jobs are not distributed strictly on the basis of personal ability; other factors influence who gets what job.

Social scientists maintain that the strongest force acting against the formation of a class system in America is the existence of strong faith on the part of the people that ambition, ability and hard work assure success; that opportunities are free and equal to all; that education and training are the key to these opportunities.

Ability and hard work will not guarantee success for all Americans. Opportunities are not free and equal to all. Education and training may not open the doors to opportunity. These situations create problems for individuals and for society and are at the heart of many of the world-of-work issues that Americans are discussing today.

Lesson in Brief

Successful people in U.S. society have for the most part followed the 4 steps in the formula for achievement. They have combined aspirations, abilities and action for achievement. There are many opportunities for the individual to apply the formula for achievement to career planning and preparation—by investing in his own human capital and by acquiring the skills needed for intelligent decisionmaking. Complete equality of opportunity does not exist in America or anywhere else. Obstacles to achievement exist, even in the relatively open society of the United States.

A revolution is occurring in the pattern of women's lives in America. In order to understand and prepare herself for this revolution, a young woman should consider that during her life she will probably be both a housewife and an employed worker—often at the same time. Young men should recognize how this new American woman will, in turn, affect their own personal, social and economic lives. If the young women of today are going to realize their fullest potential, they will have to look closely at themselves and the changing world about them. They will have to think seriously about what they want from life. Information about the changing patterns of women's lives, both in and out of the manpower market, can help young people make decisions today that will increase their chances for a meaningful life tomorrow.

The revolution taking place in the lives of American women has several dimensions. For example, the life expectancy of a female baby now is almost 74 years; in 1920 it was only 55 years. About half of today's women marry by age 21 and have their last baby by age 30. By the time her youngest child is in school, the mother may have 30 to 35 more years of active life (including work years) before her. It also is estimated that 9 of 10 girls today will be gainfully employed at some time during their lives. There are now more than 32 million women in the labor force; by 1980, it is estimated, there will be over 37 million. Two of every 5 workers today is a woman; almost 3 of 5 working women are married and living with their husbands. In 1920 the average woman worker was single and 28 years old. Today, the average woman worker is married and 39 years old.

American women have a split-level working life. The 2 periods when women are most likely to work are during ages 20 through 24 and 45 through 54. The greater economic demands on the family—such as higher cost of educating children, higher cost of health care and costs of the greater variety of goods and services considered necessary to meet the American standard of living—increasingly seem to require a 2-paycheck household. More and more, the opportunity to apply for a job or get a promotion depends on higher levels of education—and women are getting more schooling. Increasingly, women are demanding the right to choose how they will make their contribution to their family and their community.

In today's society, young women have greater freedom of choice to decide what type of life to live. This situation suggests that women should be trained to understand ideas and principles as well as develop how-to-do-it skills because many women will be returning to the labor force in their early 40s. Personal, social and economic changes are taking place in family life as a result of the wife-mother being both homemaker and income earner at the same time.

Another way to examine the change that has taken place in the old housewife/career girl division of women—a woman often used to be either one or the other, not both—is to study some typical employment situations that face young married women today across the country. What do these 3 young women have in common with one another? Are they housewives or career girls?

CAROL

"Don and I were married soon after we graduated from high school. Don got a job at the local automobile assembly plant and earned a good salary and didn't want me to work. We started our family soon after we were married since we both wanted a big family. We have 4 children; the baby is only 2 years old. Last year, Don was hurt in an accident at the plant and couldn't work any more. Although Don's paycheck was no longer coming in every 2 weeks, we were not left without income. There was the Workmen's Compensation payment [a system of insurance required by state law and financed by employers, which provides payment to workers or their families for occupational illness, injuries or death resulting in loss of income] and some money from our own insurance policy. However, we had to face it—our income wasn't enough to support the family.

"Luckily, Don was in good enough health that he could take care of the baby during the day when the older children were in school. Then, I made the rounds of the stores downtown until I got a job—selling children's wear. I know plenty about that! I don't make much for a family our size. We don't have a new car or a new TV set or a new anything as far as that goes, but at least we're all together—that's the most important thing."

DONNA

"Jim and I were married a month after I graduated from high school. He still had 2 years of college to finish so I got a job as a typist so he wouldn't have to drop out of school. We were married 3 years before our first baby came. By that time I'd had 2 promotions and was the private secretary to the vice-president of the company I worked for. When I had to quit work to have our baby, my boss told me to let him know if I ever wanted to come back to work again.

"By the time Judy was 4 and we were trying to raise enough money to make a down payment on a house, I called my old boss and asked him if he could find me a part-time job. So I went back to work, filling in part-time at the main office for the girls who were sick or on vacation. Not only did the extra money help, but I kept my skills from getting too rusty. Last fall Judy started first grade, and I found there really wasn't enough around the house to occupy my time, energy and mind, so I took a full-time job with my old employer. I go to work after Judy is in school, and she stays at a neighbor's house until I get home in the evening. By working full time, I feel like I am more than just a housewife—that I am making a personal contribution to the company that I work for. And we find plenty of uses for that extra paycheck I bring home."

JULIE

"The summer between my junior and senior year in high school I worked as a Red Cross aide in a hospital and decided that I wanted to be a doctor. However, I was afraid that the training would cost too much. After school started that fall, I decided to go to Mrs. Collucci, our school counselor, and see if she could help me figure out a way to get the education and training a physician needs. Mrs. Collucci was full of ideas. She told me about scholarships and loans and encouraged me to fill out some application blanks for colleges offering pre-med curriculums. And sure enough, by the time I had graduated I had been accepted by one of the best colleges in the state.

"After I finished college, med school and my residency, I went to work for a large hospital. I was there for 4 years before I quit because Bill and I (we were married the previous year) were going to become parents. I didn't think I could be both a good mother and full-time doctor. Our baby is now 2 and I have returned to the hospital on a part-time basis. I'm on call at the hospital for emergencies when they need help. Bill takes care of the baby at night when I have to go to work."

These case studies provide partial answers to a number of important questions: When do women make occupational decisions? Why do women work? What types of personal, social or economic stresses and strains may arise when married women seek employment?

Lesson in Brief

A revolution has been taking place in the lives of American women. This revolution affects not only women but men as well. The old way of thinking of women as either housewives or career girls is now largely obsolete. More and more women are combining both these roles at the same time during different periods of their lives. The personal, social and economic lives of everyone in society will be influenced by this new dual role of women.

Two roads diverged in a wood, and I—
I took the one less travelled by,
And that has made all the difference.

Robert Frost

Choosing a career is one of the most important decisions that an individual makes during his or her life. It is wise to approach this decision in a rational and systematic fashion. By analyzing himself and by studying the employment opportunities available, the individual should be able to increase his chances of finding a career to meet his particular needs and to provide personal satisfaction and rewards. Those who plan for the future are more likely to have a better future.

Each person makes many important decisions in his lifetime. Often these decisions involve choosing among several possible courses of action. To a great extent a person's decisions will shape his life and determine whether it will be meaningful, enjoyable and fulfilling. Four very important aspects of life are birth, death, marriage partner and career. The individual has no control over his birth and little or none over death. It seems, too, the individual has less to say about the selection of a spouse than many people believe. But the choice of a job and a career is, within fairly broad limits, in a person's own hands.

One reason why career planning is desirable in today's changing manpower market is because the margin of error young people enjoyed in the past is rapidly disappearing. At one time, students could quit school and rather easily find a job—usually as unskilled workers. But, times have changed. The number of unskilled jobs is rapidly declining. Then, too, the disappearance of the margin of error is a result of the higher level of schooling of today's labor force.

Choosing a career is serious business. A hasty decision, made in a hit-or-miss fashion, may force an individual into work which he does not like, which he cannot do well and which makes him unhappy. Yet out of the nearly 30,000 different kinds of jobs in the United States today, how does a person decide which ones offer the opportunities he wants?

Career planning and decisionmaking is a process carried out at various stages of one's lifetime, not a one-time decision. The lesson "Who Am I? What Am I Becoming?" outlined the major stages of career development. Stages 3 through 6 suggest a need to engage often in career planning and decisionmaking. If an individual has not yet begun to plan, today is the day to begin because today is the first day of the rest of his life. The kind of future a young person has will depend in large measure on the wisdom he displays in vocational planning and decisionmaking.

During career planning, a person attempts to identify which occupations are appropriate for him. Because people differ in characteristics and qualifications, they are not suited for the same types of work. However, most people have talents and abilities that are applicable to a number of occupations. The problem is to discover which of these occupations is best.

Interests

To discover which occupations are most suitable, the individual should consider his interests. What kinds of work interest him most? What work does he find enjoyable? Will he still enjoy this kind of work in the future?

Figure 5.1 may be used to determine which work areas seem most interesting. The jobs represented are not intended to be comprehensive but rather representative of broad classifications of work interests. Each job group in the left-hand column represents an interest area described in the right column. If one is interested in more than one area, he can list his various interests in order of preference. The list can be useful in developing alternative career plans.

Figure 5.1

JOBS AND INTEREST AREAS INVENTORY

Jobs	Interest Areas
Group A Auto mechanic Machine operator Carpenter	Group A jobs involve mechanical things—working with one's hands and using tools and machinery.
Group B Bookkeeper Bank teller Grocery store cashier	Group B jobs involve numerical work—handling figures and mathematical calculations.
Group C Dental technician Chemist Draftsman	Group C jobs are technical, scientific or engineering in nature.
Group D Automobile salesman Sales clerk Household appliance demonstrator	Group D jobs show a preference for working with people—the selling or promotional occupations.
Group E Secretary File clerk Receptionist	Group E jobs are clerical in nature—dealing in office work and business procedures.
Group F Musician Commerical artist Wood carver	Group F jobs deal with artistic and creative activities. Dramatic and literary (writing) jobs are included in this group.
Group G Forest ranger Truckdriver Landscaper	Group G jobs involve working out-of-doors on one's own.
Group H Lawyer Minister Teacher	Group H jobs involve working with words and ideas as well as with people.

Abilities

Another factor to consider in career planning is personal aptitudes, or natural abilities and talents. Figure 5.2 lists the abilities that most people have in differing degrees, provides a broad picture of one's own aptitudes and indicates capacity for learning and doing different kinds of work.

There are tests available to measure the abilities listed in Figure 5.2. If a person does not know enough about his aptitudes, he should check with his teacher, school counselor or State

Figure 5.2
NATURAL ABILITIES

Employment Service representative for help. In fact, these people can be valuable sources of information and help in all aspects of career planning and preparation.

An individual needs to consider which abilities he has and which he wants to develop. The degree of talent in each of these areas may vary a great deal.

Other Factors

Now let's consider what else the individual may have to offer. In addition to interests and general ability, a person has many other qualities that pertain to careers. School courses and grades, hobbies, part-time jobs, sports and extracurricular activities, personal and physical characteristics, and likes and dislikes provide clues which aid in career decisionmaking.

A personal inventory (see Figure 5.3) helps bring individual qualities and characteristics into focus. Answers to self-inventory questions will be useful for immediate and future career planning. Answers should be as objective as possible for valid results. By writing out the answers to these questions, the individual will have a useful record of his evaluation.

The next step in career planning is to find out which occupations offer the greatest opportunities. The question of job opportunity is a difficult one, for the world of work is always subject to change. New inventions, new enterprises and new industries enter the picture constantly, changing existing jobs and creating new ones. On the other hand, while industrial development creates new kinds of jobs, it may cause others to die out. As a result, some skills needed today may become obsolete, even within the span of one's working life. So, in order to make a wise occupational choice, the individual should examine the question of opportunity from all sides.

Figure 5.3

SELF-INVENTORY

EDUCATION

1. What courses have you studied?
2. In which school subjects did you do well?
3. In which school subjects did you not do well?
4. Which school subjects did you enjoy studying most? Why did you enjoy them?
5. Which school subjects did you dislike studying? Why did you dislike them?
6. What are your educational plans? In which courses and programs do you hope to enroll?
7. Which extracurricular school activities have you especially liked?

PERSONAL DATA

8. What are your outstanding abilities, talents and strong points?
9. What are your weak points?
10. How well do you get along with other people—your parents, friends, teachers, etc.?
11. What personal satisfaction would you like to get from work?
12. How much income per year do you want from a future job?
13. What hobbies and leisure activities do you especially like? Why do you enjoy these?
14. What additional hobbies or leisure activities would you like to have? Why?
15. What physical limitations do you have that may restrict your performance on a job?

JOB EXPERIENCE

16. Of the jobs you have held, which have you liked best? Why?

OCCUPATIONAL CHOICE

17. Considering all the information you have given about yourself, what 3 jobs or occupations that you can do or can learn to do would be most interesting to you right now? Which of these is your first choice, etc.? Why are you interested in these specific jobs or occupations?
18. If you could have any job, which one would you choose? Why?
19. What are your ambitions? Why do you want to achieve them?

To evaluate opportunities, a person needs the following information about occupations that interest him and that he is capable of learning:

1. The immediate and future prospects of employment
2. The educational and other skill requirements for beginners
3. The kind of additional training needed and where it can be obtained
4. The range of salaries or wages
5. The general job setting
6. The opportunities for advancement
7. The geography of employment opportunities

To locate the information needed about occupations, help is available from a number of community sources—for example, teachers, school counselors, the State Employment Service, local labor organizations, visits to places of work, the Chamber of Commerce, school and public libraries, friends and relatives, and private employment agencies.

Career planning is more than finding a job. It is discovering oneself. The important goal in career planning is not to learn merely to market oneself, but to discover oneself.

Lesson in Brief

A person's decisions shape his life. One of the most important of all decisions is choice of a career. The individual has a great deal of freedom in choosing a career. Wise use of this freedom means approaching vocational choice in a rational and systematic manner. The margin of error that existed in the past for young people who failed to plan their occupational futures is rapidly disappearing. Continuous planning increases chances of finding meaningful and rewarding work. Knowledge of oneself and the manpower market will be helpful in finding appropriate work.

296

Economic Decisionmaking and Career Planning

The steps in economic decisionmaking can be applied to a variety of economic situations, including the choice of a career. These 5 steps are valuable tools for analyzing oneself and the career opportunities that exist in the manpower market.

In Lesson 55, the 5 steps in economic decisionmaking were presented. This systematic, step-by-step approach to problem solving is useful in planning a career and preparing for participation in the manpower market. The 5 steps can be used as a framework for analyzing oneself and the information that has been gained from this book concerning the economy, the manpower market and the world of work as the case study below illustrates.

THINKING ABOUT A CAREER

Mark MacDonald is a student in Miss Svoboda's social studies class. He has been studying economics and its application to career planning. Yesterday, after class, he stopped to talk to his teacher.

"Miss Svoboda," Mark said, "I enjoyed our discussion today about the steps in economic decisionmaking, but I'm wondering how I can apply them to my own situation."

"Well, Mark" Miss Svoboda replied, "tomorrow we are going to do a planning exercise using the 5 steps to think about careers. I've developed a career planning sheet which I'll distribute to the class.

"Perhaps you would like to examine the planning sheet before tomorrow. There are a couple of things I'd like to point out. For example, don't assume you'll actually be making a career choice tomorrow or that you're somehow deciding your whole vocational future. This exercise is designed to help develop skill in planning a career. I do want you to be serious and thoughtful as you consider the ideas and information that you personally will want to weigh before you actually choose an occupation.

"This exercise takes each of the 5 steps in logical order and illustrates the concerns and types of questions you'll want to consider as you think about a career. By answering the questions that are raised, you will in fact be using the steps in economic decisionmaking. Tomorrow you'll be writing out your answers as you go through the 5 steps in class."

Miss Svoboda handed Mark a copy of the career planning sheet. He sat down and read the following outline to himself:

Planning Your Career by Using
Steps in Economic Decisionmaking

1. *Define the problem.* You are making decisions right now concerning which school curriculum to follow and which subjects to take. In a few years you will be entering the manpower market. Should you begin to plan and make decisions now regarding your future role in the manpower market and world of work? Will an understanding of manpower and the economic world increase your chances of successful employment? Here are some things you may want to consider:

1a. What are the economic and noneconomic functions of work? Which ones are most important to me?
1b. What factors affect my chances for successful participation in the manpower market?
1c. What are some personal and social benefits from career planning?
1d. My problem is. . . (Write out a definition of the problem of your career choice.)

2. *Identify goals.* You can identify your goals by asking yourself questions such as: Who am I? What do I want from life? From a job? Do I want to enter a particular field of work? Make a lot of money? Travel? Have leisure time? What are my interests and goals? Only you can decide what it is you want from life in general and your career in particular. Here are some ideas that might be helpful to you in finding out what your personal interests and goals are.

2a. Who am I? What am I becoming? (Identify some of the attitudes, values and experiences that influence who you are and what you are becoming.)

298

2b. What are my aspirations in life? Are they fame? fortune? power? happiness?

2c. What do I want from my career?

2d. My goals are... (Write out a brief statement of your personal goals.)

3. *Consider alternative methods for reaching your goals.* Employment may offer you an opportunity to achieve some of your personal goals. There are many different kinds of occupations in the economy, and jobs are available in various industries. But as you think about potential careers, you will want to consider such questions as: Do I need schooling or training beyond high school to qualify for employment? What types of work experience should I get to help obtain and keep a job? How can the jobs and occupations that interest me lead to careers?

3a. What are some of the jobs and occupations I find interesting?

3b. In what industries would I like to be employed?

3c. Which of the occupations that interest me seem to offer the best employment opportunities in the 1970s and 1980s?

3d. Which of the industries that interest me seem to offer the best employment opportunities in the future?

3e. How much and what kind of education, training and experience will I need to qualify for the various occupations I find interesting?

3f. What types of careers are possible based on my answers to 3a through 3e?

3g. Alternative methods of reaching my goals are... (Write out 2 or 3 alternative approaches to achieving your stated goals.)

4. *Study the probable consequences of the alternative methods.* This involves asking such questions as: If I decide to enter an occupation that requires college or post-high school training, what grades must I earn in school? How will I pay for my post-high school education? What types of rewards and satisfactions will I get from successfully participating in the manpower market? Many different types of satisfactions and rewards come from full participation in the manpower market. Employment will influence your whole way of life. However, competition does exist for the best jobs; obstacles have to be overcome in order to succeed.

4a.   What are the economic or monetary rewards from successful participation in the various occupations that interest me?

4b.   What noneconomic satisfactions can I get from being employed in a job that's right for me?

4c.   How will my career affect the way I live?

4d.   What type of competition will I have for the jobs that I like?

4e.   The probable outcomes of my use of the different methods are. . . (Write out a few of the probable costs, benefits and other outcomes of 2 of the alternatives.)

5. *Choose the methods that offer the best solution* to your problem in terms of the goals you have picked. You can now make a tentative choice of a course of action to achieve your career goals. This choice should reflect your own personal preferences and your understanding of what this decision requires of you. You also should be aware of what is involved in carrying out this decision. Effective participation in the manpower market is one means you can use to achieve some of your goals in life. However, your goals will probably change with education and experience. It isn't easy to know right now what occupations are best suited for your needs. Keeping in mind the results of the first 4 steps, make a tentative choice to solve your career decision-making problem. Write out a brief statement of your decision.

After Mark read the career planning sheet, he turned to Miss Svoboda and said, "This looks like an interesting exercise. I'm looking forward to going through this tomorrow in class."

All young people could benefit from the practical exercise in career planning prepared for Mark and his classmates. Practicing the steps in economic decisionmaking is a good way to learn how to use them and to begin to master the skill of problem solving.

Lesson in Brief

The steps of economic decisionmaking are useful tools to the individual who wants to plan and make decisions about his career. A person's chances of successful participation in the manpower market will be improved if he makes some tentative occupational choices early and begins planning and taking action aimed at reaching his career goals.

> Values are standards that people use to make choices and decisions about important matters. A value implies goodness or badness. People make value judgments every day. Their lives are influenced a great deal by the values they hold and use. Values are acquired from parents, schools, churches, friends and other sources. It is also possible to learn useful values through careful reasoning and a factual study of man and his social and physical world.

Frequent use of the 5 steps in economic decisionmaking has been made in this study of the economy and man's role as a worker. Step 2 of economic decisionmaking—identifying goals and underlying values—is extremely important in the decisionmaking process. Goals and values (including value judgments and value conflicts) have been discussed in other lessons. In this lesson, values will be examined more closely.

Whenever people talk about something being good or bad, they are discussing values. *Values* are defined as standards that people use to make choices about important matters. Some examples are honesty, efficiency, equality, good health and human development. A value always implies a preference based on judgments about the goodness or worth of a thing. For example, when a person chooses to buy a blue wool sweater for $10 rather than a green orlon sweater for $14, he is making a value judgment (that is, all things considered—price, quality and personal taste—the blue sweater has more goodness for him than the green one).

Many of the choices people make are far more complicated than the sweater example. Often the values used to make the choices are of social importance because the behavior which they influence may greatly affect the lives of other people.

THE VALUE OF COLOR

Paul Baxter is personnel manager of the Ace Manufacturing Company. Two men apply for a production job. Both men are high school graduates with good backgrounds, and they seem equally qualified. Howard is white. John is black. Paul decides to hire Howard rather than John because Paul prefers whites to blacks.

Paul chose a certain course of action (hiring the white worker) on the basis of a value judgment. The value of whiteness was used to make a choice concerning which man got the job.

Many people would agree that race, religion, ethnic background and sex are not good bases for making decisions in the world of work because they do not provide an appropriate measure of the skills and capability that a particular worker may be able to bring to a job. Whether a person's race, religion, ethnic background and sex will continue to influence hiring practices in the future may depend on whether Americans are willing to analyze certain values and accept responsibility for the consequences of their own actions.

ANSWERS AND QUESTIONS

Shirley couldn't help but notice that her friend and classmate, Fred, was cheating during the math test. He kept looking into his shirt pocket which contained all sorts of interesting answers neatly printed on a small card. At home that night, Shirley wrestled with her conscience. What should she do, if anything, about Fred's cheating?

By dishonestly getting a high grade, Fred might lower the grades of other students (maybe even Shirley's!). He was taking advantage of the teacher and his fellow students to promote his own self-interest. On the other hand, Shirley knew that finking (informing) was not acceptable conduct among her classmates. In this situation, Shirley's values of self-preservation and fundamental honesty were in conflict.

As a worker-consumer-citizen, an individual has to make many value judgments in his lifetime. Some of these will affect his personal situation, such as his career choice, the home he buys, etc. Other value judgments, such as the way he votes on key issues in local, state and national elections and the kinds of political candidates he supports, will affect the whole community. An individual makes value judgments about the way tax burdens are distributed; the power that is given to government agencies, labor unions and business corporations; policies to reduce pollution and poverty; and relations with other countries (war and peace, economic assistance, cooperation in space exploration).

How important are value judgments in economics? Several years ago a committee of businessmen and university presidents asked the question, What is the most important economic problem facing the United States in the next 20 years? One economist felt that the most important economic problem is that citizens know what they want, *to define useful and worthy ends*. In other words, economic life is concerned not only with how goals are achieved but also with what the goals themselves ought to be. Man does not have to drift with the current. Because man has knowledge and power, he is able to choose a wide variety of goals—based on his values—and, in fact, cannot avoid the responsibility to do so. In a statement made on educational television in 1962, former President John F. Kennedy pointed out that economic decisions are man-made decisions. The American people are to a considerable extent masters of their own economic destinies.

President Kennedy's statement implies that values are important in making economic decisions. What are the sources of values? Parents, friends, church, community, school, communications media—and sometimes one's own creative thinking. Are values fixed for all time, or do they change? Consider the value of sex equality, and contrast today's views with those held 60 years ago.

Can 2 people who disagree about a value—such as the importance that work should have in a person's life—work out their disagreement and decide which value is better? This question illustrates one of the most difficult problems that men and women face in their lives. It is a problem that no scientist, teacher, philosopher or scholar has yet solved. Knowledge of "good" has been called the ultimate purpose of all education. How can the wisest, most useful values be found? How can value differences be settled?

Consider the following suggestions drawn from many sources. They may be helpful in pursuing a rational analysis of values:

1. Keep an open mind. Even if a person is "certain" he is right, he should consider the possibility that he *might* be wrong. A value judgment is as strong as the reasons that support it and as weak as the reasons that support alternative views.

2. Try to clarify the issues, to find out exactly what the disagreement is. Frequently, after much argument and confusion, there really is no disagreement after all, only misunderstanding.

3. Look at the facts and check the accuracy of information and data. Many so-called value disputes are really disagreements about the facts; once the factual errors are eliminated, the dispute is ended.

4. Be sure that logic is sound and values are consistent. Avoid the position of the leading characters in George Orwell's famous book *Animal Farm* in which all the animals were in favor of equality, but some animals wanted to be more equal than others!

5. Avoid the trap of assuming that something is good merely because it serves one's own narrow self-interest regardless of how other people might be affected.

6. Be sure that stated values are applied to the *methods* used to achieve goals as well as to the selection of the *goals* themselves. For example, if the goal is to teach a group how democracy works but the leader orders everyone around like a dictator, he has failed to follow the value of democratic procedure.

If everyone follows these rules, will there always be perfect agreement on values? Of course not! Life is not that simple. The real question is, Will this rational approach to making value judgments produce better outcomes than the use of force, trickery, authority, unquestioned faith or tradition?

Lesson in Brief

Values are standards that people use to make choices and decisions about important matters. A value implies goodness or badness. Values play an important role in the selection of economic goals. A rational analysis of values requires keeping an open mind, clarifying the issues, verifying facts, following the rules of logic and consistency, avoiding a self-serving approach and applying stated values to the methods used in achieving goals as well as to the selection of the goals themselves.

UNIT SIX
Technology, Skills and Investment in Education

The lessons in Unit Six concern 2 themes, technology and education, whose common denominator is knowledge. When man increases his knowledge of how to make tools and use them in production, there are far-reaching effects on the economy, the world of work and the social environment in which he lives. Automation and cybernation illustrate the impact that a highly complex technology has on mass production and also on problems of human adjustment.

Ever since the Industrial Revolution, technological change has been bringing both benefits and burdens to workers and other members of U.S. society. In order to deal with technology's burdens and challenges and to make wise use of the opportunities and benefits that this form of knowledge provides, increasingly Americans depend on education. Formal schooling, on-the-job training and other programs to increase skills and understanding can all be regarded as investments that improve the quality of human resources. These investments involve costs, and they result in a variety of benefits. Some benefits are related to productivity, income and economic growth. Others, such as developing informed citizens and encouraging individuals to fulfill their human potential, may be even more important. Education is seen by many people as a possible way out of poverty and dependency for children growing up in low-income homes. It is also a means of discovering how rich and full human life can be.

In this modern, rapidly changing world, education will have to be a continuing process for men and women who want to qualify for satisfying jobs and careers. Young people who acquire a solid foundation of skills in the areas of communication, calculation, manual dexterity and group relations—and whose world-view is in harmony with a changing environment—will be better able to meet the challenges and opportunities of the future.

The Knowledge Explosion: Technology, Automation and Cybernation

Knowledge is power.

Francis Bacon

The application of scientific knowledge to production is one of the greatest "inventions" in the history of man. Rapidly improving technology makes it possible to produce new goods, more goods and better goods. Technological and economic changes also create adjustment problems for individuals and for society.

Throughout history, man has been a seeker of knowledge for many reasons. Often man wants to know simply for the sake of knowing. Just as men and women climb mountains because the mountains "are there," they also study the heavens and the earth and the creatures that inhabit the universe. Curiosity is one reason; but man is also very practical. He wants to survive on this planet and to extend his control over his environment. He wants to expand his freedom and power. And to do this, he must have knowledge.

Think of the power that man gained when he learned to make fire, to fashion cutting edges on stones, to use the lever, wheel, and bow and arrow. Man took a giant step forward in his cultural evolution when he "invented" agriculture and learned to use wooden tools and fertilizer and animal power to grow crops. He made another leap forward when he learned to harness steam, electricity and petroleum to power machines made of iron and steel.

The great American economist, Thorstein Veblen, who wrote many books and scholarly articles during the early 1900s, called technology "the life process of man." Certainly the knowledge of how to make and use tools has played a tremendously important role in the life of men and women. In the United States today, science and technology seem to dominate people's lives, creating and recreating new worlds full of opportunity and promise but also posing problems and dangers. There is perhaps no better example than atomic and nuclear energy. On one side of the coin is power; on the other is the bomb.

Why is the U.S. economy so productive? Simply stated, *advanced technology* is the answer. U.S. workers know how to make tools and how to use them in production. Without modern industrial technology, the United States would be a nation of primitive people fighting a constant struggle for bare survival. Many people would lose the struggle and starve to death, as thousands do every day in the less developed countries of Asia and Africa.

In recent years, technical knowledge has been increasing at a fantastic rate. According to a report published by the Joint Economic Committee of the U.S. Congress, "as much technical knowledge will be developed in the next 30 years as has been accumulated in the entire past history of mankind." As much new technical knowledge will be discovered (or produced) between 1966 and 1996 as in all the preceding thousands of years of man's existence on this planet combined. The report went on to say that the United States produces approximately 25,000 technical papers every week along with 400 books and 3,500 articles.

Not only is technology advancing rapidly, but also the rate of change is increasing. This should not be surprising. The more knowledge and the more tools man has, the more ways he can combine existing knowledge and tools—to create still more knowledge and tools! This is one of the most important principles of economic growth. Technology is cumulative (man keeps adding to knowledge inherited from the past), and the pace of technological progress is accelerating. Each year in the United States nearly $30 billion is spent on research and development (R & D) to assure that technical knowledge keeps expanding to meet the needs of a growing economy.

What are the consequences of technological change? The first is to *expand productivity* — the power to produce goods and services. Improvements in technology become embodied in new machines and equipment (capital goods). And through education and training, technological improvements become embodied in human resources. As the quality of capital and manpower resources improves, the economy is able to produce *more* output with a given quantity of man-hours and capital inputs. Advanced technology also makes it possible to produce *new* and *better* goods and services.

The second effect of technological progress is to *generate change.* Later, attention will be focused on the process of change and some problems created by technological advance. Now, let's take a closer look at the different forms of modern technology and the impact of technological improvements on productivity and growth.

In recent years a couple of synthetic terms—first cousins in the technology family, so to speak—have made their way into the nation's vocabulary. One is automation. The other, still strange and unfamiliar to many people, is cybernation.

Automation, formed from the words automatic and operation, is used to describe a mechanized process of production in which equipment is used to regulate and coordinate the quantity and quality of production. In other words, *automation* is the use of machines to control other machines in production. In terms of complexity, it is one step beyond mechanization. Automation is used to provide a continuous and integrated operation for a production system.

Cybernation is automation plus the electronic computer. Computers, in turn, are devices that perform, very rapidly, routine or complex logical, mathematical and decisionmaking tasks. Computers are used for calculation, control, communication and data storage.

Some writers have suggested that a "cybernation revolution" has taken place, meaning that recent changes in technology are so fundamentally different from previous industrial technology that a new era has been entered. In this evolving cybernation era, the muscle-power and manipulative skills that workers contributed to production in the past will cease to be valuable. Machines will take over much of the work that men and women do. In the future, some writers say, the only resource capability of humans that will have economic value will be brainpower.

Already, automated equipment has replaced thousands of workers in mining coal, weaving cloth, baking cakes, making steel, printing, oil refining, sorting bank checks and doing hundreds of other jobs. Fourteen glassblowing machines, each operated by 1 worker, produce 90% of the glass light bulbs used in the United States. A single assembly line operated by 2 workers produces more radios than 200 workers formerly did. A fully automated plant in the Soviet Union manufactures aluminum pistons for heavy trucks with no manual labor whatsoever. One refinery in England, using a total of 6 men on a shift, processes enough crude oil in a day to supply nearly one-third of Britain's internal consumption of oil products.

Where will it all end? Will machines take over the world and make slaves of men? Will the wise use of machines free man from toil forever? If manpower is no longer needed in production, what will man do with his leisure time? Unless people are satisfied simply to wait and see how things come out, they will want to give these questions some thoughtful attention.

Lesson in Brief

Knowledge is power. The application of scientific and technical knowledge to production is one of the greatest inventions in human history. Technological progress, automation and cybernation make it possible to produce new goods, more goods and better goods. Technological and economic changes also create problems that individuals and society must solve.

> *Technology has, on balance, surely been a great blessing to mankind—despite the fact that some of the benefits have been offset by costs. There should be no thought of deliberately slowing down the rate of technological advancement. . . . The task for the decades ahead is to direct technology to the fulfillment of important human purposes . . . and seek to make work more meaningful rather than merely more productive.*

National Commission on Technology, Automation and Economic Progress

The above quotation comes from *Technology and the American Economy*, the Report of the National Commission on Technology, Automation and Economic Progress. Appointed by the President of the United States, the Commission was made up of 14 men and women representing education, business, labor and other fields. Its job was to make a study of technological change, describe the principal effects on the economy and society, and make recommendations for programs and actions aimed at getting the greatest benefits from technological advancements and reducing the burdens of change on displaced workers.

Why was this automation commission set up? Why did the President feel that technology, automation and economic progress might be creating problems that required special attention?

There has been a widespread feeling among Americans that the pace of technological change has been quickening. Things seem to be changing so fast that people have trouble keeping up. Products and methods become obsolete almost as soon as they are unwrapped and put into use. Almost every day, new machines are installed and new production methods put into practice. Since the end of World War II, new items have become available—ball point pens, television, jet airliners, new medicines, air conditioning, transistor radios, miracle fibers for clothing, pesticides and fungicides, dishwashers, helicopters, frozen foods, space satellites, the pill, electronic computers, and the laser—to mention only a few! (Professor Kenneth Boulding, a University of Colorado economist, says that the extent of the generation gap is directly related to the rate of social and technological change.)

Moreover, there is growing recognition—to quote the Commission's Report—"of the deep influence of technology upon our way of life." The American people have seen the promise of technology. They also have seen the dangers. Concern and fear have been expressed—fear of destruction by the bomb, fear of mass unemployment, concern over air and water pollution and the destruction of the natural environment. There is even fear that technology has seized control of man's fate and threatens to destroy the essential human qualities of man.

Let's look at some of the economic *benefits* of technological advancement. In the 25 years following World War II, the gross national product increased from an annual rate of $208 billion in 1946 to $1,050 billion in 1971. The market value of U.S. output nearly quadrupled. The increase in physical output of goods and services, however, really was not this great. Inflationary price increases following World War II and during the Korean and Vietnam wars made the dollar value of GNP increase faster than actual production increased. Nevertheless, after all the proper adjustments are made for changes in the price level, real GNP more than doubled between 1946 and 1971. The average yearly increase in real GNP was about 4%.

What role did technological improvements play in the growth of GNP? Unfortunately, it is impossible to give a definite answer to this interesting question. The expansion of technical knowledge enables the economy to build better machines and design more efficient production systems. It makes workers more productive and helps businessmen increase their managerial efficiency. Technological advances make it possible to produce more goods, better quality goods and entirely new goods and services—such as television sets and TV coverage of Apollo moon missions.

At present, there is no exact way to measure the contribution that technological progress makes to U.S. economic growth. But there are some economic statistics that help tell part of the story.

First, productivity—output per man-hour—increased at an average rate of 3% a year during the past 2 decades. About two-thirds of the growth in real GNP is the direct result of increased productivity. And technological advance is one of the main reasons productivity grows.

Technology and productivity do not change at the same rate in every industry or every sector of the economy. Productivity growth in agriculture in recent years, for example, has been nearly double the increase for the overall economy. Fifty years ago, 1 farmer produced enough food and fiber to feed and clothe 8 people. Today, 1 farmer produces enough to feed and clothe 50 people! Agriculture has undergone a technological revolution, ranging from the use of giant harvesting combines and mechanized cotton pickers to chemical fertilizers and insecticides. This, in turn, has led to certain problems and *burdens* of technological progress. Farmers are becoming so productive and efficient that they are producing themselves out of jobs!

Improvements in farm technology wiped out more than 4,000,000 farm jobs in the past 25 years. The number of employed farmers and farm workers declined from 8 million in 1947 to 3½ million in 1971. Twenty-five years ago, 1 worker in 7 was employed in agriculture. Today, only one twenty-fifth of the civilian labor force is employed in farming. Between 1940 and 1971 while the total population of the United States increased from 132 million to 206 million, the farm population declined from 30 million to less than 10 million.

In the coal mining industry, technological and economic changes reduced the number of jobs from over 400,000 in the 1940s to 138,000 in 1971. One reason for this massive displacement of workers was the "Push-button Miner"—a mechanical giant 3 stories high and weighing nearly 800 tons. Manned by a crew of only 3 workers, it cuts and loads 360 tons of coal an hour.

Several years ago a committee of the United States Senate held hearings to discuss the "manpower revolution." One of the businessmen who spoke to the committee, the board chairman of a large corporation that produces automation machinery, had this to say:

From a technological point of view automation is working; but the same thing cannot be said so confidently from the human point of view. [There are many] myths about automation. The first myth is that automation is not going to eliminate many jobs. Personally, I think automation is a major factor in eliminating jobs in the United States at the rate of more than 40,000 a week.

A second myth is that automation will create jobs for workers, not only in running the machines but in maintaining and building them. [But if workers were not replaced by automation] there would be no point in automation.

A third myth that needs to be laid to rest is the belief that those who lose their jobs to automation can be retrained and put into other jobs requiring higher skills and paying more money. [But] studies have shown . . . many workers are just not retrainable, due to their levels of intelligence, education and age.

Still another myth is that workers replaced by automation in one part of the country can find jobs in other areas. The truth is that the workers thrown out of jobs are usually just those who are least able to move. They are the lower paid, the older, the unskilled. Either they cannot afford to move from an economic standpoint or they are psychologically incapable of beginning a new life in a strange area.[1]

Today many manpower specialists might disagree somewhat with this businessman's opinions about the third and fourth myths. But most people would agree that his views on the first and second were correct, with certain reservations.

Where does all this discussion leave us? Is automation good or bad for the American economy and the American people? The answer, of course, is that technological advance, automation and cybernation have both advantages and disadvantages. Automation increases ability to produce goods and services, yet it also displaces particular workers and forces people to change the way they work and the way they live. One important fact to note, however, is that automation has definitely not caused unemployment to increase over recent years. As a matter of fact, a careful look at

---

1. U. S. Senate, *Nation's Manpower Revolution*, p. 1650.

the economic statistics will show that the unemployment rate in 1969—after all the technological advance and automation in the 1950s and 1960s—was 3.5%, the lowest level in 16 years! (Higher unemployment rates in 1970, 1971 and 1972 generally were caused by factors other than the rate of technological change.)

Consider again the quotation at the beginning of this lesson. Note the words of wisdom and guidance regarding technological change. "The task for the decades ahead is to direct technology to the fulfillment of important human purposes . . . [and] seek to make work more meaningful rather than merely more productive." This may prove to be the most difficult challenge the American people face in the 1970s and beyond.

Lesson in Brief

Technological advance is an important source of productivity growth and increased GNP. But technology and automation also displace some workers. In the past 25 years, more than half of the farm work force has been eliminated by technological and economic change. Members of the National Commission on Technology, Automation and Economic Progress feel that technological advancement should be encouraged, but special attention should be given to solving the human problems created by technological change.

The future belongs to those who prepare for it.

Anonymous

Good health, education and a realistic world-view oriented to the future all contribute to effective participation in economic life and successful living in a general sense. This world-view must accept the fact that many things are changing, including technology, resources and institutions. The individual who can adjust effectively to a changing world will avoid many problems, fears and burdens and should benefit more fully from the opportunities that change may offer.

The word *philosophy* means the love of wisdom and refers to the study of knowledge. Most people have a philosophy of life that includes their beliefs about the meaning of life and what things are most important in their lives. Let's explore some ideas concerning an individual's *world-view* (the way he looks at the world and interprets what he sees) and the subject of change. Consider the following story about a cow.

THE SHAFTER COW

At exactly 5:13 a.m. on the 18th of April, 1906, a cow was standing at 123 degrees, 20 minutes west longitude, 37 degrees, 58 minutes north latitude—somewhere between the main barn and the milking shed on the old Shafter Ranch in California, minding her own business. Suddenly, the earth shook, the skies trembled and, when it was all over, there was nothing showing of the cow above ground but a bit of her tail sticking up.[2]

The San Francisco earthquake of 1906—that swallowed up the Shafter cow and started fires that virtually destroyed the city—symbolizes the powerful forces of change at work in the world. Individuals may choose to explore and understand these forces in order to help solve technological, economic and social problems before they get out of hand. Or, like the cow, they may

---

2. Don Fabun, "The Dynamics of Change, Kaiser Aluminum and Chemical Corporation."

ignore what goes on until they are overwhelmed by reality. Some people seem to be unaware of what is happening in their world. Some men and women play the game "Ain't It Awful"—talking, complaining, but not doing anything. Mature people not only try to understand their situation but also try to do something constructive about it.[3]

How people view economic change in today's world will affect the world of the future, because the way people think about events—such as technological change, problems of disadvantaged minorities, overpopulation and pollution of the environment—will make a difference in what they actually do about them. In fact, the overall view that a person has of the economic and social world around him may be the most important part of his entire economic thought pattern. If he believes that the tendency to bargain and trade is basic human nature; if he thinks that rational search for pleasure and the avoidance of work and pain are the source of human activity; if he believes that market forces do and should determine the way income is distributed—then he holds one outlook on the economic world. His viewpoint may influence beliefs about government manpower policies, poverty and pollution. If another individual believes that capitalism is an evolving institution that developed out of earlier ways of organizing production and distribution; that man is only partly a rational animal; that the work done and things consumed are directed by institutions rather than the individual's rational search for pleasure—then this person has a world-view which may lead him to interpret economic and social conditions quite differently. Such differences in world-view and attitude can affect public opinion, elections and governmental policies.[4]

Just as no one knows what the future will bring, neither does anyone know what the proper world-view is for a given individual. The individual's world-view is a matter of personal philosophy that

---

3. Two excellent books dealing with attitudes and personal behavior are Eric Berne's *Games People Play* (New York: Ballantine Books, 1973) and Thomas A. Harris's *I'm OK--You're OK* (New York: Avon Books, 1973).

4. Some of the ideas expressed in this paragraph are based on *Economics and Man* (Homewood, Illinois: Richard D. Irwin, 1959) by John S. Gambs and Sydney Wertimer, Jr.

develops and grows as he learns more about the world and his place in it. There are, however, certain facts that might be helpful in searching for a useful world-view. It can be predicted with a great deal of confidence, for example, that life in the year 2023 will be a lot different from life in 1973. The work that men and women do, the goods and services they consume, the methods of production will all be vastly different. Moreover, since the rate of change in technology and economic life seems to increase each year, life 50 years from now will be much different, with changes even greater than those which occurred between 1923 and 1973.

How will it be possible to keep pace with change? How can people renew themselves and adjust to the new demands that will be placed on them as workers, consumers, citizens and human beings? Is it better to face the future with optimism and hope rather than with pessimism and fear?

Previous lessons in this book have suggested partial answers to these questions. It will be easier to face the future if the individual acquires understanding and skills that are basic and durable, versatile, transferable to new work, and instrumental so that learning can continue throughout life. The maintenance of good health, both physical and mental, will certainly make adjustment to the future easier. And, finally, *knowing that change will come* and *being oriented to the future rather than the past* will promote attitudes and a world-view that make adaptation to change much smoother.

Approaching the future creatively and enthusiastically can help make it serve individual needs and desires. When a person knows what to expect and deals with the facts, he is less likely to feel that he (like the Shafter cow) is a helpless victim of huge forces outside his understanding and beyond his control.

Lesson in Brief

Technology, economic resources and the institutions of the U.S. society have changed a great deal in the past 50 years. The world can be expected to continue changing in the future. In order to meet the challenges of change and take advantage of opportunities provided by technological progress and economic growth, workers will need to develop skills and understanding, good mental and physical health, and a world-view oriented to the future rather than to the past.

In the dynamic economy of the United States, changes are always taking place in the number and nature of jobs. Technology and other forces cause some old jobs to disappear while creating new jobs. The changes that will take place in the manpower market during the next 50 years will mean that each person is likely to have 6 or more different types of jobs during his or her years of employment. Continuing education and training will be necessary to improve work skills so that workers can take advantage of changing employment opportunities.

In many cases, the parents of today's youth did not have the opportunities for education and training when they were in school that are available to young people today. Yet, many have been able to get and hold jobs without a great deal of additional education or training. It is not safe, however, to assume that what was good enough for Mom and Dad will be good enough for tomorrow's workers.

The future will be different from the past. The labor force composition is changing rapidly, and the amount of education and training is increasing for nearly every type of worker. Nevertheless, because of the rapid nature of change, it is hard to predict the exact type of education and training that will provide the specific skills needed for jobs of the future. The fact is that not even a panel of vocational education experts set up by the President of the United States a few years ago could determine what skill training people should have so they could be usefully employed 10 years hence. The nation has reached a point in its economic life where it is not possible to tell whether a given form of training will be adequate for a man or woman as much as 10 years in the future.

Let's look at the future of education and training for the changing labor force through the experiences of a girl named Laura. The story could very well concern itself with Mike, Ken or José because what happens to Laura in tomorrow's manpower market could happen to any man or woman in America.

LAURA VOSS

In the spring of 1973 Laura Voss, a 9th grade student in Everytown Junior High School, went to the office of Mrs. Rosenberg, her guidance counselor, to discuss a high school program for the fall.

In talking with Laura, Mrs. Rosenberg recalled that the girl's stepmother had asked, "What's going to happen to Laura when she graduates from high school? Is she just going to rush into marriage because she has nothing else to do? I hope she gets a chance to develop her own future and takes time to decide what she wants to be."

Mrs. Rosenberg kept in mind what Laura's stepmother said as she pointed out that in Everytown one of the best jobs a girl could get was in an office. She explained that business firms need people who can type, keep books and run offices. "If you take the business education courses, I don't think you'll have any trouble getting a job when you graduate," Mrs. Rosenberg said.

"Well, that sounds great," said Laura. "What subjects do you think I should take?"

"You are required to take social studies, science, physical education, math and English. You should also take some home economics and business education courses like general business, business English, typing, shorthand and office practice." So Laura and her counselor developed a program in which about one-third of her high school time would be spent on business subjects.

In 1976 Laura graduated from high school. Since she received excellent grades in high school her parents said, "We don't think you should go to work yet. Why don't you enroll in a vocational-technical school or business college?"

So Laura attended a private business school which offered a 2-year program in office management. She spent about two-thirds of her time on business subjects. She was good at them, and she liked them. Her good spirits and readiness to learn made Laura well-liked by teachers and fellow students and a genuine credit to the school.

In 1978 Laura graduated with honors and took a job with the K. L. Wohlford Real Estate Agency. There, too, Laura did well. At the end of the second month she got a pay raise and, at the end of the fourth, another.

As the months went by, Laura received additional pay raises. She was successful on her job and happy with life. Then in 1980 she met

Jim. She was 21 years old. She fell in love and wanted to marry Jim immediately.

But Mr. Wohlford said, "Laura, don't do anything rash. You've got a good job here, with a great future. Don't just throw it away!"

Laura took Mr. Wohlford's advice and waited a whole year. Then she married Jim. After their marriage, Laura continued to work. She enjoyed working for the agency, and K. L. Wohlford continued to value her as a model employee. But after 2 years, Laura told Mr. Wohlford that she would soon have to stop working because she was pregnant. So, at age 24 Laura quit work to become a full-time housewife and mother.

Gail was born in 1983. Laura had a second child, Jack, who was born when she was 28 years old. Two years later Gail started school. Laura didn't miss her too much because Jack kept her busy. But 4 years later in 1993, when Laura was 34, Jack too started school.

Laura then found she had more free time. She thought about going back to work and talked to her husband about it, but Jim said, "No wife of mine is going to work when she doesn't have to. Why don't you join a garden club or something like that?"

So Laura joined a garden club but decided gardening and going to meetings weren't worthwhile activities and gave them up. She became a Girl Scout den mother but didn't like that either. She joined a church group and did volunteer work at the hospital, but she found none of these things really satisfying. Laura became unhappy and restless. She even considered divorce as a possible answer to her problems.

Years went by, and Gail entered high school. With Gail in high school, Laura began to worry about Gail's future education. Laura told Jim, "Gail ought to go to college. And if she does, we're going to need about $5,000 or $6,000 a year more than you're earning now. It won't be long before Jack too will be ready for college. Don't you think I should try to find a job?" Jim finally agreed. So in 1998 at the age of 39, Laura decided to return to work.

Laura went to the Wohlford Real Estate Agency to try to get her old job back. K. L. Wohlford had retired, so she introduced herself to the new owner and said, "I used to work for Mr. Wohlford about 16 years ago, and I would like to work here again."

He said, "Well, that's great. What can you do? What do you have to offer us?"

"I can do bookkeeping."

"Bookkeeping? Did Wohlford hire bookkeepers in your day? We don't have a bookkeeping job in this office; that work's now done by a machine. This is 1998!"

"Well, I can take shorthand," Laura went on.

"Did the agency hire stenographers in your day? I always thought that was done with dictating machines."

"I can type. Surely you can use a good typist. I have done some personal typing in the last few years, and I am almost as fast and accurate as I use to be."

"We use the voice typewriter now," the owner replied.

"Well, I can manage an office. I even completed a 2-year business school program in office management and have a certificate."

"Look, Laura, did you see those 3 women in the other room when you came in? Each of them has 25 years seniority with this agency. They literally are charity cases. The only reason I keep those women is because they have seniority. Any one of them could manage this office with half her brain."

"Then what kinds of work do you have available?"

"Can you program a cybernetic calculator or computer?"

"What's that?"

"Can you use binary numbers?"

"What are they?"

"Laura, do you have an education?"

"Of course I have! I went through high school and business school!"

"Well, it doesn't sound as if you are really educated. Perhaps you'd better do some checking."

So Laura returned to her old business school and told them she just learned that her training won't get her a job. She needed to learn some new skills valuable in the 1998 manpower market.

The school's admissions director looked up her records. "You know," he said, "we don't teach those subjects you took in the 1970s any more. It's good that you took typing, though. We don't give credit for typing courses any more, but we still require all our students to type their class assignments. The teachers don't have the time to figure out students' handwriting. However, I'm not sure we can admit you to the school right now."

"What do you mean I can't get back into school?" Laura asked. "I've already had 2 years. I've got a certificate here which says I graduated from this school with honors."

"Yes, but this business school today isn't the same as the old business school," the admissions director replied. "Our students are required to prove their ability to study our courses before we enroll them. They take exams in communication skills, both spoken and written; human relations; science; and computation skills. There is also an examination on general cultural knowledge. If you like, we can arrange for you to take the exams next month."

Laura was stunned. It had been many years since she took any examinations. But she needed some training to qualify for a job, so she signed up for the exam. When she got her exam grades, she was crushed. She barely passed the communication and human relations tests. Her scores were not high enough on the computation, science or general cultural background examinations. The admissions officer informed her that she would have to study at night school or by TV classroom-on-the-air to prepare to take the exams again.

"You mean I have to go back to high school or study by TV," Laura said. "Why that's silly. I'm a grown woman who has already had 14 years of formal education and training." As Laura left in a huff, she wondered how she ever got into such a mess. She decided to look up Mrs. Rosenberg, her old school counselor.

Mrs. Rosenberg was living in retirement. But when she answered Laura's ring at her door, she recognized her immediately. "Laura, it's wonderful to see you. Come in. What brings you to see me?"

"Mrs. Rosenberg, I have a real problem. I don't see how I can possibly solve it." She told Mrs. Rosenberg the trouble she'd been having. "How could anyone have such a great beginning in work and end up in such a jam?"

The old woman nodded. "Laura, I want to show you something I kept for many years and cherished." She got up and showed her a framed letter hanging on the wall:

March 10, 1979

Dear Mrs. Rosenberg: I've just gotten my third raise. I want you to know that I believe my progress comes directly from what you and the school did for me. I can never adequately repay you and the school for giving me the means to achieve success. Thank you from the bottom of my heart.

Gratefully,

Laura

"I was so happy when I received that letter, Laura. But even then I wondered how well-equipped you would be for a work career in 10 or 15 years. Everything changes so fast."

Laura's case suggests that in the future middle-aged women will have difficulties getting back into the labor force or even into school. Their present job skills, no matter how excellent, may become obsolete. Laura's situation points to the need for additional education to avoid becoming an obsolete human resource. After all, new machines and equipment are required by industry as technology advances. In the same way, the economy needs human resources with new skills and know-how. To obtain the skills needed to compete for tomorrow's jobs, *continuing education will be essential.* This education and training will require time, energy and, in some cases, money. But the result of continuing investment in personal skills and abilities will greatly increase the chances for success in the manpower market.

Lesson in Brief

Many of today's specific occupational skills will not be good enough for tomorrow's jobs. Young people entering the manpower market in the 1970s can expect to have 6 or more different jobs during their productive lifetimes. Only through continuing education and training can they prepare themselves to meet the challenge of change in the world of work.

The men and women in the nation's labor force increasingly are better educated. Today, the average worker is a high school graduate. The increase taking place in the years of schooling completed by members of the labor force will continue. Some employment experts feel that to enter the job market without at least a high school diploma is now economic suicide.

Will it take a good education to get tomorrow's jobs? The answer to this question may be found by using some of the information and analysis presented in Unit Three. The discussion of supply and demand in the manpower market pointed out that the education of workers was one of the factors affecting the supply of workers. And manpower requirements—the need for employees with certain skills—was one of the factors affecting the demand for workers. Therefore, if both the supply of and demand for workers in the manpower market is examined, it should be possible to answer the question posed at the beginning of the lesson.

In our discussion of the manpower market, we noted that the labor force was the pool or supply from which employers could draw workers. Let's look at Table 6.1 to see the amount of schooling that workers have now and are likely to have in the future. For example, the number of men and women in the civilian labor force who completed exactly 4 years of high school will increase from 36.4% during the period 1967-1969 to 42.4% in 1980, and the number of college graduates will increase from 13.7% to 16.9%. By 1980, 7 of every 10 workers will have at least a high school education.

Table 6.1 reviews the education of today's workers and the potential *supply* of manpower for 1980. Now let's turn to the *demand* for workers during the decade of the 1970s. By examining the amount of schooling that different occupational groups have today and the relative increase in demand for workers in these occupations, some insight into the relationship between education and employment opportunities can be gained (see Table 6.2).

328

Table 6.1
YEARS OF SCHOOLING COMPLETED BY CIVILIAN LABOR FORCE

Years of Schooling Completed	Average 1967-1969 (% distribution)	Projected 1980
ELEMENTARY:		
Less than 8 years	10.3%	5.8%
8 years	11.0	6.1
HIGH SCHOOL:		
1 to 3 years	17.6	16.8
4 years	36.4	42.4
COLLEGE:		
1 to 3 years	11.0	12.0
4 years or more	13.7	16.9
TOTAL Labor Force	100.0%	100.0%
SUMMARY:		
Less than 4 years of high school	38.9	28.7
4 years high school or more	61.1	71.3
TOTAL Labor Force	100.0%	100.0%

Source: U.S. Department of Labor, Bureau of Labor Statistics, *The U.S. Economy in 1980*, 1970, p. 42.
Note: In this study, data are for men and women 25 years and over.

Table 6.2 suggests that the occupations that are growing the fastest in employment opportunities are generally the same ones that require the most education. Professional and technical workers, sales workers, and clerical workers are examples. Service workers represent an exception. Job opportunities for them will rise sharply even though the average worker in that occupational group has less than a high school diploma. Managers, officials and owners are another exception—in this case having more schooling yet showing less employment growth.

Table 6.2

YEARS OF SCHOOLING AND PROJECTED EMPLOYMENT GROWTH, BY OCCUPATIONAL GROUP

Occupational Group	Average Number of Years of Schooling Completed in 1971[a]	Rank by Number of Years of Schooling Completed	Rank by Percentage Increase in Projected Employment 1970-1980
Professional & technical	16.3	1	1
Managers, officials & owners	12.8	2	6
Sales workers	12.7	3	4
Clerical workers	12.6	4	3
Craftsmen & foremen	12.2	5	5
Service workers	11.9	6	2
Operatives	11.4	7	7
Laborers	11.1	8	8
Farmers & farm workers	10.0	9	9

Source: U.S. President and U.S. Department of Labor, *Manpower Report of the President, 1972*, p. 207.

[a]Average here is the median, which is the middle number in a distribution of numbers ranging from the highest to the lowest. Half the people have more than the median number of years of schooling, and half the people have less.

Some insight into the relationship between education and employment may be gained by looking at what happens to men and women who do not have the "credentials" (a high school diploma) to match the majority of American workers. Table 6.3 shows the employment situations of school dropouts and compares them with high school graduates. The statistics show, for example, that 50.5% of high school graduates are white-collar workers, while only 23% of the high school dropouts and 10.1% of those who dropped out before they reached the eighth grade have white-collar jobs. More than half the high school dropouts are employed in blue-collar jobs.

These statistics show that over 70% of the men and women in the labor force in 1980 will be high school graduates. These are the workers that today's youth will be competing against for jobs. The relative demand for workers for tomorrow's jobs in almost every case will be greatest for those occupations where high school graduation is already the norm. To drop out of school before completing high school may seriously limit a person's employment opportunities in the future.

It is important to be cautious in interpreting the data presented in this lesson. While the educational level of the labor force will rise in the 1970s and many of the occupations that will grow the fastest are those requiring the most schooling, it does not follow that everyone should rush off to college in order to guarantee himself a good job. Being a high school graduate or having a college degree never has "guaranteed" anyone a good job. This fact has surprised many high school and college graduates during the last few years.

The U.S. Department of Labor estimates that, in the 1970s, 8 of every 10 jobs to be filled will be open to people who have not completed 4 years of college. However, Labor Department experts also note that more job training will be required of young people in the 1970s as industrial processes, technology and business procedures become more complex. Although many occupations that do not require a college degree can be learned on the job, training requirements will continue to rise during the 1970s. Young women and men with occupationally-oriented education

Table 6.3

OCCUPATIONAL EMPLOYMENT OF WORKERS
IN MARCH 1971, BY LEVEL OF SCHOOLING

Occupational Group	Less than 8 Years	High School Dropouts	High School Graduates
WHITE-COLLAR WORKERS	10.1%	23.0%	50.5%
Professional & technical	.7	1.7	6.7
Managers, officials & owners	5.2	7.6	10.8
Clerical	2.3	9.0	26.2
Sales	1.9	4.7	6.8
BLUE-COLLAR WORKERS	56.8%	52.1%	34.5%
Craftsmen & foremen	14.7	17.7	14.5
Operatives	29.8	27.6	16.3
Laborers	12.3	6.8	3.7
SERVICE WORKERS	23.2%	19.6%	12.5%
FARMERS & FARM WORKERS	10.0%	5.3%	2.6%
TOTALS, All Workers	100.0%	100.0%	100.0%

Source: *Monthly Labor Review*, November 1971, p. 34.
Note: In this study, workers were 18 years and older. Because of rounding, sums of individual items may not equal totals.

"High School Dropouts" refers to those who completed 8 years of elementary school to 3 years of high school.

beyond high school may be in a better position to compete for good jobs.

Lesson in Brief

American workers have a great deal of schooling, and the amount of education that they will have in the future will be even greater. While it may not be economic suicide to enter the manpower market without a high school diploma, it will almost certainly be a handicap.

The individual does not have an education unless he has occupational skills.

Grant Venn

Skill—the ability to use knowledge effectively—is essential to successful participation as a worker and income-earner in the economic life of American society. One of the most important facts of modern economic life is that workers cannot get tomorrow's jobs with yesterday's skills. New kinds of skills are needed in the nation's constantly changing human resources economy. These skills are developed through education, training and work experience.

Skill is the ability to use knowledge effectively. Skill is technical proficiency. Skill is knowing how to get the job done and actually being able to do it.

Manpower skills are the most valuable resource that an economy can have. As pointed out earlier in this unit, the application of scientific and technical knowledge to the production of capital goods (such as machinery, buildings, equipment) and consumer goods and services (such as cars, TV sets, medical treatment, haircuts) is a vitally important factor in the development of an economy of abundance. Men and women in their capacity as human resources—are the factors of production that apply knowledge to get the job done. This is the most important difference between advanced economies—such as the United States, Britain, the Soviet Union and Japan—and the less developed economies of Asia, Africa and Latin America. The richer countries have a more advanced technology spread throughout the economy along with a vast supply of highly skilled manpower, while the less developed countries are lacking in skilled manpower and modern technology.

Manpower skills certainly are important to the economy as a whole and a major cause of economic growth. How important are manpower skills to individual members of the economic society?

Of course, the answer is that skills are extremely important. Workers with the highest skills generally qualify for the best paying and most satisfying jobs. Workers without job skills not only get low wages but also often have trouble finding a job. In 1971, the unemployment rate for experienced professional and technical workers was 2.9%. For experienced, unskilled nonfarm laborers, the unemployment rate was 10.8%. In other words, the unemployment rate was almost 4 times as high for unskilled laborers as for the highly-skilled professional and technical workers. Lifetime earnings for college graduates are more than double the earnings of workers having only 8 years of schooling. Education, training and skills will continue to bring bigger payoffs in the human resources economy of the future.

Acquiring skills is like putting money in a bank account. The more and better the skills, the greater the degree of employability and earning power. Just as a healthy checking or savings account makes individuals and families feel more secure, a healthy *skill bank* makes a worker feel more confident and secure in terms of the role he can play in economic life. Putting skills to work involves something more. It is also necessary to learn where the opportunities exist in the manpower market and to be willing and able to adjust to the demands of employers. This may require a worker to move to a different community and perhaps even adopt a somewhat different way of life.

Let's identify some basic skills valued in the manpower market and study the characteristics of these valuable manpower skills.

Years ago, the U.S. economy was built on muscle power. Today, it is built on brainpower. There are 4 types of skills needed for today's and tomorrow's jobs:

> *Communication:* Using words—both written and oral
> *Computation:* Using numbers
> *Manual dexterity:* Using one's hands
> *Group organization:* Working effectively with other people

Let's examine each of the CCMG skills more closely.

Because the U.S. economy is becoming more and more specialized and interdependent, increasingly *communication* is relied upon to get work done. Books, pamphlets, training manuals, reports, instruction sheets, business forms—the printed page—tell people what work to do and how to do it. Instructors and on-the-job supervisors use the spoken word to explain how a job is done. For example, a teacher must be able to communicate effectively in order to teach successfully. People read newspaper ads to inform them of job opportunities. (And people also write these ads). Application forms must be filled out when applying for a job. Reports must be written, distributed and read in order to keep managers and officials informed about what is going on in their organizations.

Today, more than ever before, the American worker is required to read, write, speak and listen effectively in order to get a job and perform it successfully.

A second important skill is *computation* or calculation—being able to work with numbers quickly and accurately. A worker who can keep records, perform simple operations such as adding and multiplying, and make change accurately at the cash register has skills that are very much in demand by today's employers. Mistakes due to carelessness or inability to process numerical data can be costly for a business firm—and sometimes even cost the inept worker his job.

The third basic skill is *manual dexterity*, which is the ability to work effectively with one's hands. The ability to use tools, operate office equipment, wrap packages, assemble parts of a machine, stamp invoices and do similar jobs is extremely important in the production process. It is not enough to know how a job is done. What counts is being able to do the job. For example, the department head in a company's bookkeeping operations may know how a piece of electronic equipment is supposed to be assembled, but she may lack the manual dexterity or motor skills required to perform the work.

Finally, the fourth basic skill needed in the modern economy is *group organization* because it involves interpersonal relations and the ability to work effectively with other people. This is especially important in service-producing industries—the sector of the economy that is expanding most rapidly. Today, few people in the economy work alone as individual producers. For the most part, they work in groups. Social or human relations skills are required to work effectively with other people and to perform a job in such a way that it contributes smoothly and efficiently to the overall task at hand.

The following case studies show how the basic CCMG manpower skills apply in specific instances.

BETTY MURPHY'S SKILL BANK

Betty Murphy, who has never worked for a mail-order firm before, decides to fill out a company job application form which requires her to read the instructions and write the proper information. Afterwards, she has a personal interview in which she listens to a personnel assistant explain the job requirements and then demonstrates her own oral communication skills by answering questions and discussing her qualifications for the job. Because she can read descriptions in a catalogue, is good with numbers and can speak clearly and distinctly, she is hired as a telephone order clerk and becomes a valued employee. Eventually, she may be promoted to supervisor.

MARTHA WALKER

Martha Walker applies for work as an assembler in a local factory specializing in transistor radios and electronic equipment. She has trouble understanding what is required on part of the application form and leaves several items blank. Her handwriting is unclear, and she spells 7 words incorrectly on a single page. The company representative who interviews Martha notices her long, pointed fingernails and the button that is missing from her jacket. Martha says she does not enjoy working with people, is a slow reader, did not do very well in arithmetic in school and resents having people tell her what to do. The interviewer recommends that Martha not be hired.

The 4 kinds of manpower skills identified as being of greatest importance for tomorrow's workers—communication, computation, manual dexterity and group organization—are not exactly new. Everyone is familiar with the 3Rs—Reading, 'Riting and

'Rithmetic. And vocational education programs have always stressed "hands-on" skill training (manual dexterity). But in the future, reading and writing (communication skills) will be more important than ever. Arithmetic (computational skill) will continue to grow in importance. Some of the older manual training skills have become outdated, though others continue to be extremely valuable. Group organization and personal relations skills will gain in importance in a highly organized society.

What is important about the CCMG skills for the manpower revolution of the second half of the 20th century is that they all must be open-ended. These 4 skills are important because they are *basic, durable, transferable* (to new and different jobs), *versatile* (can be used in a wide variety of specific occupations and jobs) and *instrumental* (can be used in acquiring new and different specific job skills in the future).

Manpower experts say that the average young worker today can expect to change occupations 6 or 7 times or more during his lifetime. Young men and women who build up a basic skill bank in school and through work experience will be able to draw on those skills for the rest of their working lives. Through continuing education and training, these workers will be able to keep up with changing manpower requirements year in and year out. On the other hand, the worker who fails to build a solid base of manpower skills and acquires only a limited, narrow, specific job skill will face high risks of unemployment, insecurity, low earnings and personal dissatisfaction throughout his working life.

Lesson in Brief

In order to participate effectively in economic life, a worker must have manpower skills—the ability to use knowledge effectively on the job. Skills that are basic, durable, versatile, transferable and instrumental will prove most valuable for a worker's personal skill bank. The 4 basic manpower skills are communication, computation, manual dexterity and group organization.

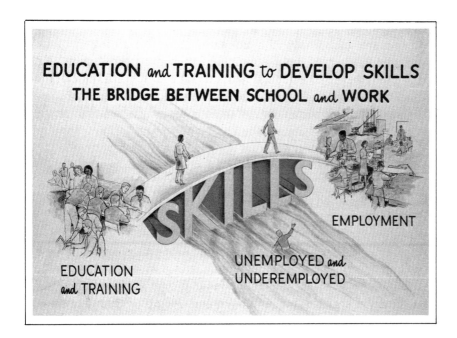

How to Get the Skills Needed for Tomorrow's Jobs

68

Most of tomorrow's jobs will require more skills and different skills than jobs required in the past. In order to acquire the needed skills, men and women can enroll in a variety of training programs available in many areas of the country. A knowledge of these educational opportunities will be valuable to young people preparing for entry into the manpower market of the 1970s and 1980s.

Before examining the educational and training programs available to provide young people with occupational skills, let's find out where experienced workers already in the labor force actually got their formal job training. Workers have acquired formal job training in many different types of schools and training programs. Table 6.4 shows the source of formal training for adult workers having such training at the time the survey was made. The table indicates, for example, that 1 of every 9 workers (11%) who received formal job training got his training in the Armed Forces. Of women workers having formal job training, 28% received their training in special schools such as business, nursing and beauty schools.

Let's begin an examination of available training programs by looking at those offered in public high schools. Most of the nation's high schools offer vocational programs for their regular day students and also for employed and unemployed out-of-school youth and adults. Training opportunities are also provided by a growing number of post-secondary vocational schools and 2-year community colleges. Ten million people are enrolled in these programs, one-third of whom are adults. Vocational education programs are designed to train both men and women for useful employment in skilled trades and industry, agriculture, home economics, office occupations, and retail trade. These vocational courses prepare students for such occupations as automobile mechanic, apprentice carpenter, farmer, practical nurse, salesman, secretary and machine operator.

Table 6.4
SOURCES OF FORMAL TRAINING PROGRAMS
TAKEN BY SELECTED WORKERS

Source of Training	Total	Men	Women
High School	38%	30%	55%
Special School (business, nursing, beauty, etc.)	19	15	28
Armed Forces	11	16	1
Apprenticeship	8	12	1
Company School	7	7	5
Correspondence Courses	6	8	2
Technical Institute	6	8	2
Junior College	5	4	6
TOTALS, All Sources	100%	100%	100%

Source: U.S. Department of Labor, Office of Manpower, Automation and Training, *Formal Occupational Training of Adult Workers*, December 1964, quoted in S. Wolfbein, *Education and Train- for Full Employment*, 1967, p. 71.

Note: Includes all workers in the civilian labor force 22-64 years of age having less than 3 years of college; data for April 1963.

Some students who are enrolled in a general or college preparatory program arrange to include individual vocational courses in their studies in order to gain occupational skills. Many high schools now include work experience or "cooperative" programs in their curriculum. These programs are usually a part of the vocational curriculum of the school and combine study in the classroom with work experience on a job. The general purpose of these work experience programs is to prepare students for useful employment while they are completing their high school education.

About 15% of the workers in the civilian labor force received their formal occupational training by attending a college or university for 3 or more years. (This group is *not* reported in Table 6.4.) There are many different types of programs in colleges and universities that provide skills—especially communication, computation and group organization—needed for employment in professional and other types of occupations. Two-year community junior colleges offer many types of programs such as computer programming, nursing, and automotive and aircraft mechanics. These institutions have expanded greatly in recent years.

Special schools and technical institutes—both public and private—offer a variety of programs for technical, office, industrial and personal-service occupations. These were the sources of training for 25% of the workers reported in Table 6.4.

In the remaining 3 types of training programs to be discussed, the worker gets his training on the job. This form of training involves learning a job by actually practicing the skills needed to perform the work. It is the oldest type of program for learning occupational skills. For centuries, craftsmen and tradesmen have been recruited and trained on the job. The men who shaped and laid stone for the pyramids in Egypt, who wove silk in northern Italy during the Renaissance, who built ships on Scotland's River Clyde in the 18th century, who set type for Benjamin Franklin in Philadelphia were selected and trained at the work place for their highly skilled work. Training and manpower experts estimate that in the past about 60% of the workers just "picked up" the skills (either on the job or off the job, without formal training) needed to do their current jobs.

Formal on-the-job training (OJT) is provided by many employers, sometimes in cooperation with the U.S. Department of Labor. Most OJT in American industry is sponsored by private business firms, but OJT training is also financed under the government's Manpower Development and Training Act (MDTA).

This act creates training programs involving a partnership between cooperating employers and the federal government. In 1971, about 90,000 workers were enrolled in OJT programs, nearly one-third of whom were women. Two-thirds of all trainees were being prepared for skilled or semiskilled blue-collar occupations.

The U.S. Department of Labor sponsors additional training programs aimed primarily at disadvantaged workers who do not have the skills needed to get today's jobs. MDTA Institutional Training programs, for example, are operated by public or private training institutions with supervision from the vocational education agencies of the state government. In recent years, enrollment in these programs has been between 50,000 and 60,000 trainees. Men received training in such occupations as automotive mechanic, baker's apprentice, printing typesetter and electrical appliance serviceman. Women—who make up 40% of trainees—were being prepared to work in such occupations as key-punch operator, psychiatric aide, receptionist and x-ray technician.

Apprenticeship programs are available for young men and women to learn the skills they need for such specific occupations as bookbinder, dental technician, plumber, carpenter, and tool and die maker. What are *apprenticeship* programs? They are formalized on-the-job training for learning skilled crafts, usually sponsored by labor unions, employers, and federal, state and local governments. Approximately 350 different skilled trades can be learned through apprenticeships. Most of these trades are in the construction, printing and metalworking industries. Of the 270,000 apprentices registered in 1970, half were in the building trades (carpenters, electricians, plumbers, etc.).

The training of an apprentice involves learning a wide range of skills on the job over a period of 2 years or more, training under a written agreement with an employer and usually a labor union, and going to job-related classes at a school. Requirements for apprenticeship training vary among states and occupations. The basic qualification for this type of training is that the apprentice be capable of learning the skills necessary to become a *journeyman* (fully qualified craftsman) at the end of his training period.

The programs described above reflect a growing need for

343

workers with new and better skills. These skills are necessary to perform the jobs being created by the process of technological change and economic growth.

Lesson in Brief

There are many different educational and training programs available to provide the skill training needed for tomorrow's jobs. Vocational education programs, some of which involve actual work experience, are available in many high schools. Colleges, universities and junior colleges as well as public and private technical, business and trade schools offer many different programs for learning work-related skills. On-the-job training is provided by many employers. Federal and state governments sponsor MDTA training programs. Apprenticeship programs are also available to learn skilled trades. Whatever the chosen occupation, there usually will be a variety of education and training programs for obtaining the skills needed to qualify for employment.

Education: An Investment in Human Resources

69

One of the most important economic discoveries of the 1960s was that education and other forms of investment in human resources provide vast benefits to individual workers and to the economy as a whole. Research studies have shown that manpower can be made more productive by investing in a worker's knowledge and skills—sometimes called his "human capital"—in the same way that the economy gains from investments in nonhuman capital such as machines, buildings and equipment. Knowledge about investment in human resources will be valuable in planning a career and making personal and social decisions.

Human resources, the subject for this lesson, is one of the newest and most exciting fields of economic research. The study of human resources puts man and manpower at the very center of the new theory of production and economic growth. In this sense it can be said that, in economic theory, man is replacing the machine—in contrast to what many writers on automation and cybernation have said about the machine replacing man on the production line!

Writing in the late 1700s, Adam Smith, the father of economic science, whose ideas were discussed in Unit Two, pointed out that the division of labor helped increase productivity by improving manpower efficiency and also by making it possible to develop specialized machines. Smith and other economists after him created a theory of economic growth that placed much emphasis on investment to increase the supply of capital equipment. For nearly 200 years—until the 1960s—most economists believed that investment in *nonhuman capital* (such as machines, factory buildings, railroads) was the best way for business to make profits and also promote economic growth (higher GNP, year after year) for the nation. In order to understand the new theories of investment in human resources, it is helpful to study the older theories of investment in nonhuman resources.

Let's begin with the term investment itself. An earlier lesson in this book defines investment—one of the 4 components of gross national product—as "spending by business firms to buy new equipment and buildings." Actually, *investment* is the use of resources (manpower, natural resources and previously-produced capital goods) to make capital goods that, in turn, can be used in further production. The amount of investment that takes place is measured by counting the dollars spent to purchase newly-produced capital goods.

There are 2 very important economic results of investment—money is spent to pay for the production of new capital goods, and the quantity of capital goods in existence increases. Investors (individuals, business firms or government agencies) are willing to spend money to obtain capital goods because they expect to get some form of return on their investment. (This return is sometimes called a "payoff.") Suppose a corporation invests $100,000 in a new machine that will produce $30,000 worth of goods annually for 10 years (total value: $300,000). Then the machine is worn out and has to be junked. The average cost of the machine is $10,000 per year. Average return or payoff (above the cost of the machine) is $20,000 per year. This is a 20% annual rate of return on the original investment (Note: $20,000 is 20% of the original investment of $100,000.) Some corporations get returns on investment as high as 30% a year. The average rate of return on investment for all business firms, however, is closer to 10% per year.

Now let's apply the concepts of investment, capital and rates of return to human resources. First of all, note the similarity between investment in nonhuman capital and investment in *human capital*. Money is spent to employ manpower, materials and machines needed to produce buildings and new equipment. This is an investment. When money is received from the sale of the goods and services made with the new capital goods, this is a return on investment. In the case of education—which is an important form of human capital—it takes manpower (teachers), natural resources (land, fuel, electricity) and capital goods (school buildings, books, pencils, paper) to produce educational services. Money is spent—mostly by governmental units in the case of public education—to employ the inputs that are used to "produce" educated men and women. This is an investment in human resources. When these men and women enter the work force and begin using the human capital they have acquired to help produce goods and services, there is a return on the investment that was made in their education. This return comes in the form of personal earnings and also shows up in the increased production of the economy.

What is the payoff from education in terms of increased output for the *economy as a whole?* According to economist Edward F. Denison, improvements in the quality of the labor force contributed 23% of the total growth of national production during the period 1929-1957. This sizable contribution was the direct result of workers' having more years of schooling than members of the labor force had before this period. Denison projected that education would contribute almost the same proportion of economic growth during the period 1960-1980.[5]

What is the payoff from education in terms of increased earnings for the *individual worker?* Male workers who complete from 1 to 3 years of high school can, on the average, expect to earn $95,000 more during their lifetimes than men who complete less than 8 years of schooling. Male high school graduates will earn about $57,000 more than men who drop out before graduating. Male workers who complete 5 years or more of college (the equivalent of a master's degree or more) earn approximately 70% more income than male high school graduates who do not go on to college. (See Table 6.5 in the next lesson.)

From the viewpoint of the economy as a whole, which is a better investment—using resources to produce more nonhuman capital or investing in human resources? Of course, this is not a simple question of either-or. The economy must invest in both kinds of resources, human and nonhuman. The important question is, How can the economy balance investment appropriately between nonhuman capital and human capital?

There are many factors to consider before arriving at an answer. Investments in human resources will affect the man or

---

5. *Sources of Economic Growth in the United States,* pp. 73-74.

woman not only as a worker but also as a citizen, a consumer and a human being. And there are differences in who gets the payoff from investments in machines and investments in people. A corporation can own a machine and keep all the money that it earns (after taxes). But a corporation cannot own a worker and, therefore, may not be able to capture the total returns from investing in the education and training of its employees. However, putting aside these complications for now, let's consider some economic facts that might be helpful in maintaining a wise balance between investment in nonhuman capital and investment in human capital.

Economists who have studied investment in schooling in the United States estimate that the rates of return for the eighth year of school are about 30%—approximately 3 times as high as average returns on nonhuman capital. Rates of return on the fourth year of high school (leading to a diploma) are estimated to be about 15%. And rates of return on investments in the fourth year of college also are 15%.[6] These rates of return, based on estimates as measured by earnings, suggest that in the future it might be wise to place more emphasis on investment in human resources than in machinery and equipment—exactly what many economists and manpower experts are recommending today. A word of caution— the estimates reported are still being checked and are subject to change. Nevertheless, the tentative judgment clearly is that investment in human capital is a wise use of economic resources promising big payoffs, both for the individual and for the economy as a whole.

Another point to consider is that investments have to be financed. Somebody must pay for resources that are used. For certain reasons, it may be harder to finance investments in human capital than investments in nonhuman capital. The family next door might prefer to invest $500 in new shares of Tenpenny Nail Company stocks—helping the company to raise money needed for building a new plant—rather than vote to raise school taxes by

---

6. Jon T. Innes et al., *The Economic Returns to Education*, pp. 25-30.

$50 per year for the next 10 years in order to expand the school's career education program.

In 1972 Christopher Jencks, a Harvard University professor, questioned some widely-held beliefs concerning the importance of educational attainment as an explanation of differences that exist in the level of incomes among Americans. In his book *Inequality: A Reassessment of the Effect of Family and Schooling in America*, Jencks maintains that education contributes much less to a person's economic success in adulthood than other factors such as personality, on-the-job competence and luck.

The contention seems to be that educational attainment is not nearly as important as some people had thought for explaining differences in income distribution. This challenges the conventional belief of many manpower specialists, economists and educators. Professor James S. Coleman has questioned Jencks's conclusion, arguing that every research project done on the determination of income shows that the level of educational attainment is the most powerful factor determining income.

We believe that education is an important factor in determining income and that the individual's and society's investment in education and training produces results which can improve personal economic and social well-being as well as benefit society. Obviously, educational attainment is not the sole factor determining income levels. Perhaps it is not even the most important one. Questions of economic and social determination are difficult for social scientists to deal with. But education is one factor over which *the individual has some control* that can influence his or her chances of economic success. More and better education and training—especially if it is appropriate not only in terms of today's jobs but also tomorrow's occupational opportunities—will increase the chances of achieving a higher income and more satisfying career. For millions of boys and girls growing up in the United States, education is the most likely escape route from poverty and dependency.

Lesson in Brief

During the 1960s economists began to pay increased attention to the economic value of investing in human resources. Early research findings indicated that nearly one-fourth of U.S. national economic growth was the direct result of improved education of the work force. Statistics also show that workers with more human capital—more education, knowledge, skills and other productive abilities—receive higher earnings than workers having less education. Rates of return on investment in human resources (as indicated by years of schooling) are estimated to be higher than average rates of return on many investments in nonhuman capital such as machinery and equipment. Recently, a dispute has arisen about the importance of educational attainment in determining income distribution.

350

Let ignorance talk as it will, learning has its value.

Jean de La Fontaine

One of the rewards for successful participation in the manpower market is the pay that a worker receives. How much money a worker earns depends on many factors including the amount of schooling he has completed. The cash value of completing high school compared with being a dropout amounts to more than $50,000 in the lifetime of the average male worker.

In previous lessons, the 4 functions of work were listed:

1. To help produce goods and services
2. To earn the dollars needed to buy goods and services and maintain a standard of living
3. To satisfy certain personal and social needs that workers have as human beings
4. To develop and conserve a worker's skills and fulfill his human potential

In this lesson, we will focus on function number 2—the economic rewards that workers receive—and see how investments in education affect cash earnings.

We have already noted that wages and earnings vary greatly for different categories of workers. In 1972, the average production worker in manufacturing made $3.80 an hour and worked a 40-hour week. If this "average worker" were able to work full time for the entire year, his annual earnings would amount to $7,904 ($3.80 x 40 hours per week x 52 weeks). Actually, many manufacturing employees do not have the opportunity to work full time for the entire year. During some weeks their hours of paid employment are reduced, and at other times they are laid off the job entirely.

Many construction workers earn over $200 a week when they are working. So do school teachers. Physicians often make between $500 and $1,000 per week. Unskilled laborers seldom earn as much as $100 a week.

There are many factors that influence the pay that a worker receives for his labor. Basically, wages are determined by the operation of supply and demand forces in the manpower market. Sometimes wages are set by collective bargaining agreements that employers and labor unions make. And minimum levels of wages are established for some classes of workers by the federal government or state government. A *minimum wage* of $1.60 per hour, for example, means that it is against the law for an employer to hire a worker and pay him less than $1.60 an hour. Of course, the employer can always pay more. But if he paid less than $1.60 he would be breaking the law and could be punished—even if the worker were willing to accept less. The federal minimum wage was increased from $1.40 to $1.60 an hour in 1968 and further increases have been proposed. Many workers, however, are not covered by this law. State governments may also set minimum wages. In 1972 the District of Columbia approved a minimum wage of $2.46 an hour, effective in 1973.

So much for institutional factors and the general forces of supply and demand. Now let's examine the specific connection between education and earnings.

Table 6.5 shows the estimated lifetime earnings for men according to the number of years of schooling they completed. These are averages and will not, of course, be accurate for every male worker. Moreover, the figures will probably be revised upward as the years go by. The data indicate that a worker who completes 4 years of high school can expect to earn about $341,000 in his lifetime. This is $57,000 more than school dropouts are expected to earn. Note that a worker with less than 8 years of schooling earns only 55% as much income as a high school graduate, while a college graduate will earn 49% more than a high school graduate.

The statistics in Table 6.5 show that higher earnings are associated with more years of schooling. Of course, there are many exceptions to this rule. Everyone has heard of the self-made man who dropped out of school at the age of 16 and then went on to become head of his own business firm, earning $200,000 a year! On the average, though, it appears that a person's chances of earning a higher income are much better if he has more education.

Is this because more schooling always makes people more productive? Not necessarily! The truth of the matter is that educational attainment is often used as a convenient method of discriminating in favor of certain people for jobs, training opportunities, promotions, etc. Employers give preference to high school graduates over dropouts in hiring. Labor unions sometimes require a high school diploma to qualify for apprenticeship training.

Table 6.5
ESTIMATED LIFETIME EARNINGS, FOR MALES,
BY YEARS OF SCHOOLING COMPLETED

Years of Schooling Completed	Lifetime Earnings	Difference In Lifetime Earnings[a]	Earnings as % of H. S. Graduates
Less than 8 years	$189,000	—	55%
8 years	247,000	+$56,000	72
1 to 3 years of high school	284,000	+ 37,000	83
4 years of high school	341,000	+ 57,000	100
1 to 3 years of college	394,000	+ 53,000	115
4 years of college	508,000	+114,000	149
5 or more years of college	587,000	+ 79,000	172

Source: U.S. Bureau of the Census, *Current Population Reports,* Series P-60, No. 56, p. 9.
Note: Subjects range from 18 years to death; estimates are based on 1966 dollars.
[a]Compared with group listed immediately preceding.

Let's assume, however, that individuals with more education actually are more productive. Can one be absolutely sure that it was the additional years of schooling that made these persons more productive? Or is it possible that people of higher intelligence tend both to obtain more education and be more productive? If these 2 tendencies go together—and it is almost certain that they do—then the amount of credit to give each factor in explaining higher earnings really cannot be determined.

There are many other influences on earnings, too, such as family income and the educational attainment and occupations of parents. But even after looking at all of these factors, it remains true that people with more schooling, on the average, consistently have higher incomes. Why?

According to the theory of human capital, the investment of resources (manpower, capital and natural resources) to educate a future worker has the effect of increasing that worker's productive capacity. The process of education increases a worker's knowledge and skills—his ability to communicate, compute, work with his hands and cooperate in group activity. These are forms of "productive intelligence" that are highly valued in today's manpower market.

Table 6.6
AVERAGE WEEKLY, MONTHLY AND YEARLY
EARNINGS, FOR MALES, BY LEVEL OF SCHOOLING

	8 Years of Schooling	High School Graduates	College Graduates
Total lifetime earnings	$247,000	$341,000	$508,000
Average yearly earnings	5,040	6,960	10,370
Average monthly earnings	420	580	805
Average weekly earnings	100	135	205

Source: Computed from data in Table 6.5.

Now let's look at Table 6.6. We have made simple calculations to show how much would be earned weekly, monthly and yearly by a man with only 8 years of schooling, a high school graduate and a college graduate. Looking at earnings in this way makes it easier to think about the things that a high school graduate, for example, could buy with the extra income he earned as compared with a worker having only 8 years of schooling.

Statistics on the estimated lifetime earnings of women workers are shown in Table 6.7. Women who work full time, year-round on the average will earn about $184,000 from age 25 to death if they have completed 8 years of schooling. This is $65,000 less than women workers with 4 years of high school are expected to earn.

Table 6.7
ESTIMATED LIFETIME EARNINGS, FOR FEMALES,
BY YEARS OF SCHOOLING COMPLETED

Years of Schooling Completed	Lifetime Earnings	Difference In Lifetime Earnings	Earnings as % of H. S. Graduates
Less than 8 years	$167,000	—	67%
8 years	184,000	+$17,000	74
1 to 3 years of high school	213,000	+ 29,000	85
4 years of high school	249,000	+ 36,000	100
1 to 3 years of college	312,000	+ 63,000	125
4 years of college	326,000	+ 14,000	131
5 or more years of college	436,000	+110,000	175

Source: U. S. Bureau of Census as quoted in Herman P. Miller, *Rich Man, Poor Man*, 1971, p. 178.
Note: Lifetime earnings calculated from age 25 to death for year-round, full-time women workers. Estimates are based on 1966 dollars.

There are 3 things to keep in mind about these statistics on expected lifetime earnings:

1. They do show that, in general, more education leads to higher earnings.
2. They do not predict what any particular individual will earn in his lifetime (they only indicate what the chances are of earning a certain amount).
3. The figures are subject to modification as the economy grows and changes over time.

As an illustration of this third point, estimates of lifetime earnings for male Negro college graduates made in 1960 probably will turn out to be incorrect in the long run. The Census Bureau reported that expected lifetime earnings of male, nonwhite college graduates amounted to $185,000 compared to $395,000 for white college graduates and compared to $191,000 for white males who completed only 8 years of schooling. However, incomes of Negroes have been rising relative to incomes of whites recently. In 1970, median family income of Negroes was 61% of the median family income of whites, an increase of 7 percentage points from the 1964 figure of 54%. Annual earnings by Negro men in 1969 ranged from 64% to 76% as much as whites having comparable education. In 1968, median income for a white male with an eighth grade education was $5,184, which is considerably below the median of $7,511 for a nonwhite male with 1 or more years of college.

Much of the data presented on lifetime earnings is concerned with high school and college education. There is a shortage of information about other types of education and training and differences in the quality of schooling. Economists have only begun to study the payoff from education. Much research remains to be done. There have been some studies done on the short-run payoffs of vocational and technical education. One study found that graduates of high school vocational education programs earned $3,456 more in their first 6 years of work than did academic high school graduates who did not go to college. Another study showed that a year after completion of a post-high school technical course in North Carolina graduates were earning $553 a year more than their high school classmates. Generalizations about the economic value of vocational education, however, are difficult to make. In *Work in America*, a controversial government report published in 1973, serious doubts are expressed about the utility of vocational education programs.

Education provides many benefits to individuals and to the whole society. It can help free man from ignorance, strengthen democracy and make the economy more productive. Education provides a cash payoff to the individual worker who invests in his own human capital by getting more schooling and training. This is an important lesson for young people to learn, especially those who are growing up in low-income homes. Education can increase the chance of getting a better job and provide a possible escape from poverty and deprivation.

Lesson in Brief

Workers who are successful in the manpower market get both economic and noneconomic rewards. The economic or financial rewards depend on the supply and demand for workers with particular qualifications and on institutional factors in the manpower market. Statistics show that workers with more schooling on the average get better-paying jobs and have higher earnings than workers with less schooling. One reason is that education is an investment in human resources that often increases a worker's knowledge, skills and productivity. Education offers a possible way out of poverty, deprivation and dependency for young people growing up in low-income families.

> Economic growth, one of the most important goals of the American people, is caused by increases in the quantity of productive resources, by technological progress and by greater efficiency in production. Recent research shows that new technology and increased education of the labor force stand out as major sources of American economic growth.

The following 6 economic goals that most Americans would rank high on a list of national priorities were discussed in Unit Two:

1. Full production—full employment and efficient use of manpower and other available resources
2. Stable growth—steady increases in gross national product per person each year without inflation
3. Freedom of choice—for workers, consumers and business enterprises—with reasonable equality of opportunity
4. Economic security—to assure freedom from want for every American
5. Distributive justice—a fair and reasonable division of income among families and between workers and property owners
6. International balance—having harmonious economic relationships with other nations of the world

The first 2 goals focus specifically on the *overall level* of output and income. American people want to produce as much as they can in any particular year (full production). And they want to increase their ability to produce more goods and services year after year (economic growth, as reflected in a higher gross national product each year). These 2 goals are especially important because, as history shows, the nation does a better job of pursuing all other goals when the economy is operating at high levels.

How well has the U.S. economy been performing with respect to the goals of full production and growth? Between 1966 and 1969 the economy operated very close to full production. On the average, more than 96% of the labor force was employed. Manufacturing capacity was expanding rapidly, and the utilization rate was reasonably high. From 1965 to 1969, real GNP increased at an average rate of 4½% a year.

Then came the recession of 1970. GNP fell by $5 billion. The unemployment rate jumped to 5.4%. The utilization rate of manufacturing capacity dropped under 80%. While 1971 and 1972 registered increases in GNP, the economy continued to operate below full production.

Interesting things were happening in the economy, however, besides failure to achieve high employment and full production. Inflation was causing all sorts of problems. Between 1967 and 1972, the consumer price index rose by 25% and the purchasing power of the dollar fell to 80¢. In August 1971, wages and prices were frozen in an effort to halt the inflation and policies were followed that worsened the unemployment problem.

Despite the ups and downs, growth has occurred over the long run. Between 1909 and 1957, total GNP quadrupled and real GNP per person doubled. Since 1950, real GNP (expressed in constant 1958 prices) has more than doubled while real GNP per person increased from $2,300 to nearly $4,000. Median family income, after adjusting for inflation, rose from a little over $5,000 in 1950 to about $10,000 in 1971. Why has there been a rising trend of production and income over the years?

In Unit Two we pointed out that the productive capacity of the economy is limited by the quantity and quality of available resources and by the level of technology. Economic growth is possible only when 1 or more of the following changes takes place:

1. Increases in the *quantity* of productive resources (manpower, capital, natural resources)
2. Improvements in the *quality* of resources (such as new and better machinery and workers who have more education and training)

3. Advances in *technology* (including automation and cybernation)
4. Greater *efficiency* (better management, economies of large-scale production and marketing)
5. Higher levels of resource *use* (by reducing unemployment and increasing the utilization rate of capital plant and equipment)

Every economic change that increases the nation's ability to produce goods and services can be set within this framework. For example, if a million and a half workers were added to the civilian labor force each year, the total productive capability would increase. When business firms invest an additional $60 billion in new plants and equipment, the productive capacity of the American economy goes up. In similar fashion, the economy also grows when the quality of resources improves, when technological progress is made, and when business management and workers find more efficient methods of production.

Economists have estimated that the potential ability to produce goods and services in the American economy is increasing at an annual rate of about 4% each year because of all the additions and improvements in resources and methods of production. So long as jobs are provided for manpower and productive uses for capital goods and natural resources, the growth of the *actual* GNP can keep up with the growth of the *potential* GNP. In 1966, 1967 and 1968, this is exactly what happened in the U.S. economy.

And now comes the big question: What specific factors have caused the growth of the U.S. economy? What are the "engines" of economic growth that provide the thrust and the drive for the ever-increasing GNP?

Before the 1960s economists used to assume that most of the growth was caused by investment in tangible capital goods along with certain improvements in production methods. Now, however, economists are finding that growth depends to a very great extent on technological advance and improvements in the quality of human resources.

Earlier we mentioned Edward Denison's research finding—that increased education of the labor force contributed 23% of the growth in national production between 1929 and 1957. Why? Because more schooling had the effect of improving the quality of human resources, raising the *productivity* of workers—enabling them to produce more goods and services for every hour worked.

The study concluded that increases in nonhuman tangible capital goods, such as buildings and machinery, contributed only 15% of the growth in output. Improvement in the *quality* of manpower was given 1 1/2 times as much credit (23%) for expanding national production as increases in the quantity of physical capital. When it came to changes in the *quantity* of manpower, more than 30% of total growth was explained by the enlarged labor force that resulted mainly from population growth. Technology and other factors, such as economies of large-scale production and marketing, accounted for the remaining growth.

Note that education *directly* contributed 23% of the nation's economic growth. Education also makes *indirect* contributions to growth by advancing knowledge and making improvements in the organization and methods of production. Other research studies have all reached similar conclusions:

- Education has directly contributed approximately one-fourth of the growth that the American economy has made in recent years.
- Education contributes indirectly to economic growth by increasing knowledge which can be applied to production.
- The returns from educational expenditures (investment in human resources) are equal to or greater than returns from other investments in the American economy.

Because education helps to improve the quality of the nation's human resources, it is an important source of economic growth.

All of these findings suggest that using time, effort and other resources in education may be a wise economic investment. This does not imply that the only purpose of education is economic. Education may very well provide *noneconomic* benefits that are more important than the extra production and extra income that result from higher-quality human resources. Education may help men and women become better citizens, happier and more fully developed as strong, sensitive and creative people. To the extent that education also helps men and women become more productive in their capacity as human resources, this may be viewed as an important bonus of the educational process.

Lesson in Brief

Because education helps to improve the quality of the nation's human resources, it is an important source of economic growth. Education also contributes indirectly to growth by helping expand knowledge which can be used in production. Finally, increased education provides certain noneconomic benefits, such as helping develop better-informed citizens.

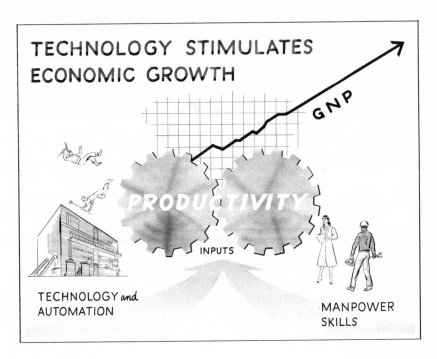

An affluent democratic society can grow [in strength] if it has the wisdom and the courage to invest in the development of its people.

Eli Ginzberg

Education is an investment in human resources that yields benefits to individuals and to society as a whole. But there is no such thing as a free lunch. Educational investments involve costs. Public and private schools and colleges spent $86 billion in the 1971-72 school year, 8% of the GNP.

In earlier lessons, the benefits of education from the viewpoint of individuals and society as a whole were discussed. Some of these benefits are economic in nature while others relate to personal fulfillment and the quality of life.

Some of the most important benefits that result from education are these:

1. Investments in education can add to a worker's skills or human capital, increasing his employability, productivity and earning power.

2. Workers with more schooling generally have higher earnings. Studies have shown that expected lifetime earnings of male high school graduates are more than $50,000 higher than earnings of dropouts. Earnings of college graduates are $167,000 more than lifetime earnings of high school graduates.

3. Rates of return on investments in the education of human resources frequently are higher than rates of return on investment in nonhuman capital such as machinery, buildings and equipment. Rates of return on the eighth year of schooling have been estimated at about 30%; returns on the fourth year of high school at 15%; and returns on the fourth year of college at 15%. Rates of return on investments in nonhuman capital are often below 10%.

4. Increased education of the work force contributed about one-fourth of the total growth in real national production between 1929 and 1957.
5. The so-called noneconomic benefits of education—including personal fulfillment, wisdom and understanding, better citizenship, and improvements in the quality of life—may be more important than the extra output and income that result from increased productive capacity of human resources.

These returns on investments in education are not, of course, a windfall or free gift from nature. There is no such thing as a free lunch. Output—in this case, the increased knowledge and skill resulting from educational investments—can come about only in response to the use of resources in some productive way. Costs are involved. These costs can be measured in terms of the manpower (3 million teachers and administrators plus other employees and school board members) and the nonhuman resources (land, buildings, equipment) that could have been used in the production of other goods and services. Or the costs may be measured in dollars. During the 1971-72 school year, the nation's public and private schools and colleges spent an estimated $86 billion (8% of GNP) to provide educational services to some 60 million students. Additional billions of dollars were spent by private industry, labor unions, the Armed Forces and students themselves for education and training outside the schools.

Table 6.8 shows how much money was spent by local, state and federal government and by other sources to support the nation's schools from kindergarten through the university level. A total of $55 billion was spent for the schooling of 52 million elementary and secondary school students, a little over $1,000 for each student. Nearly $32 billion was spent for 8 million students ($4,000 per student) enrolled in colleges and universities. Since most college-age students normally would be active in the nation's labor force, the real cost of higher education probably comes closer to $8,000 per student per year counting the opportunity cost of each student's foregone earnings. Between 1960 and 1972, total school expenditures more than tripled, from $25 billion to $86 billion and from 5% to 8% of the expanding GNP.

Table 6.8
SCHOOL EXPENDITURES IN 1972
(billions of dollars)

Source	Total Spending All Levels of Schooling	Spending for Elementary and Secondary Schools	Spending for Higher Education
Local[a]	$28	$27	$ 1
State	26	18	8
Federal	10	4	5
All Other[b]	23	6	17
TOTALS, All Sources	$86 bil.	$55 bil.	$31 bil.

Source: *Statistical Abstract of the United States 1972,* p. 106, and *Saturday Review*, December 18, 1971, p. 68.

Note: Totals may not add up because of rounding. Estimates are for 1971-72 school year, ending June 30, 1972.

[a]Includes nearly 18,000 school districts.

[b]Schools supported by religious organizations, private persons, etc.

Where do the various units of government obtain the money for school expenditures? Mostly, the money comes from property *taxes*, sales taxes and income taxes.

More than 90% of *local* school revenues comes from the *property tax.* This is a tax levied on the dollar value of real estate—such as land, homes and industrial buildings—and to a much smaller extent on such "personal property" as automobiles, machinery and equipment, and business inventories. In 1970 (when school expenditures totalled "only" $71 billion) local governments collected $34 billion in property taxes. *State* governments obtain most of their tax revenues from *income taxes* on individuals and corporations and from *sales taxes*. More than 80% of the $48 billion collected in 1970 came from these sources. The *federal* government, which is the smallest spender for education among the 3 levels of government, gets more than 80% of its revenue from individual and corporate *income taxes*.

The real estate property tax plays such an important role in financing local schools that many people simply refer to property taxes as *school taxes*. Most homeowners pay hundreds of dollars a year in property taxes. In the early 1970s serious questions were raised about the fairness of this tax, from the viewpoint of both local taxpayers and students. In a famous California court case, *Serrano* v. *Priest* (1971), questions were also raised about the legality of linking the quality of a child's education to the amount of wealth that his parents and neighbors have. Proposals have been made to reduce the inequalities in school expenditures and educational opportunity by having the state and federal government pay a much larger share of the costs of operating the nation's schools.

What are some of the implications of these facts about benefits and costs of education? As individuals, members of a local community and citizens of a large and powerful nation, how can people use the knowledge that they have gained concerning the economics of education?

Because knowledge tells people about the consequences of certain actions, they are able to make more intelligent plans and decisions—such as the amount of schooling to complete. Knowing the results of actions helps citizens make wiser judgments about how to use resources to achieve economic and noneconomic goals. Research discoveries in the 1960s suggest that the nation can achieve the goal of increased national production by investing in the education of workers. Individual workers can improve their chances of achieving personal goals of increased earnings and economic security by accumulating more human capital. Unemployment and poverty can be reduced by improving the education of the work force.

In addition, education can bring satisfaction and pleasure to a person as well as increase his productivity and earnings. Education can open up new areas of human development such as the ability to appreciate good music, paintings, literature and poetry, and engage in philosophical or spiritual reflection. These are consumer-type and humanistic benefits. In other words education not only can improve the economy's ability to produce but also can help people make wiser decisions about what to consume and how to consume, including the "consumption" of leisure time.

Beyond these individual benefits, there are also benefits that spill over from educated individuals to improve the well-being of other members of society. These are called *social benefits*. One example is the direct contribution that education makes to increased national production. Another is the indirect contribution that education makes to the advancement of knowledge. There are also social benefits that lie outside the usual boundary lines of economics. For example, citizens who can read and write and understand economic and social issues are able to vote more intelligently in local, state and federal government elections. An educated population is a basic requirement for political democracy. Moreover, parents with more education are able to give their children certain cultural advantages in their family life.

We must put up a warning flag. Education alone is not the solution to all of the world's problems or to all of the problems that individual men and women will face. It is not the golden key to economic success or to personal happiness and fulfillment. But education is too important to ignore as many economists did until the 1960s. Education is also too important to dismiss as having only limited influence on economic and social success in American life.

Lesson in Brief

Investments in education can increase a worker's productivity and earnings and also contribute to the growth of national output.

There are always costs involved in the educational process. During the 1971-72 school year, the nation's schools and colleges spent $86 billion to provide educational services to 60 million students. Most of this money comes from taxes, including the real estate property tax which has been called an unfair and unconstitutional way to finance local schools. While it would be a mistake to consider education as the solution to all of the world's problems, schooling does provide many economic and other types of benefits to individuals and to society.

Postscript

In these final pages, we would like to share with readers some additional thoughts about the changing world of work and prospects for achieving personal satisfaction and human fulfillment.

Careful study of the 6 units in this book—on Work, the American Economy, the Manpower Market, Career Opportunities, Decisionmaking and Knowledge—hopefully will be useful to young people preparing for full participation in American economic life. We have tried to provide a road map into the future—identifying opportunities, obstacles, alternative routes, economic and personal rewards. The next "chapter" and the ones following will of course be written in real life by individual readers interacting with their constantly changing socioeconomic environment. The physical capabilities, understanding, skills, values, determination and self-discipline that each man and woman actively invests in personal career development will have a major impact on the quality of employment and quality of life that he or she will experience.

Unless one is a technological-economic determinist (whether pessimistically or optimistically so), the future can be anticipated not in terms of Utopia or Despair but on the basis of how well the individual can cope with day-to-day opportunities and challenges inherent in modern life *and* what influence he can exert to help shape the environment in which he works and lives.

Recalling the 3 economic roles that individuals play—consumer, worker and citizen—it is well to consider that men and women are not simply means of production. Nor are they merely insatiable consumers, compulsively vacuuming up an expanding abundance of whatever goods and services the economic system happens to spew out. Each American can be a *whole person*, sensitive and capable of feeling, thinking, valuing and acting. Together, the American people can change and improve the world in which they live. As John Gardner so fervently argues, self-renewal *is* possible, both for individuals and for whole societies. Consider, for example, the implications of the following

369

ideas and attitudes in terms of improving the *quality of employ-ment* for workers in the United States:

Traditionally, manpower problems have been defined and measured mainly in the *economic* terms of employment, unemployment and income. The gradual refinement of these economic measures has sharpened the objectives of policy and program planning. Still largely absent in the evaluation of manpower problems, however, is an adequate assessment of the many *other dimensions* of work and employment that affect worker wellbeing.

This broad, more qualitative orientation requires attention not only to how well the economic system absorbs individuals into employment and meets their financial needs, but also to *the adequacy with which it satisfies quite different kinds of needs— physical, psychological and social.* These dimensions of employ-ment are not easily defined or measured, but they are essential to a full understanding of the conditions of work and how satisfactory these are to workers.

[In defining] "the quality of employment," some essential features of the concept may be noted:

(A)   It is concerned primarily with the extent to which employment satisfies the *needs of the individual*, rather than those of the employer and the economy generally. This is not to say that conflict between these different interests is inevitable; obviously there are many points of convergence. But the furtherance of worker interests and worker satisfactions stands as a legitimate social goal in its own right.

(B)   It requires that work and employment be viewed and evaluated in the *total scheme of life*, rather than in the isolation of the work environment. An individual's experiences as a worker obviously have varied and complex interrelationships with his roles as *family member, social participant* and *political decision-maker*. And the available data suggest that, while generally positive, the impact of employment experience on nonwork life can, under some circumstances, have pronounced negative effects. Thus, *the quality of employment has a major effect on the quality of American life in general.*

(C)   [The concept of the quality of employment] has two major dimensions which, although interdependent, require sep-arate consideration.

1.   The first [dimension] relates to the *deleterious effects of work experience*. The ways in which various forms

and conditions of work adversely affect the physical health of employees have long been recognized. Statistics on the incidence of occupational injuries and illnesses testify to this negative aspect of employment. But even here, the data are incomplete. Far greater attention must be given to the ways in which employment contributes to *mental,* as well as *physical,* ill health.

2. The second dimension is the extent to which the quality of employment is, and can increasingly become, a truly *positive and developmental experience.* The goals and functions of employment should go beyond the avoidance of poverty, insecurity and illness and purposively and progressively advance worker wellbeing—in keeping with the continuously rising aspirations and expectations throughout our society.[1]

In the first lesson of this book, we presented 3 alternative sketches of what the world of work might be like in the future. We personally believe that the future of work in the coming decades will resemble the more humanized system of Sketch # 3. But the pattern that evolves will not simply be a matter or chance or fate. Women and men are agents of change. Their values and actions will influence the actual shape of the future. President John F. Kennedy observed more than a decade ago: "Economic decisions are man-made decisions. We are to a considerable degree masters of our own economic destiny."[2]

If the American people desire to contribute to improving the quality of their lives, in part by making the quality of employment better, we believe they have the power to do so. But do they have the *will* and know a *way* to bring about the necessary institutional renewal?

An encouraging development in U.S. society is the nation's current involvement with career education in the schools. If career

---

1. From *1968 Manpower Report of the President,* page 47, with minor editorial changes and italics added.
2. John R. Coleman and Kenneth O. Alexander, *Study Guide for the American Economy* (College of the Air Television Production). New York: McGraw-Hill, 1962, p. xvii.

education is to be more than a glittering label—if, for example, it can become a serious and sharply-focussed effort to increase the understanding and competence of young people with respect to the role of human resources in the U.S. economy—then we can be more optimistic about the future of work in America.

In order to *do* something, one has to *know* something. Manpower understanding and manpower development can help individuals achieve success and satisfaction in the world of work. But equally important, they can qualify young men and women to become agents of change and help bring about not just a healthier economy but a better society.

* * *

During the past 10 years we have been personally and professionally involved with students, educators and the community in developing world-of-work economic education programs. Out of this experience has come positive reinforcement of our conviction that man—the whole man—is indeed the heart of manpower and economic education and should be the focus of career education. We sincerely hope the ideas explored in this book will have a favorable impact on the lives of those thousands of young men and women who have shared the experience with us.

Describing and analyzing the socioeconomic institution of work—new territory both in terms of social science and educational curriculum—is an exciting challenge replete with pitfalls. We invite criticisms and suggestions from the students, teachers, counselors, manpower specialists and others who may have occasion to read this book.

References

This section includes complete citations on all publications that we have mentioned in footnotes, tables and narrative material. Since book titles are listed here, they are *not* repeated in the index. Selected titles for some of the authors mentioned in the text are also included in this list of references. References are entered sequentially according to the page on which they appear. When the same publication is cited more than once, a referral is made to the page where the publication was first cited. In cases where more than one publication is cited on a page, the letters "A" and "B" are used to identify the first and second references on that particular page.

****

Page Number	Citation
21	Denis F. Johnston. "The Future of Work: Three Possible Alternatives." *Monthly Labor Review*, Vol. 95, No. 5 (May 1972), pp. 3-11.
42	Adapted from: *Profiles in Success: Forty Lives of Achievement*, by Lily Jay Silver, pp. 47-53. Copyright 1965. Library of Congress Catalog Card No. 64-22452. Published by arrangement with Fountainhead Publishers, Inc., New York City, New York.
47	Table 6.10 of *Americans View Their Mental Health*, by Gerald Gurin, Joseph Veroff, Sheila Feld. Copyright 1960 by Basic Books, Inc., Publishers, New York. Reprinted by permission of the publisher.
48	Norman R.F. Maier. *Psychology in Industry*, 3rd Edition. Boston: Houghton Mifflin Company, 1965. Selected data reprinted by permission of the publisher.
51	Arthur Kornhauser. *Mental Health of the Industrial Worker, A Detroit Study*. New York: John Wiley and Sons, Inc., 1965. Selected data reprinted by permission of the publisher.
87	John Stuart Mill. *Principles of Political Economy*, 5th London Edition. New York: D. Appleton and Company, 1884 (p 257).
92	Adam Smith. *An Inquiry into the Nature and Causes of the Wealth of Nations*. Modern Library Edition. New York: Modern Library, 1937.
101	Pp. 4-5 in same publication cited on p. 92.
106	John Maynard Keynes. *The General Theory of Employment, Interest and Money*. New York: Harcourt, Brace and Company, 1936.
108	Darrell Huff. *How to Lie with Statistics*. New York: W.W. Norton and Company, 1954.
109	U. S. Department of Commerce. *Survey of Current Business*, Vol. 52, No. 7 (July 1972), p. 7.
112-A	U. S. Department of Labor, Bureau of Labor Statistics. *Monthly Labor Review*, Vol. 95, No. 5 (October 1972).
112-B	U. S. President and U. S. Department of Labor. *Manpower Report of the President 1972*. Washington: U. S. Government Printing Office, 1972.
123	Same citation as p. 109.
124	*Road Maps of Industry*, No. 1526. New York: National Industrial Conference Board, 1965.
127	President's Commission on National Goals. *Goals for Americans, Programs for Action in the Sixties*. New York: Prentice-Hall (Spectrum Book), 1960.

References

Page Number	Citation

134-A   U. S. Department of Commerce, Bureau of the Census. *Statistical Abstract of the United States 1972*. Washington: U. S. Government Printing Office, 1972 (p. 469).

134-B   *The Fortune Directory*. Chicago: Time, Inc., May 15, 1969 (p. 2).

140   U. S. Department of Commerce, Bureau of the Census. *Government Finances in 1970-71*. GF71 No. 5. Washington: U. S. Government Printing Office, October 1972 (p. 22).

144-A   U. S. Department of Commerce, Bureau of the Census. *Historical Statistics of the United States*. Washington: U. S. Government Printing Office, 1960 (p. 97f).

144-B   P. 241 in same publication cited on p. 134-A.

148   John Kenneth Galbraith. *The Affluent Society*. Boston: Houghton Mifflin Company, 1958.

156   U. S. Department of Commerce, Bureau of the Census. "Income in 1970 of Families and Persons in the United States." *Current Population Reports*, Series P-60, No. 80. Washington: U. S. Government Printing Office, October 4, 1971 (p. 28).

184   U. S. Department of Labor, Bureau of Labor Statistics. *Handbook of Labor Statistics 1972*. Washington: U. S. Government Printing Office, 1972 (p. 32).

191-A   U. S. Department of Commerce, Bureau of the Census. *Statistical Abstract of the United States 1966*. Washington: U. S. Government Printing Office, 1966 (p. 247).

191-B   P. 244 in same publication cited on p. 134-A.

196   U. S. Department of Labor, Bureau of Labor Statistics. *Occupational Outlook Handbook*. 1972-73 Edition. Washington: U. S. Government Printing Office, 1972.

212   P. 21 in same publication cited on p. 196.

213   P. 175 in same publication cited on p. 112-B.

215   P. 179 in same publication cited on p. 112-B.

232   U. S. Department of Labor, United States Employment Service. *Dictionary of Occupational Titles*. 3rd Edition. 2 Volumes and Supplement. Washington: U. S. Government Printing Office, 1965.

235   P. 25 in same publication cited on p. 196.

237   P. 283 in same publication cited on p. 196.

241   P. 367 in same publication cited on p. 196.

246-A   P. 16 in same publication cited on p. 196.

246-B   P. 14 in same publication cited on p. 196.

248   Pp. 17 and 840 in same publication cited on p. 196.

251   Pp. 171-172 in same publication cited on p. 112-B.

254   U. S. Department of Labor, Women's Bureau. *The Myth: Male Workers Are More Equal Than Female Workers, The Reality: All Workers Are Equal* (3-page leaflet). Washington: Women's Bureau, April 1971.

257   P. 259 in same publication cited on p. 112-B.

259   P. 19 in same publication cited on p. 196.

262-A   U. S. Department of Labor, Bureau of Labor Statistics. *The U. S. Economy in 1980, A Summary of BLS Projections*. Bulletin 1673. Washington: U. S. Government Printing Office, 1970 (p. 49).

262-B   U. S. Department of Labor. *U. S. Manpower in the 1970s. Opportunity and Challenge*. Washington: U. S. Government Printing Office, 1970.

Page Number	Citation

267   "Geographic Mobility in the Sixties." *Road Maps of Industry*, No. 1666. New York: The Conference Board, May 15, 1971. Selected data reprinted by permission of the publisher.

269   U. S. Department of Labor, Bureau of Labor Statistics. *Employment and Earnings for States and Areas 1939-1970*. Washington: U. S. Government Printing Office, 1971 (p. xv).

271-A   U. S. Department of Labor, Bureau of Labor Statistics. *Employment and Earning Statistics for the United States, 1909-66*. Washington: U. S. Government Printing Office, October 1966 (p. xvi).

271-B   P. 215 in same publication cited on p. 112-B.

273-A   *The Economic Almanac 1964*. New York: National Industrial Conference Board, 1964 (p. 44-45). Selected data reprinted by permission of the publisher.

273-B   P. 259 in same publication cited on p. 112-B.

305   George Orwell. *Animal Farm*. New York: Harcourt, Brace and Company, 1946. (Reissued in paperback.)

309   Thorstein Veblen. *The Instinct of Workmanship*. New York: The Macmillan Company, 1914. (Reissued in paperback.)

313   National Commission on Technology, Automation and Economic Progress. *Technology and the American Economy*. 6 Volumes. Washington: U. S. Government Printing Office, 1966.

316   John J. Snyder, Jr. In *Nation's Manpower Revolution, Hearings before the Subcommittee on Employment and Manpower of the Committee on Labor and Public Welfare, U.S. Senate*, 88th Congress, 1st Session, Part 5, p. 1650. Washington: U. S. Government Printing Office, 1963.

318   Don Fabun. "The Dynamics of Change, Kaiser Aluminum and Chemical Corporation." *Kaiser NEWS*, 1967. Reprinted by permission of the publisher.

319-A   Eric Berne. *Games People Play*. New York: Ballantine Books, 1973.

319-B   Thomas A. Harris. *I'm Ok–You're Ok*. New York: Avon Books, 1973.

329   P. 42 in same publication cited on p. 262-A.

330   P. 207 in same publication cited on p. 112-B.

332   William V. Deatermann. "Educational Attainment of Workers, March 1971." *Monthly Labor Review*, Vol. 94, No. 11 (November 1971), p. 34.

341   U. S. Department of Labor, Office of Manpower, Automation and Training. *Formal Occupational Training of Adult Workers*, December 1964. Quoted in Seymour L. Wolfbein, *Education and Training for Full Employment*. New York: Columbia University Press, 1967 (p. 71).

347   Edward F. Denison. *The Sources of Economic Growth in the United States and the Alternatives before Us*. Supplementary Paper No. 13. New York: Committee for Economic Development, January 1962 (pp. 73-74).

348   Jon T. Innes, Paul B. Jacobson, Roland J. Pellegrin. *The Economic Returns to Education*. Eugene, Oregon: University of Oregon, 1965 (pp. 25-30).

349   Christopher Jencks. *Inequality: A Reassessment of the Effect of Family and Schooling in America*. New York: Basic Books, Inc., 1972.

353   U. S. Department of Commerce, U. S. Bureau of the Census. *Current Population Reports*, "Annual Mean Income, Lifetime Income and Educational Attainment of Men in the United States, for Selected Years, 1956 to 1966." Series P-60, No. 80. Washington: U. S. Government Printing Office, October 4, 1971 (p. 9).

References

Page Number	Citation

355   Unpublished U. S. Bureau of Census data as quoted in Herman P. Miller, *Rich Man, Poor Man*. New York: Thomas Y. Crowell Company, Inc., 1971 (p. 178).

357   *Work in America: Report of a Special Task Force to the Secretary of Health, Education and Welfare*. Cambridge: Massachusetts Institute of Technology Press, 1973.

365-A   P. 106 in same publication cited on p. 134-A.

365-B   *Saturday Review*, Vol. 54, No. 51 (December 18, 1971), p. 68.

370   John W. Gardner. *The Recovery of Confidence*. New York: W. W. Norton & Company, Inc., 1970.

371-A   U. S. President and U. S. Department of Labor. *Manpower Report of the President 1968*. Washington: U. S. Government Printing Office, 1968 (p. 47).

371-B   John R. Coleman and Kenneth O. Alexander. *Study Guide for the American Economy* (College of the Air Television Production). New York: McGraw-Hill Book Company, 1962 (p. xvii).

Index